Luxury FEVER

*Money and Happiness
in an Era of Excess*

ROBERT H. FRANK

PRINCETON UNIVERSITY PRESS
PRINCETON AND OXFORD

Published in the United States and Canada
by Princeton University Press,
41 William Street, Princeton, New Jersey 08540

Originally published by the Free Press,
A Division of Simon & Schuster Inc.

Library of Congress Cataloging-in-Publication Data
Frank, Robert H.
    Luxury fever : money and happiness in an era of excess / Robert H. Frank.
        p. cm.
    Originally published: New York, NY : Free Press, © 1999.
    Includes bibliographical references and index.
    ISBN 0-691-07011-3 (pbk. : alk. paper)
        1. Wealth—United States. 2. Luxury. 3. Consumption (Economics)—
    United States. 4. Competition—United States. I. Title.
HC110.W4F7 2000
305.5'234' 0973—dc21   00-038499

Designed by Carla Bolte

The paper used in this publication meets the minimum requirements of
 ANSI/NISO Z39.48-1992 (R1997) (*Permanence of Paper*)

www.pup.princeton.edu

Printed in the United States of America

10 9 8 7 6 5 4
ISBN-13: 978-0-691-07011-7 (pbk.)

ISBN-10: 0-691-07011-3 (pbk.)

FOR JANIE MAE LEE

CONTENTS

ACKNOWLEDGMENTS

I thank Philip Cook, Gerry Cox, Bruce Fitzgerald, Tom Gilovich, Kristin Goss, Ben Hermalin, Shelly Kagan, Ellen McCollister, Bruce Nichols, Dennis Regan, Larry Seidman, and Rafe Sagalyn for helpful comments on earlier drafts. I am grateful as well to participants in the Political Economy Workshop at the University of Western Ontario, the Legal Theory Seminar at Yale, the Russell Sage Foundation Seminar, and The Center on Philanthropy Faculty Seminar. And for their invaluable research assistance, I thank Jeremy Chua, Aaron Chatterji, Rajib Das, Zulfi Khan, Nadja Marinova, Rupal Patel, Lisa Shenouda, Giorgios Vlamis, and Andrea Wasserman.

CHAPTER 1

MONEY WELL SPENT?

The propane grill I bought during the 1980s has been on a downhill slide for several years. First to go was its ignition button, the crude mechanical spark generator that normally fires up the gas. Lighting the grill is now a delicate operation. I turn on the gas, wait a few seconds, and then throw a match inside. Throw it in too soon, and it goes out before it reaches the burner below. Wait too long, however, and it sets off a small explosion. A second problem is that the metal baffle atop the burners has rusted through in the middle. This concentrates an enormous amount of heat over a small area near the center of the cooking surface, but very little elsewhere. I am still able to cook reasonably good chicken and small steaks if I quickly rotate pieces in and out of the hot zone. But grilling a big fish filet has become impossible.

My grill's various deficiencies could surely be repaired, but I have no idea by whom. And even if I did, the cost would almost surely exceed the $89.95 I originally paid for it. And so, reluctantly, I find myself in the market for a new one.

If you have searched this market yourself recently, you know that the menu of available choices is profoundly different from what it was 10 years ago. I vaguely remember models available then with built-in storage cabinets and shelf extensions on either side. But even with these embellishments, the most you could spend was a few hundred dollars. There was nothing—absolutely nothing—like today's Viking-Frontgate Professional Grill.

Powered by either natural gas or propane, it comes with an infrared rotisserie that can slowly broil two 20-pound turkeys to perfection while you cook hamburgers for 40 guests on its 828-square-inch grilling surface. It has a built-in smoker system that "utilizes its own 5,000-BTU burner and watertight wood chip drawer to season food with rich woodsy flavor." Next to its grilling surface sit two ancillary rangetop burners. Unlike the standard burners on your kitchen stove, which generate 7,500 BTUs, these burners generate 15,000 BTUs, a capability that is useful primarily for the flash-stir-frying of some ethnic cuisines and for bringing large cauldrons of water more quickly to a boil. If you have ever longed to throw together a Szechwan pork dish on your backyard patio, or feared getting off to a late start when you have guests about to arrive and 40 ears of corn left to cook, the Viking-Frontgate has the extra power you may need. The entire unit is constructed of gleaming stainless steel, with enamel and brass accents, and with its fold-out workspaces fully extended, it measures more than seven feet across.

The catalog price of the Viking-Frontgate Professional Grill, not including shipping and handling, is $5,000. If that's more than you want to pay, many cheaper models are available. For instance, the all-stainless Weber-Stephens Summit Grill, which the company touts in four-page spreads in *Forbes* and *Vanity Fair,* and which has almost as many bells and whistles as the Viking-Frontgate, sells for only $3,000. And for shoppers who feel they can get by with an 18 by 24 inch grilling surface and only one ancillary rangetop burner, Frontgate offers a model for $1,140 that delivers "professional results at a great value."

Even Frontgate's stripped-down model, however, sells for considerably more than most of us would have dreamed possible a mere decade ago. And indeed, most of the 12 million charcoal and gas grills sold annually in the United States still cost less than $700, a category that will surely include my own next grill as well.[1] Yet grills costing more than $2,000 are by no means rare in the current market. On the contrary, they have become by far "the hottest growing sector in the $1.2 billion-a-year industry."[2]

The evolution of spending patterns in the gas-grill industry is part of a much broader change that has been occurring in recent decades. Popular impressions of what's been happening may be misleading since only the most spectacular examples tend to capture media attention. In one typical recent piece, for instance, the *New York Times* interviewed Alan Wilzig, 32, a Jersey City banker, about the lavish, medieval-style castle he and his brother had just built in the Hamptons.

> Q: This place cost you nearly $10 million to build. Why build something so opulent?
>
> A: To build. It's like having the biggest erector set in the world. It takes about the same amount of effort to buy a $200 million bank as it does to buy a $20 billion bank. Same with a house. You might as well buy the biggest one that you can handle responsibly. We built 14,000 square feet in 14 months. What would have been different if we had built an 8,000-square-foot house with half as many fun things to do? . . .
>
> Q: You have an underwater sound system in your swimming pool, indoor and outdoor hot tubs, a tennis court, 80 gilt mirrors and six suits of armor. If you could add one toy or feature to the castle, what would it be?
>
> A: [pauses] Nothing. If we would have thought of it, we would have built it.[3]

The spending habits of people like the Wilzigs, so remote from what most of us experience, may seem to have little relevance for our own lives. And indeed, the spending of the superrich, though sharply higher than in decades past, still constitutes just a small fraction of total spending. Yet their purchases are far more significant than might appear, for they have been the leading edge of pervasive changes in the spending patterns of middle- and even low-income families. The runaway spending at the top has been a virus, one that's spawned a luxury fever that, to one degree or another, has all of us in its grip.

Thus, although it is the mansions of the superrich that make the news, the far more newsworthy fact is that the average house built in the United States today is nearly twice as large as its counterpart from the 1950s. And although it is the $250,000 sticker price of the 12-cylinder

Lamborghini Diablo that prompts the finger-wagging of social critics, the more telling observation is that the average price of an automobile sold in the United States now exceeds $22,000, up more than 75 percent from just a decade earlier.

No matter where you stand on the income scale, no matter how little you feel you are influenced by what others do, you cannot have escaped the effects of recent changes in the spending environment. Among other things, they affect the kinds of gifts you must give at weddings and birthdays, and the amounts you must spend for anniversary dinners; the price you must pay for a house in a neighborhood with a good school; the size your vehicle must be if you want your family to be relatively safe from injury; the kinds of sneakers your children will demand; the universities they'll need to attend if you want them to face good prospects after graduation; the kinds of wine you'll want to serve to mark special occasions; and the kind of suit you'll choose to wear to a job interview.

At one level, the recent upgrades in what we buy might seem a benign symptom of the fact that we are more productive, and hence richer, than ever before. Our cars are not only faster and more luxuriously appointed, but also safer and more reliable. And although social critics may lampoon the frills of modern appliances, which of these critics would trade their current appliances for the ones they owned 20 years ago? Although we seem to concede that money does not always buy happiness, most of us remain steadfast in our belief that having more of it would be a good thing. For example, when people were asked what single factor would most improve the quality of their lives, the most frequent answer in one American survey was "more money."[4]

But there is also a dark side to our current spending patterns. Whereas those at the top of the economic totem pole have done spectacularly well, the median American family has gained virtually no ground at all during the past two decades, and those in the bottom fifth have actually suffered earnings losses of more than 10 percent in real terms. Similar changes have occurred in the United Kingdom, and this pattern has begun spreading elsewhere as well. With static or declining incomes, middle- and low-income families have thus had to finance their higher spending through lower savings and sharply rising debt. In the process, our personal savings rate has fallen steadily and is now significantly lower than that of any other major industrial nation. Personal bankruptcy filings are at an all-time high.

Even among those who can easily afford today's luxury offerings, there has been a price to pay. All of us—rich and poor alike, but especially the rich—are spending more time at the office and taking shorter vacations; we are spending less time with our families and friends; and we have less time for sleep, exercise, travel, reading, and other activities that help maintain body and soul. Because of the decline in our savings rate, our economic growth rate has slowed, and a rising number of families feel apprehensive about their ability to maintain their living standards during retirement. At a time when our spending on luxury goods is growing four times as fast as overall spending, our highways, bridges, water supply systems, and other parts of our public infrastructure are deteriorating, placing lives in danger. Our parks and streets are becoming dirtier and more congested. Poverty and drug abuse are on the rise, and violent crime, though down from its recent historical peaks in some cities, continues at high levels. A growing percentage of middle- and upper-income families seek refuge behind the walls of gated residential communities.

Is this pattern something we ought to be concerned about? And if so, is there anything we can or should try to do about it? We have long grown accustomed to hearing social critics carp about how much better society as a whole would be if we could somehow manage to spend our money a little differently. And indeed, common sense seems to confirm that at least some of the spending by the superrich could be put to better uses. The barstools aboard the late Aristotle Onassis's yacht, *The Christina,* were covered with the buttery soft—and jarringly expensive—foreskin of the sperm whale penis. The vessel's faucets were of solid gold, and at the flip of a switch its swimming pool could be covered by a retractable, mosaic-tiled dance floor. *The Christina* was just one salvo in Onassis's costly battle to outdo rival shipping magnate Stavros Niarchos, whose own yacht, the 375-foot *Atlantis,* was designed by an architect whose explicit instructions were to make it 50 feet longer than the Onassis vessel. Can anyone truly doubt that it would have been better to build each boat a little smaller, and use the money thus saved to provide school lunches for hungry children?

Yet only the lunatic fringe would empower our government to confiscate money from whoever bureaucrats may feel is spending it unwisely. As conservatives are correct to remind us, the very incentives that led people like Onassis and Niarchos to accumulate such vast wealth have also resulted in millions of new jobs and dramatically improved levels of overall prosperity. If our high and rising living standard rests on the continued willingness of the rich to work hard and take risks, what does it really matter if they sometimes seem to spend their money in frivolous ways?

Telling points all, and ones that critics of our current spending patterns have consistently failed to address. To say that the world we live in isn't perfect is simply not an interesting claim. The real question is whether there is any *practical* way to make things better.

My central premise is that the answer to this question is unequivocally yes. There are not only alternative ways of spending our time and money that we would strongly prefer to our current patterns but also simple and practical ways to get there.

The first part of this claim has been made by many others. But whereas social critics in the past have relied mainly on their own intuitions and personal prejudices about how money is best spent, my approach is to examine evidence from the large scientific literature on the determinants of human well-being. A host of careful studies suggest that across-the-board increases in our stocks of material goods produce virtually no measurable gains in our psychological or physical well-being. Bigger houses and faster cars, it seems, don't make us any happier. But other studies identify a variety of categories in which extra spending would promote longer, healthier, and happier lives for all. For example, we could expect such improvements if we spent more to alleviate traffic congestion, or spent more time with our families and friends, or provided cleaner air and drinking water for our cities.

The more novel and provocative element of my claim is that we can actually achieve such changes without having to compromise other important values. We will not need to empower bureaucratic commissions to make judgments about which specific forms of consumption are wasteful. Nor will we need to engage in detailed, prescriptive regulation of individuals and corporations. Nor will we need to engage in painful acts of self-denial. Nor will we need to risk crippling the incentives that lead talented and industrious people to create new wealth. And nor will we need to curtail any of the economic and social freedoms that we currently enjoy. Rather, I will suggest a simple revision of our existing spending incentives that will make it possible for each of us to pursue our respective visions of the good life more fully and effectively, no matter what (within reason) those visions might be.

On its face, this may seem a preposterous claim. The obvious question it raises is that if better living conditions were so easily achieved, why haven't we already achieved them? If we would be happier working shorter hours and spending more time with our families, even though that would mean living in smaller houses and buying less expensive cars, why don't we just do it? The easy answer that interesting 30-hour-a-week jobs aren't widely available simply won't do, for even though employers might be happy with the workweek just the way it is, they would surely feel pressure to accommodate if enough of us felt strongly about it.

Over the past several years, the so-called voluntary simplicity movement has spawned dozens of popular self-help books that urge us to scale back, telling us we'll be happier if we adopt simpler, less harried lifestyles. The brisk sales of these books suggest that their authors have struck a resonant chord. Their upbeat message is that more comfortable, stress-free living patterns are ours for the taking. All we need do is control our appetites.

Skeptics can be forgiven, however, if they find this a naively optimistic view. After all, people have always been on the lookout for ways to improve their situations. If we would really be happier with simpler lifestyles, it seems a safe bet that we wouldn't need self-help manuals to discover this. It would simply have been part of our shared cultural wisdom all along.

The fact that we are working more hours and buying more goods than ever before has led champions of the status quo to conclude that our current spending patterns, for all their apparent shortcomings, must reveal what we truly value most. Sure, it would be nice to have bigger houses *and* more time for our families; but when forced to choose, we seem to opt overwhelmingly for the former. This is a powerful rejoinder, and social reformers are destined to continue losing their debates with defenders of the status quo until they can come up with a persuasive response to it.

Yet the plain truth, as even the most ardent free-marketeers have known all along, is that the choices of rational, well-informed people simply do not always add up to a whole that meets their approval. One of the clearest examples involves activities that pollute. The fact that millions of motorists voluntarily drive to work in Los Angeles does not mean that they approve of the resulting smog that enshrouds their city. On the contrary, smog tends to be excessive in many cities because any individual who endured the inconvenience of car pooling or riding the bus would end up breathing essentially the same dirty air as if he drove. Making these sacrifices might easily be worth it *if everyone else also made them,* for then we'd get significantly cleaner air. But individuals can control only their own choices, not the choices of others.

The incentives we confront as individual consumers are often problematic in precisely analogous ways. As a 17-year-old Detroit high-school senior, Terrell Garner saved his earnings from a part-time job for several months to be able to buy an $875 pair of alligator shoes to wear to his senior prom. Many social critics would object that he did so because he was duped by sophisticated marketing tactics. Yet so brisk is the demand for these shoes that the Detroit retailers who sell them see no reason to bother advertising. Garner's choice is more plausibly understood if we assume that he perceived correctly that these shoes would create just the impact he wanted: "Once I stepped in the door [at the prom], it was like 'Pow!'" he said, describing the "shoes' mythical, almost explosive appeal."[5]

This appeal would not exist except for the fact that his shoes stood out relative to the shoes worn by others. Garner had no reason to feel concerned that the combined effect of his and others' purchase decisions made it considerably more expensive for someone to stand out from the crowd. But as he moves on to higher paying jobs, he will discover that the cost of achieving similar impact from a new pair of shoes will rise accordingly. Detroit attorney Thomas Marshall, for example, now owns 10 pairs of alligator shoes, including a pair that cost him $3,000; and Cecil Fielder, the baseball player, reportedly owns several hundred pairs in 26 different colors.[6]

The irony is that if, within each social group, everyone were to spend a little less on shoes, the same people who stand out from the crowd now would continue to do so. And because that outcome would free up resources to spend in other ways, people would have good reasons to prefer it. Each individual, however, can choose only the amount that he himself spends on shoes, not the amounts spent by others. Similarly, Onassis and Niarchos might not have minded if *both* of their yachts had been a little shorter (since it's hard, after all, to find docks that can accommodate vessels that long); but each could choose only his own yacht's length, not the other's.

Adam Smith's celebrated invisible hand—the claim that society as a whole does best when individuals pursue their own interests in the open marketplace—rests on the assumption that each person's choices have no negative consequences for others. Yet even the most ordinary individual spending choices frequently do have negative consequences for others, just as the presence of a preschooler with the chicken-pox has negative consequences for others. If I buy a 6,000-pound sport-utility vehicle, I increase the likelihood of others dying in a traffic accident; and in the process, I create an incentive for them to buy heavier vehicles than they otherwise would have chosen. If I buy a custom-tailored suit for my job interview, I reduce the likelihood that others will land the same job; and in the process, I create an incentive for them to spend more than they had planned on their own interview suits. When I stay an extra hour at the office each day, I increase my chances for promotion; but in the process, I reduce the promotion prospects of others, and thereby create an incentive for them to work longer hours than they otherwise would have chosen. In situations like these, individual spending decisions are the seeds of a contagious process.

And situations like these are by no means exceptional. H. L. Mencken once defined a wealthy man as one who earns $100 a year more than his wife's sister's husband, and considerable evidence strongly confirms the wisdom of his observation. People who earn $40,000 a year may be happy or sad, but they are far more likely to be satisfied with their material standard of living if their associates earn $35,000 rather than $60,000.

As a young man fresh out of college, I served as a Peace Corps volunteer in rural Nepal. My one-room house had no electricity, no heat, no indoor toilet, no running water. The local diet offered little variety and virtually no meat. Yet, although my living conditions in Nepal were a bit startling at first, the most salient feature of my experience there was how quickly they came to seem normal. Within a matter of weeks, I lost all sense of impoverishment. Indeed, my $40 monthly stipend was more than most others had in my village, and with it I experienced a feeling of prosperity that I have recaptured only in recent years.

At no time during my stay in Nepal was I ever conscious of taking satisfaction from the fact that I had things that others lacked. But even though I felt completely satisfied with my living conditions there, I would experience a crushing sense of poverty if I were to live in the United States or any other prosperous country under those same conditions. Not a day would pass in which I would not be keenly aware of the extent to which my circumstances fell short of community standards. Things I did not feel I needed in Nepal I would feel I needed here.

The poor are not the only ones who experience pressure to spend more when community consumption standards rise. It is natural for people at all income levels to experience new desires in the presence of others who spend more than they do. And even apart from any changes in what we consciously desire, our individual spending decisions are often influenced by the fact that our menu of available choices is so strongly shaped by what others spend. For example, when I tell salesmen that I want to replace my old propane grill with something roughly like it, they respond that the old models have been discontinued, and that, in any event, I really ought to consider a grill with substantially more features.

"I was sad because I had no on-board fax until I saw a man who had no mobile phone."
Warren Miller (1993) from The New Yorker Collection. All rights reserved.

The real significance of offerings like the $5,000 Viking-Frontgate Professional Grill, for most of us, is that their presence makes buying a $1,000 unit seem almost frugal. As more people buy these upmarket grills, the frame of reference that defines what the rest of us consider an acceptable outdoor grill will inevitably continue to shift. I could easily spend $1,000 on a new grill tomorrow, and few people would notice that I'd done anything strange. More troubling still is the possibility that, with ready opportunities to spend five times that amount and more, *I* might fail to notice anything strange about spending $1,000 to replace my $90 gas grill.

In short, both the things we feel we need and the things available for us to buy depend largely—beyond some point, almost entirely—on the things that others choose to buy. When people at the top spend more, others just below them will inevitably spend more also, and so on all the way down the economic ladder. And as this happens, simpler versions of products that once served perfectly well often fall by the wayside.

This diagnosis of why our current spending patterns are problematic suggests the possibility, at least in principle, of reducing the speed of the consumption treadmill, thereby freeing up resources that can be put to various uses that would make more of a difference in our lives.

For now, I will say only that this can be accomplished in a simple and painless way. My case for change is purely pragmatic, one based on self-interest alone. It rests not at all on the social critic's claim that luxury consumption is self-indulgent or decadent, but rather on detailed and persuasive scientific evidence that if we adopt a simple change in the incentives we face, all of us can expect to live longer, healthier, and more satisfying lives.

Yet it would be a mistake not to acknowledge that the case for changing our current consumption patterns entails a moral dimension as well. In our rush to balance federal, state, and local government budgets, we have slashed funding not only for bridge and highway maintenance but also for hospitals that serve the poor, the Head Start program, the school lunch program, drug rehabilitation programs, homeless shelters, and a host of other low-overhead programs that make life more bearable for our neediest citizens. These programs are being cut not because they do not work, not because they destroy incentives, but because we say we cannot afford them.

Yet the balanced-budget agreement of 1997 prescribed not only deep program cuts but also nearly $150 billion in tax cuts, many of them targeted toward middle- and upper-income families. With the federal budget deficit now in temporary remission, free-marketeers in and out of Congress have mounted a concerted effort on behalf of the so-called flat tax, which would further reduce the taxes paid by top earners by more than half. And to what end? So we can spend $10,000 on our outdoor cooking grills instead of $5,000?

The average taxpayer's annual contribution to Head Start and other programs for needy citizens is small—far less than many upper-middle-class couples spend on wine for a single dinner party. As by far the richest country in human history, we should be doing more, not less, to provide better opportunities for others less fortunate. And as we shall see, the only cost required to take these steps is a *small and temporary* across-the-board reduction in the rate of growth of material goods consumption by middle- and upper-income families. In the face of this truly negligible cost, our current policies become all the more difficult to defend.

Again, however, my aim is to not to scold but to describe a striking new set of possibilities. In the fact that our current consumption patterns entail a substantial measure of waste lie the seeds of a golden opportunity. By a simple and easily achieved rearrangement of our current consumption incentives, we can effectively enrich ourselves by literally trillions of dollars a year. Seldom in our history have our moral imperatives and our naked self-interest been so closely aligned.

CHAPTER 2

THE LUXURY SPENDING BOOM

The economist Thorstein Veblen's term *conspicuous consumption* was inspired by the spectacular excesses of America's Gilded Age—roughly, from 1890 until the beginning of World War I. Among the most visible players of that era were the high-living descendants of railroad tycoon Commodore Cornelius Vanderbilt. By 1900, the clan had constructed eight lavish mansions between 51st and 59th Streets in Manhattan—including One 57th Street, whose 137 rooms made it the largest house ever built in an American city.[1] The Vanderbilts also built 10 major summer estates, including Newport, Rhode Island's Marble House, an $11 million birthday present from Cornelius Vanderbilt II to his wife Alva in 1892.[2] (During the 1890s, a construction foreman earned about $1.25 a day and a common laborer could be hired for as little as 2 cents an hour.)[3] To this day, George Vanderbilt's Biltmore Estate in Asheville, North Carolina, a 250-room Renaissance-style chateau completed in 1895, remains the largest private house ever built in America.[4]

Of these grandiose expenditures by the superrich, Veblen wrote that "since the consumption of these . . . excellent goods is an evidence of wealth, it becomes honorific; and conversely, the failure to consume in due quantity and quality becomes a mark of inferiority and demerit."[5] It was Veblen's view, in other words, that the rich often spent lavishly merely to demonstrate to others that they could afford to do so.

THE CURRENT BOOM

We are today in the midst of another luxury fever. In some ways, it is less spectacular at the very top, owing largely to the fact that concentration of wealth was considerably higher during the earlier era. For example, John D. Rockefeller's net worth at its peak was more than 2 percent of America's annual income, whereas the $40 billion net worth of Bill Gates, today's richest American, amounts to roughly one-half of one percent of current national income.[6] Yet our national income is also considerably higher now than in the last century, and there are pockets of excess to match even the most florid ones of the Gilded Age. Far more important, the current consumption boom affects a vastly larger number of people.

Whereas most families in the Gilded Age had to struggle to make sure their children were adequately clothed, nourished, and sheltered, these needs are no longer at issue for all but a tiny fraction of today's families. The bottom 20 percent of earners now spend just 45 percent of their incomes on food, clothing, and shelter, down from 70 percent as recently as 1920.[7] For most families, the current economic challenge is to acquire not the goods they need but the goods they want. The goods that fill this bill are different in different social circles. For some, a recreational vehicle is the treasured possession; for others, a summer house at the shore. But whatever one's station in life, the quest to move up is currently in full swing.

Unfortunately, no prepackaged government data chart the current spending boom. To get a feel for what is happening, we must compose a picture from assorted bits and pieces. In many cases, it appears that we're simply buying bigger or better versions of existing goods. In others, we're buying things that previously didn't exist. And in still other cases, we're paying higher prices for the most desirable versions of goods we've bought all along. Our focus for the moment will be on the changes in spending at the top of the income pyramid. These have not been the only significant changes in our recent spending patterns, or even—in terms of their direct effects—the most important ones. Far more important, as we shall see, are the indirect effects that increased spending at the top has spawned throughout the rest of the economy.

Because this is a book about waste, however, it behooves us to take at least a cursory look at the expenditures of the rich, among which we find by far the most vivid examples of outlays that achieve little.

The Patek Philippe Wristwatch

Cecil Harvell, a 39-year-old Morehead City, North Carolina, attorney is the proud owner of a $17,500 Patek Philippe wristwatch, a gift from his wife. The company, fearing its potential customers might think that an unreasonable sum to spend, runs ads that encourage them to think of their purchase as creating a family heirloom: "because of the exceptional workmanship, each one is a unique object. Which is perhaps why some people feel that you never actually own a Patek Philippe. You merely look after it for the next generation." The pitch seems to work: "with a seven-year-old son, Mr. Harvell said he viewed the watch as a keepsake that could be passed down through the family."[8]

Still, $17,500 is a lot of money. (It is more than the annual income an urban family of four must have in order not to be officially classified as poor in the United States.) And yet Harvell's is by no means the most expensive watch Patek Philippe offers. Its more elaborate models are more costly not because they are encrusted with precious stones but because they feature additional "complications"—complex mechanical performance options. The most elaborate of these is the "tourbillon," essentially a gyroscope that turns once every minute to compensate for gravity's distorting effects. (The accuracy of my $30 battery-powered quartz watch is unaffected by gravity, and hence does not require a tourbillon correction.) Each complication can add up to $120,000 to the cost of the watch.

The most elaborate Patek Philippe ever made is the Calibre '89, which has 900 parts and 33 complications. Only four Calibre '89s were made to mark the company's 150th birthday. The first was sold at auction for $2.7 million, and the remaining three fetched even higher prices. In a world without the Calibre '89, it might seem wildly absurd to spend $17,500 on a wristwatch. But in a frame of reference that includes the vastly more expensive model, it is easy to see why owners of the $17,500 version might find it difficult to conceive of themselves as spendthrifts.

For buyers who feel the $17,500 model doesn't make a strong enough statement, yet don't want to spring for the Calibre '89 model, Patek Philippe also offers a limited edition model that sells for $44,500. Demand for this model is so brisk that it is available only on backorder.[9]

Sales of Patek Philippe and other high-end timepieces costing at least $2,000 rose 13 percent in 1997, to $1.1 billion.[10] And although the absolute number of people who can afford these watches remains small, their significance is far out of proportion to their number. Except for the growing presence of Patek Philippe and other similar products in the marketplace, many fewer upper-middle-class buyers would have purchased wristwatches costing $1,000.

Top Prices and Still Sold Out

A standard proposition of introductory economics texts is that supply and demand for any good inexorably tend toward a balance in which buyers are able to buy as much of that good as they choose to at the prevailing market price. Shortages are the exception to this rule, and they tend to occur for goods and services whose demand has been growing (or whose supply has been shrinking) rapidly. Perhaps the clearest evidence that we are in the midst of a luxury consumption boom is that, despite the unprecedented high prices of luxury goods, waiting lists for them have grown increasingly common.

Suites costing from $750 to $1,800 a night at The Four Seasons Resort in Palm Beach are booked months ahead,[11] as are $5,000-a-night suites at Little Nell in Aspen.[12] All 84 seats on Tavoca World Tours' $38,000-per-person 1996 world tour sold out six months in advance.[13] First-class air transportation to the Caribbean sold out so far in advance of the 1997 Christmas season that Bill Fischer, a travel agent specializing in six-figure vacations, chartered a specially equipped Boeing 727 to transport his clients. The plane featured "59 fully reclining leather seats, a bar section and a chef to prepare omelets during the three-hour flight."[14]

Salvatore Ferragamo now imposes an eight-pair limit on buyers of its richly detailed leather shoes.[15] Porsche's new roadster, the Boxster, has a waiting list of almost one year, and the few used models available

sell at a premium of as much as $10,000 over the sticker price of new
ones. Someone who bought one of the 150 limited-edition Patek
Philippe Pagoda wristwatches issued in 1997 for only $24,000 could sell
the same watch a year later for more than $50,000.[16] A Fifth Avenue
jeweler reports more than a dozen backorders for various models of its
Cartier Tank Française wristwatches, which sell for as much as
$20,500.[17] Yacht manufacturers report a large backlog of factory orders,
and the recent demand surge has caused used vessels, normally priced
considerably below new ones, to sell for close to their original prices.[18]
At a recent boat show in Fort Lauderdale, the more than 20 boats offered at prices of $18 million and higher sold out in a mere five days.[19]
Prada's $400 gray flannel pants have a waiting list of three months.[20]
Many Lexus dealers report substantial delays in filling orders for the new
LX450 sport-utility vehicle, sticker-priced at $48,000 and up.[21] Even the
$14,000 Hermés Kelly handbag is available only on backorder.[22]

Waiting lists are common as well at many of the nation's poshest
restaurants. At Manhattan's Restaurant Daniel, for example, reserva-
tions are taken up to one month in advance, and the prime-time blocks
are typically booked by noon on the first day of each month.[23] Le
Cirque 2000, which has only 42 tables, receives several thousand reser-
vation requests each day.[24]

When Intrawest Corporation offered new condominiums priced
up to $500,000 (Canadian) at its Whistler Village development outside
Vancouver, all 90 units sold out in less than an hour and a half, with at
least three backup offers on each sale.[25] In mid-1997, Gulfstream Corporation reported backorders for 98 of its luxury jets, chief among
them the Gulfstream V, which sells for more than $37 million.[26] Sea-
gram's head Edgar Bronfman, Jr., is reported to have earned a princely
profit by selling his place on the Gulfstream V waiting list to Walter An-
nenberg, former owner of *TV Guide*.[27]

Tracking Luxury Spending

Luxury spending in the United States is currently growing more than
four times as rapidly as spending overall. Thus total U.S. spending on
luxury goods—defined by retail trade associations as goods in each cat-

egory exceeding a given price threshold, such as $200 for a pair of shoes—increased by 21 percent between 1995 and 1996, compared to an increase of only 5 percent in overall merchandise sales during the same period.[28] Luxury travel (trips with per-diem spending of at least $350) grew 130 percent between 1990 and 1995.[29] The occupancy rates for luxury hotels, which stood at 69 percent a decade ago, now stand at 76 percent.[30] Luxury cars (those selling for more than $30,000 in 1996 dollars) accounted for about 12 percent of all vehicles sold in the United States in 1996, up from 7 percent in 1986.[31] Although mult-millionaires are clearly prominent among the purchasers of luxury cars and many other luxury products thus defined, recent large sales volumes imply that the vast majority of buyers must have less than six-figure incomes.

Recent sales changes for German luxury cars suggest that the trend toward luxury auto purchases may even be accelerating. Thus Audi's sales grew by 53.6 percent between 1995 and 1996, Porsche's by 26.3 percent, Mercedes's by 23.9 percent, and BMW's by 14.4 percent.[32] In 1997, the total number of cars sold in the United States fell by 3 percent, but the number of luxury cars sold rose by 6.5 percent.[33] Mercedes sold 35 percent more cars in the United States in 1997 than in 1996, Porsche 79 percent more, and BMW 16 percent more.[34]

The luxury auto sales figures do not include sales of sport-utility vehicles, which are classified as trucks. Sales of these vehicles, many with sticker prices well over $30,000, grew from 750,000 units in 1990 to almost 1.5 million in 1995,[35] and grew by 260 percent between January 1995 and October 1997.[36] Sales in the new luxury sport-utility segment, which includes entries from Mercedes, BMW, Lexus, Infiniti, Lincoln, and now Cadillac, tripled between 1996 and 1997.[37] And as standard-size sport-utility vehicles have grown increasingly common, many families have turned to the larger super-haulers such as the Chevy Suburban and the Ford Expedition. Fully equipped versions of these vehicles, which tip the scales at more than 6,000 pounds and get about 8 miles per gallon, sell for over $40,000. Many of these vehicles are more than 18 feet long, requiring many who buy them to have their garages remodeled.

Vacation Homes

Another indication that we are in the midst of a luxury spending boom is the sharp increase in second-home ownership over the last two decades. One measure of this is the decline in the proportion of dwellings occupied year-round in many exclusive resort communities. For example, the year-round occupancy rate for private dwellings in Jackson Hole, Wyoming, now stands at only 50 percent, down from 83 percent in 1980.[38]

As with luxury car sales, the trend in second-home sales seems to be accelerating, with most major ski areas reporting record rates of new housing construction. In one typical high-end project, the 93 building lots in Vail's Bachelor Gulch Village sold out on offering for an average price of $776,000.[39] In Snowmass Village, Colorado, the 21 new units in the Owl Creek project recently sold for an average price of $2 million for four-bedroom, 4,000-square-foot Norman-style houses featuring 10-foot ceilings, stone fireplaces, Sub-Zero refrigerators, and Viking gas ranges.[40]

The boom in second-home construction is by no means confined to the superrich. The newly constructed three- and four-bedroom houses at Elkhorn near Sun Valley, Idaho, for example, offered a more modest 2,700 square feet of living space, and were priced between $545,000 and $640,000.[41] And even the relatively down-market resorts of the northeast are upgrading. Pennsylvania's Whitetail Mountain, for instance, recently built 48 Federal-style town houses priced up to $280,000. "We didn't spend a lot of time studying the real-estate market in the area," says Stephen K. Rice, president of Whitetail Ski Company, the developer. "We had so many requests from our skiers that we knew there was a lot of pent-up demand."[42]

Bigger and Better Equipped Homes

Not only are more of us buying second homes, the main homes we build and live in are becoming much larger and more elaborately equipped. For example, as the *New York Times* writer Patricia Leigh Brown described the computerized electronic control equipment in the home of one Silicon Valley CEO, "In place of the maids, there is a night mode, a day mode, an at-home mode, and an away mode. [The owners] can change the setting on alarms, water heater, air conditioning, or lighting by e-mail from a laptop, whether they're on vacation in Scotland, or at work. A tiny camera at the door takes a snapshot of a guest, and then, like the doddering butler announcing a visitor, generates a picture that can be sent via Internet to their office PC."[43]

Although family sizes have become steadily smaller during the postwar era, our houses have grown steadily larger. Whereas houses built in the United States in the 1950s averaged roughly 1,100 square feet, by 1996 that average had grown to more than 2,000.[44] Nearly half the houses built today have more than 2.5 bathrooms, as compared to only 20 percent in 1975.[45] In 1996, almost 14 percent of new homes built had more than 3,000 square feet of living space.[46] National Association of Home Builders data didn't even include that category in 1986, when the largest category was 2,400 square feet. Whereas only 18 percent of new homes built in 1986 were 2,400 square feet or larger, a decade later 30 percent were.[47] Scottsdale, Arizona, builder Larry Kush notes that the largest houses in his developments now measure 6,000 square feet, up from 4,000 in 1993.[48] Of the huge, mass-produced houses built in popular new luxury subdivisions springing up in the suburbs of New York, Alexander Garvin, professor of architecture and planning at Yale, said, "They call them McMansions."[49]

Existing data categories conceal the explosive growth in the construction of so-called trophy homes—mansions with more than 10,000 square feet of living space. In Beverly Hills, for example, 17 such houses were sold in 1997, up from only 9 in 1994.[50] Along one short stretch of the Florida coast near Palm Beach, 19 private residences ranging from 23,000 to 64,000 square feet have been built in the last several years; and in 1996 alone, 22 houses in the area exchanged hands in the market for prices above $10 million.[51] Indeed, many of the mansions constructed in recent years, although smaller than the 1895 Biltmore Estate, threaten to alter the current threshold for what counts as a trophy home.

By one estimate, the total construction cost of Microsoft Chairman Bill Gates's 45,000 square-foot house on the shores of Lake Washington, just east of Seattle, may top $100 million, including $6.5 million for the swimming pool alone. When estimating the cost of constructing a house, contractors use numbers like $125 per square foot for a high-quality middle-class house and $200 per square foot for luxury construction. The Gates mansion came in at more than $2,000 per square foot.

Microsoft cofounder Paul Allen recently built a 74,000-square-foot house, also in the Seattle area. (Allen also owns a 200-foot Feadship, *The Medusa,* complete with its own helicopter, recording studio, and movie theater.) Oracle CEO Laurence Ellison is in the process of building a $40-million, 23-acre estate in Woodside, California. Even the hired help has gotten into the act, albeit on a slightly smaller scale. For example, Microsoft's chief programmer, Charles Simonyi, has just moved into his 20,500-square-foot house, which features a 60-foot indoor swimming pool.

These are *very* big houses. The Paul Allen compound, for example, is approximately the same size as the building that houses Cornell's Johnson Graduate School of Management, in which roughly 100 faculty and administrative staff have offices and in which more than 600 students attend classes each day.

People who part with more than $10 million for a house naturally tend to be particular about getting exactly what they want. It has thus been the tradition for almost all new homes in this segment to be custom-built according to the plans of specific buyers. A further indication of the current luxury boom is that we are now beginning to see trophy homes built on speculation.[52] In 1996, for example, builder Alvin Weintraub began construction of a $12 million Mediterranean-style mansion in Beverly Hills with no buyer in sight.[53] That same year, contractor Frank McKinney dug ground for an $11.9 million oceanfront spec chateau in Delray Beach, Florida.[54] These developers explain that busy entrepreneurs often don't have time to scout for choice sites and oversee a two-year design and construction project.

Even in wealthy communities, the trend until recently had been for residential properties to be subdivided into ever smaller lot sizes. Further evidence of the current luxury consumption boom may be seen in an apparent reversal of this trend whereby owners in many wealthy communities have attempted to enlarge their estates by buying adjacent properties. For example, Rick Goldstein, a retail consultant who paid $1.2 million for an 1842 farmhouse in Bridgehampton, New York, in 1990, spent the next three years trying to persuade his neighbors to sell him the parcels on either side. Having purchased these parcels for $750,000 each, he now has a 4-acre estate: "All lawn plus a guest house," as he describes it.[55]

Such transactions, it appears, are becoming increasingly common.[56] The violinist Itzhak Perlman, already the owner of two East Hampton parcels totaling almost four acres, paid $2.2 million in 1990 for a 3.5-acre lot next door. Michael Schulhof, former chairman of Sony Corporation of America, paid $1.9 million in 1988 for his house on almost an acre of land, then paid $875,000 in 1990 for an adjoining 1.1-acre parcel. Designer Oscar de la Renta, owner of a 200-acre retreat outside Kent, Connecticut, bought the adjacent 168-acre estate in 1996 for $1.25 million.[57] And a Manhattan financier just extended the bedroom of his Central Park West apartment by paying a neighbor $200,000 for about 100 square feet space between them "so he could, in Jim Morrison's immortal words, break on through to the other side."[58]

Pleasure Craft

Although sales of both motor and sailing yachts were no higher overall in 1997 than they had been a decade earlier, the most recent sales figures represent a much smaller number of significantly more expensive boats. The world's stock of pleasure craft longer than 100 feet, for example, is currently more than 5,000, about twice what it was 10 years ago.[59] (About half are owned by Americans.) In addition to their multimillion-dollar purchase prices, these vessels can cost upwards of $1.5 million to run and maintain each year—including $500,000 for crew, $200,000 for fuel, $100,000 for insurance, and $225,000 for maintenance and repairs. Simply to repaint the hull of a vessel this size, which must be done every four years, costs about $400,000.[60]

Despite these outlays, most owners spend only a few weeks each year on their yachts, and the typical ownership tenure is roughly two years (after which many owners trade up to larger vessels).[61] Including the forgone interest on the money used to purchase these vessels, the

cost of time actually spent on board is more than $10,000 an hour for
many owners.

Professional Home Appliances

Every era has its status symbols. In the 1950s, it was the stay-at-home
mom; in the 1980s, the Porsche 911. In many communities, the status
symbol of the 1990s has been the restaurant stove. Whereas burners
on standard residential stoves generate less than 8,000 BTUs, those on
commercial stoves generate 15,000 BTUs and more. As with the high-
output ancillary burners on the Viking-Frontgate Professional outdoor
cooking grill, this is a capability that is useful primarily for flash stir-
frying of Chinese dishes.

Many buyers of such stoves choose them less for their technical
specifications than for their handsome appearance. "I cook maybe
seven times a year—the rest of the time you look for places where you
can get takeout—but I have a $7,000 stove," said Carol Burnett, a Cal-
ifornia executive. "You think of it as a painting that makes the kitchen
look good."[62]

As the number of people owning stoves with 15,000-BTU burners
has grown, it was perhaps inevitable that at least some buyers would
begin to ask: Why only 15,000 BTUs? Why, indeed? Cypress Semicon-
ductor CEO T. J. Rodgers, described in one press account as "a man
whose own dog bites him," recently purchased a stove with a 35,000-
BTU wok, halogen burners, and a ceramic pizza oven.[63]

Noting that high-end appliances have higher markups than models
further down in the price range, some commentators have characterized
the proliferation of performance features in recent years as a clever marketing tactic whereby manufacturers lure people into parting with more
of their money. *New York Times* economics reporter Louis Uchitelle, for
example, notes that manufacturers add "some gadget or twist that millions of consumers are willing, or can be persuaded, to pay extra to have.
. . . In each of these higher prices, an extra profit is embedded."[64]

The first manufacturers to introduce new and improved models
do indeed enjoy padded profit margins in most cases, but it would be
a mistake to view the high-end appliance boom as a phenomenon

whose primary consequence is a transfer of wealth from consumers to producers. After all, it takes real resources to build more elaborate versions of existing appliances and other products, resources that could have been put to other uses. Now that the innovating firms have proved that offering 15,000-BTU burners is a good way to appeal to buyers with spare cash in their pockets, more and more rival manufacturers have begun to offer this feature, and its price premium has fallen more closely into balance with the added cost of producing it.

The general pattern is that, as time passes, products embody more and more costly new features. Today's high-end models become tomorrow's base models, whose prices, even with no padded profit margins, fully reflect the cost of their additional features. The producer's quest for higher profits is an important facilitator in this dynamic, to be sure. But the prime mover is the consumer's desire to own bigger and more highly differentiated versions of existing products.

Further indications that this desire has become increasingly widespread can be seen in the proliferation of high-end products offered by retailers in their recent Christmas catalogs. The 1997 Christmas issue of *The Robb Report,* for example, listed a 200-foot motor yacht, still under construction, and quickly received nine serious inquiries despite its $32 million price tag.[65] Williams-Sonoma offered a $13,000 custom commercial stove, promising delivery "within four months." Neiman Marcus quickly sold out its recent offering of 70 new Jaguar convertibles at more than $80,000 apiece. Victoria's Secret offered a Diamond Dream Bra, designed by Harry Winston and modeled by Tyra Banks, priced at $3 million. (Its previous year's diamond-studded Miracle Bra, modeled by Claudia Schiffer, sold for only $1 million.) And Hammacher Schlemmer tempted its customers with its $139,000 bionic dolphin: a one-person water craft that dives 150 feet, goes 35 mph underwater, 85 mph on the surface.[66]

Cosmetic Surgery

Cosmetic surgery has been another high-growth luxury consumption item. The American Academy of Facial Plastic and Reconstructive Surgery reports that the number of face-lifts performed by its members rose 178 percent between 1988 and 1993.[67] Approximately 2 million cosmetic procedures were performed in 1991, more than six times the number just a decade earlier,[68] and demand has been growing steadily in the years since.[69]

Once the almost-exclusive province of women 55 and older, an increasing proportion of cosmetic procedures now involve men, and almost half involve patients between the ages of 30 and 49.[70] Howard Klavin, a plastic surgeon in Santa Monica, California, reports that the average age of his face-lift patients is now 44. "It used to be women in their 60s who came in for face-lifts. Now if you haven't done it by 60, you're not going to."[71]

Male patients tend to explain their surgery as an attempt to hold their own in an increasingly youth-oriented corporate world. "A 49-year-old male South Florida newscaster had a face lift last year to stay competitive in a young person's arena. In his career, you'd *better* look good. Or at least not old."[72]

Much of the new surgery appears motivated not by a desire to erase the ravages of time but by a desire to conform to ideals of physical perfection. "They're in a mad rush for nose jobs and liposuction on their necks, tummies and butts," says Dr. Robert Guida, a plastic surgeon at New York Hospital. "They've now got the cash and want to look like Jack Armstrong, the All-American Boy, so they can attract more clients."[73] For example, as George Kapanos, a 30-year-old Wall Street broker, described his recent rhinoplasty, "I feel more comfortable now that I got rid of my Greek nose. When I sit with my clients, I feel 100 percent correct." He notes that his income rose 40 percent in the year following his surgery, compared with only 10 to 15 percent in previous years.[74] Iowa City plastic surgeon John Canady perceives a sense of urgency in these younger patients that he didn't see in the previous generation. "But it's not surprising," he adds. "It's a more urgent time."[75]

Although many who turn to cosmetic surgery are motivated by the expectation of higher incomes, others seem driven by the hope of finding a mate. Crow's feet and sagging jawlines were not terrible handicaps during an era when most people remained married to the same spouse for a lifetime. But with divorce rates at an all-time high, there are record numbers of middle-aged people now in the marriage market. And many of them believe that the surgeon's knife will give them just, so to speak, the edge they need.

The Charm Premium

Another manifestation of the current luxury spending boom is the sharply higher premium one must pay to obtain higher-quality versions of many existing goods. Even among goods that serve essentially the same function, buyers typically face a choice among numerous quality levels. In the real estate market, for example, houses of a given size may be ranked by quality or desirability according to various features such as privacy of location, architectural charm, length of commute, and so on. Other things being the same, houses with more of these features will sell for higher prices than those with fewer. For convenience, I will call this difference in price the "charm premium."

For houses, as for many other goods that cannot be easily transported from one place to another, the charm premium will tend to be larger in high-income communities than in low-income communities. Most people, after all, would prefer to live in a house with architectural charm or a sweeping view, and in high-income communities the bidding for these desirable features will naturally be more intense.

My wife and I were forcefully confronted with this reality several years ago while considering a move from Ithaca to Evanston, Illinois. Ithaca is a small city in upstate New York in which university professors, although not at the top of our modest local economic pyramid, are not far below it. Evanston, by contrast, is a wealthy suburb of the nation's third-largest city. It and the tony adjacent suburbs to the north are home to many of the wealthiest executives and professionals of the entire metropolitan Chicago area. The handsome 1911 Arts and Crafts–style house that we have carefully restored in Ithaca commands only about a 20 percent charm premium over architecturally less interesting but otherwise similar houses. And even though Evanston has much more wealth than Ithaca, we found that we could buy an architecturally undistinguished house of about the same size there for only a

little more than what we could get for our Ithaca house. But it would
have cost us literally three times that amount to buy a house with a
comparable amount of charm in Evanston. Some examples of the escalating charm premium in recent years:

THE PREMIUM FOR A VIEW. One important dimension of the charm premium
in the real estate market is the extent to which a homesite commands a
view of the water, city lights, mountains, or some other desirable topo-
graphical feature. Evidence suggests that the prices of homesites with
views have been escalating sharply in recent years. For instance, buyers
now pay premiums of 50 to 100 percent for lots that overlook water and
20 to 50 percent for lots that overlook city lights—as much as 10 percentage points higher than the corresponding premiums just five years
ago.[76] In Pelican Hill, a new development in Newport Coast, California,
the 266 lots with views of the ocean sold out quickly at an average price
of $1 million each, whereas the developer has had difficulty selling a
handful of lots without views priced at only $600,000.[77] Even a view of a
golf course now commands a premium of 20 to 25 percent.[78]

THE PREMIUM FOR CHOICE LOCATION. Further indirect evidence of the rising
premium for a choice location in the real estate market is the increasing
frequency with which buyers are willing to demolish existing luxury
houses to build even larger ones. In 1994, Chicago attorney Mario Cirig-
nani bought and demolished a $235,000 house in Hinsdale, Illinois, and
then spent $1 million to build a much larger, French-style chateau in its
place. The prime attractions of Hinsdale are its quiet, tree-lined streets
and its easy 21-minute rail commute to downtown Chicago. More than
10 percent of the 4,500 houses in Hinsdale have been demolished during
the last decade and replaced by bigger ones.[79] Not even places like Mission Hills (a small suburb of Kansas City, Kansas) are exempt: 14 houses
have been torn down there since 1994 to make way for upgrades.[80]

Real estate agents call these houses "scrapers," and there is an especially brisk trade in them in the communities of Silicon Valley. For
example, Roger Rickard, president of Foster City's Cornish & Casey
Real Estate, said his agents had sold literally dozens of scrapers in

1996.[81] Brian Pinkerton was 32 years old and fresh out of the University of Washington when America Online, the Internet access provider, offered him an executive position in its Silicon Valley office, plus a payment of $1.4 million and stock options for his unfinished Ph.D. thesis. He then bought and demolished a $600,000 scraper in the elite enclave of Atherton so that he could build a house large enough to entertain his friends.[82] "It was definitely livable," said Pinkerton of the house he tore down. "I just wanted something a little bigger."[83] At a party to demolish a 1950s house on the site of Intuit co-founder Tom Proulx's 10-acre estate, also in Atherton, "guests were issued hard hats. There was cyber-baronial exultation in the air. 'The first thing we did,' Mrs. Proulx said, 'was hit golf balls through the picture windows.' "[84]

Sometimes even the teardowns themselves are architectural treasures. For example, to win the Woodside Planning Department's approval to build his proposed $40 million, 23-acre Japanese retreat, Oracle CEO Lawrence J. Ellison had to promise to airlift an existing house by Julia Morgan (the architect of San Simeon, the William Randolph Hearst castle) to Stanford University.[85]

PRICES FOR ULTRAPREMIUM WINES. The wine market provides another clear instance of escalating charm premiums. Although total wine consumption in the United States is actually down slightly from its peak in 1986, sales of ultrapremium wines—those selling for at least $14 per bottle—have grown at an annual rate of 23 percent since 1980, with 1996 sales of 3.4 million cases.[86] With this shift in demand has come a parallel shift in relative prices. As collector Bruce Toll, president of a large home-building company in Pennsylvania, observes, "I have cases today that are worth $5,000 to $7,000 that I paid $500 to $700 for in the last seven years."[87]

The Wine Spectator's auction index—based on the auction prices of wines from a variety of top producers and vintages—climbed more than 40 percent in 1996 alone.[88] The price trajectory of a smaller set of the most sought-after wines has been even steeper. Included in this group are the classed growths of Bordeaux, the best wines produced from grapes grown on the slopes surrounding the Gironde River and estuary in western France. The auction price of a 750 ml bottle of 1989 Chateau Latour, for example, jumped 45 percent in the fourth quarter of 1996 to $164.[89] A bottle of the 1990 Chateau Latour, considered a marginally better vintage, now sells for $400, up five-fold from its release price of $80. And if you want a single bottle of Chateau Petrus from the 1961 vintage, regarded by many connoisseurs as the star of the best of the postwar Bordeaux vintages, you'll have to write a check to the auctioneer for $2,696. A recent auction produced the first six-figure price for a single case of wine—$112,500 for a 1945 Chateau Mouton-Rothschild.[90]

The best wines from California, although priced lower than the best from Bordeaux, have experienced similar growth in demand and prices. For example, 4,000 people are on the waiting list to buy the next release of Helen Turley's Napa Valley Marcassin Cabernet Sauvignon, priced conservatively at $100 per bottle.[91] Turley also makes a cabernet for Colgin-Schrader Cellars, whose owner reports offers of up to $5,800 for a 12-bottle case, 11 times its initial retail price.[92] Opus One, another prestigious Napa Valley producer, saw the price of its fabled 1987 cabernet sauvignon more than double in 1996.[93] The winery sold 27,000 cases of its latest cabernet within six weeks of its release in 1996. "It was easier than it was to sell 10,000 cases six years ago," said the firm's marketing director.[94]

We see similar patterns in the market for premium spirits. Sophisticated scotch drinkers, for example, have turned their backs on traditional blends in favor of substantially pricier single malts. A favorite single-malt scotch at The Canteen in Birmingham, Alabama, is The Balvenie, which is aged from 10 to 15 years and sells for $9.20 per shot.[95] But even single-malt prices pale in comparison to what connoisseurs of fine brandy are willing to pay. At Bernard's in the Los Angeles Biltmore, for instance, a snifter of 1928 Sempe Armagnac currently goes for $195.[96]

PREMIUM CIGARS. As in the wine market, the lion's share of demand growth in the cigar market has been accounted for by premium grades, cigars that sell for from $3 to as much as $20 apiece and more. These cigars are often filled with tobacco grown from seeds developed in Cuba and then hand-wrapped with half tobacco leaves. Whereas overall growth in cigar sales has averaged less than 10 percent per year since 1992, sales growth for premium cigars has averaged more than 40 percent.[97] Premium cigar sales in 1996 ran nearly 60 percent higher than in 1995.[98]

Although Cuban cigar sales have been banned in the United States since 1962, demand is so intense that premium brands like Cohiba or Montecristo are often available, at very steep prices, on the black market.[99] But even perfectly legal premium cigars have grown surprisingly expensive. For example, a single Don Ramon from Partagas 150 sells for $50 at the Cigarbar at Hamilton's in Beverly Hills.[100] It comes in an 18-year-old Cameroon wrapper signed and numbered by the employee who rolled it. Patroon, a Manhattan restaurant, rings up as much as $5,000 a day in cigar sales alone.[101]

Industry observers attribute the premium cigar's success to "the association of cigar smoking with a lifestyle of quality."[102] This link is promoted by magazines like *Cigar Aficionado,* whose covers portray cigar-smoking celebrities such as Arnold Schwarzenegger, Madonna, and Demi Moore. Put out by the publisher of *The Wine Spectator, Cigar Aficionado* had more than 400,000 paid subscribers in 1996, more than twice as many as a year earlier.[103]

Along with the swift growth in demand for premium cigars has come an expansion in exclusive establishments that cater to cigar smokers. One of these is The Grand Havana Room in Beverly Hills, which opened in 1995. It has no sign outside, its telephone number is unlisted, and its celebrity-studded membership roster has a waiting list of several hundred. Access to the club is via a special elevator operated by keys given only to members, who pay $2,000 to join and a monthly fee of $150. In the center of the club is a glass-walled room with 450 cedar humidors in which members can store their cigars at the optimal combination of 70 percent relative humidity and 70 degrees Fahrenheit.[104]

New York and Washington branches of The Grand Havana Room opened in early 1997, and owner Harry Shuster has plans to open in San Francisco, Dallas, and Las Vegas as well.[105] Similar, if less exclusive, cigar bars have recently opened in most major cities, according to Robert Langsam of the International Association of Cigar Clubs.[106]

Only in America?

The world's purveyors of luxury goods have long recognized the United States as their most lucrative market by far. But Americans are not the only ones with voracious and growing appetites for luxury goods. Japan, with fewer than half as many people as the United States, consumes more than half the U.S. volume of luxury goods.[107] Popular press accounts in Asia, Europe, and elsewhere describe a growing appetite for such goods in recent years.[108] Even Russia has become a hotly contested market by the manufacturers of luxury goods. Rolls-Royce, for example, has recently opened its first dealership in Moscow, and Mercedes-Benz describes Russia as its fastest growing market.[109]

A Puzzling Change

Fragmentary and anecdotal though much of the evidence we have seen may be, it is consistent with the widespread impression that a large and growing share of spending in the United States has been flowing toward high-end goods and services. We are driving more expensive cars and buying more vacation houses, more designer clothing. Our living spaces are larger and more elaborately equipped; we are drinking better wines and spirits; and we are buying more sophisticated appliances. More and more of us are having cosmetic surgery and having it at ever younger ages.

In one sense, these changes are a simple continuation of a pattern that began with the industrial era more than two centuries ago. With our fundamental needs for food and shelter now largely satisfied, it is only natural that we spend more and more on luxuries as our incomes continue to grow. What is puzzling, however, is that whereas spending on luxuries has been sharply accelerating in recent decades, prevailing trends in productivity and income growth have been moving in precisely the opposite direction.

CHAPTER 3

WHY NOW?

The past quarter century has been a period of slow growth for the American economy. Whereas real per-capita incomes rose at an average annual rate of almost 3 percent between 1950 and 1973, the corresponding average for the years since has been only half that. The median household income in the United States was $34,100 in 1995, actually down 2 percent in real terms from 1990.[1] Why, then, has our spending on luxury consumption goods been escalating so rapidly in recent decades? The simple answer is that, despite slow growth in average income levels, those near the top of the income ladder have enjoyed unprecedented prosperity. And as we shall see in the next chapter, the behavior of these top earners appears to have influenced the spending decisions of millions of others.

Incomes of the top 1 percent of U.S. earners have more than doubled in real terms since 1979.[2] To be in the top 1 percent of U.S. earners in 1995 meant to have annual earnings of more than $150,000 in 1995 dollars. The number of people with earnings that high nearly doubled between the 1980 and 1990 censuses.[3] Whereas in 1979 the 95th-percentile U.S. earner received 10 times as much as the 5th-percentile earner, the corresponding ratio for 1993 was more than 25.[4] The income gains have been even more spectacular for those near the very top of the income pyramid. CEOs of America's largest companies, for instance, earned 35 times as much as the average worker in 1973; today they earn some 200 times as much.[5] Including his gains from exercising stock options, Disney's Michael Eisner took home more than $565 million in 1997.[6] The 1997 Forbes 400—the celebrated annual tally of the 400 richest people in America—included 170 billionaires, up from only 13 in 1982.[7] Almost 5 million Americans had a net worth of at least $1 million in 1996, more than double the number just four years earlier.[8] In 1994, 9.6 percent of all tax returns filed with the IRS reported adjusted gross incomes of at least $200,000, up from 8.4 percent in 1992. In 1970, only 3.2 percent of American households had incomes of at least $100,000 in 1996 dollars.[9] In short, people who had a lot of money to begin with have considerably more now, and there are also many more people with a lot of money than there used to be.

That the current luxury fever is supported in part by the spectacular rise in top incomes is a recurrent theme in popular press accounts. "This place is churning out millionaires," said one Silicon Valley real estate mogul to explain the record sales of his brokers, who recently sold $300 million worth of property in a single month, much of it above asking prices.[10] As in the real estate market, so too in the market for fine wines. Prices for these wines are soaring less because American palates have grown more sophisticated than because they are being bought up by people with a sudden excess of cash in their pockets. "Wall Street has a lot to do with it," complained one collector about the spiraling prices of classed-growth Bordeaux. "They get their bonuses at the end of the year and it ruins the market. . . . I've sat next to people at auction who turn to me and say, 'Is that a good buy?' "[11]

Wall Street firms paid out more than $8.1 billion in bonuses in 1997, an average of $54,000 per employee. Checks ranged from $10 million or more for the biggest winners to only a few thousand for clerks.[12] Roughly a thousand Wall Street professionals received bonuses in excess of $1 million in 1997–98.[13] Goldman Sachs alone made roughly $3 billion in fiscal 1997, the bulk of which is apportioned among its 190 most senior directors. Although their "current compensation," is typically less than $4 million annually, many of these directors take away nearly four times that amount in bonus money.[14] One layer down in the hierarchy, Goldman's 215 managing directors can expect to take home an average of $1.5 million in 1998 bonus money.[15]

The timing of these checks correlates closely with luxury spending bursts in several areas. For example, New York area exotic car dealers report that the bulk of their sales go to Wall Streeters during the peak bonus months from December through March.[16] During those months in the winter of 1997, Pray Porsche in nearby Greenwich, Connecticut, depleted its large inventory of 911 Turbos, many with sticker prices as high as $160,000.[17]

The recent boom in summer rentals in the Hamptons has also been attributed to soaring bonuses on Wall Street. "You have a young couple in their 20s who both have significant income and they just bought a city co-op and they'll come out and rent a house for $60,000, $70,000 for the summer," explains Diane Saatchi, president of the Dayton-Halstead real estate agency in East Hampton.[18] Soaring Wall Street bonuses also help account for the increased demand for cosmetic surgery in New York, according to an area physician whose operations on young male stockbrokers have risen six-fold since the current bull market began.[19]

The same stock market boom that has produced the record brokers' bonuses has also increased the wealth of millions of citizens across the country. By mid 1998, for example, the Dow Jones Industrial Average was about nine times higher than it had been just 20 years earlier. With portfolios that have more than doubled in the last several years alone, many more families can easily afford to part with $50,000 for their new BMW 540i sedans.

Yet another explanation of recent luxury consumption growth is the changing demographic profile of the postwar baby boomers. The leading edge of this huge population cohort is just entering its 50s, traditionally the peak earnings years. And many have begun to savor additional spending power as their children finish college and take jobs of their own.

But although these demographic shifts matter, they account for only a small proportion of the recent surge in luxury spending. Far more important has been the unusually rapid growth in the incomes of top earners in every demographic category. When people at the top earn more, they spend more; and little of the extra spending goes for necessities, since these people have long since acquired everything they might be reasonably said to need.

WILL CURRENT TRENDS CONTINUE?

If growing disparities in the distribution of income are indeed the primary explanation for the recent surge of spending on luxury goods, those who would forecast how spending patterns will evolve must look to the forces that have been driving the recent growth in income inequality. What are these forces, and are they likely to continue? Or will we revert to earlier patterns, in which income grew at roughly the same rate up and down the income ladder?

Although much has been written about the recent growth in income inequality, there remains considerable disagreement about its causes. Some commentators, for example, mention changes in public policy, citing tax cuts for the wealthy and program cuts for the poor. Others emphasize the decline of labor unions, the downsizing of corporations, and the growing impact of foreign trade. Economists stress changes in the amount of, and rate of return on, people's "human capital"—an amalgam of education, training, intelligence, energy, and other factors that influence individual productivity. Commentators on the left often see darker causes, citing market imperfections that allow the rich to set their own terms in a world increasingly insulated from competition and social inhibitions against greed.

But even though there may be an element of truth in most of these claims, each misses something essential. Lower tax rates on the rich have undoubtedly made the distribution of income less equal than it would have been, for example, but the explosive growth of top salaries was well under way even before the major tax cuts enacted in 1986. Increased competition from abroad may also have played a role, but only a supporting one. Thus competition from low-wage workers in other lands may have dampened wage growth among the least skilled workers in the United States, but this cannot explain why inequality is growing sharply even within occupations—such as dentists—that are virtually unaffected by foreign competition. Nor has competition from the most skilled workers in developing countries—software engineers in Mumbai, for instance—prevented their American counterparts from enjoying brisk salary growth.

Education, training, and the other components of human capital are obviously important determinants of salary differences, just as the conventional economic wisdom insists. Yet even these factors cannot explain the recent growth in top earnings, for as best we can measure, the population from which today's economic superstars are drawn is neither better trained nor more intelligent than its predecessors. There is some evidence that the rate of return to education has risen during the last 15 years, but that cannot explain why income inequality has also grown sharply even among college graduates.

Growing social tolerance of acquisitiveness and greed may be a contributing factor, but similar attitudes prevailed in the 1920s and 1950s, and a much smaller share of our national income went to top performers during those periods. And if any one thing is certain, it is that growing income inequality has not resulted from any weakening of market forces. On the contrary, global and domestic competition has never been more intense than now.

THE SPREAD OF WINNER-TAKE-ALL MARKETS

In our recent book, Philip Cook and I argued that the recent surge in earnings inequality stems, in large part, from the growing importance of what we call "winner-take-all markets"—markets in which small differences in performance often give rise to enormous differences in economic reward.[20] Long familiar in entertainment, sports, and the arts, these markets have increasingly permeated accounting, law, journalism, consulting, medicine, investment banking, corporate management, publishing, design, fashion, and a host of other professions. To understand the recent surge in earnings inequality, and hence to predict future income and consumption patterns, it is helpful to look briefly at the forces that give rise to winner-take-all markets. (The material that follows is developed in much more detail in *The Winner-Take-All Society*, whose readers may wish to skip this chapter and move directly to chapter 4.)

Winner-take-all markets have proliferated in part because technology has greatly extended the power and reach of the planet's most gifted performers. At the turn of the century, when the state of Iowa alone had more than 1,300 opera houses, thousands of tenors earned adequate, if modest, livings performing before live audiences.[21] Now that most music we listen to is prerecorded, however, the world's best tenor can be literally everywhere at once. And since it costs no more to stamp out compact discs from Luciano Pavarotti's master recording than from a less renowned tenor's, most of us now listen to Pavarotti. Millions of us are each willing to pay a little extra to hear him rather than other singers who are only marginally less able or well known; and this explains why Pavarotti earns several million dollars a year even as most other tenors, many of them nearly as talented, struggle to get by.

Although the details of the transformation differ from arena to arena, the essence of the story remains fundamentally the same. For example, the tax-advice industry, once the almost exclusive domain of the small-scale local practitioner, has gone through at least two similar waves of upheaval during recent decades. First came the national accounting franchises, such as H & R Block, which discovered how to delegate many of the routine chores to part-time nonprofessionals. And now, tax software for the masses. Although the move from the solo-practitioner era to the franchise era increased the concentration of industry earnings at the top, the market was still able to provide a good livelihood for a large number of players. In the software era, by contrast, developers compete intensively to develop the most comprehensive, user-friendly software, whereupon the market chooses only a handful of winners—most notably, Intuit's TurboTax® and MacInTax® programs. The people who oversaw these projects may have been only marginally better than their nearest competitors, yet the difference in their rewards has been dramatic.

Similarly, the able lawyer who once sued for $10,000 on behalf of a client with a stiff neck now heads a team that battles for several billion in a class-action suit. The gifted portfolio manager who once guided a small firm's pension fund now oversees a global consolidated trust. And just as the printing press enabled a handful of the world's best storytellers to replace millions of village raconteurs centuries earlier, electronic newswire services and regional printing facilities today allow a small number of syndicated columnists to displace thousands of local journalists. The common thread in these transformations is that technical forces have enabled top performers to serve broader or more valuable segments of their respective markets.

In all these markets, small differences in relative performance give rise to enormous differences in income. The celebrity columnist who appears on a weekly television news panel and earns $15,000 per appearance on the corporate lecture circuit is often only slightly more talented, or lucky, than his peers who live on modest local newspaper salaries. Likewise the class-action attorneys who collect 40 percent of their clients' multimillion-dollar judgments are often only slightly more able than the lawyers who contest five-figure lawsuits. And the portfolio manager who earns millions overseeing a global trust may be only marginally better informed than her modestly paid rivals who supervise the pension funds of small companies.

The dependence of economic reward on performance ranking is, of course, nothing new. What is new is the rapid erosion of the barriers that once prevented the top performers from serving broader markets. In the music industry, the driving force was the arrival of breathtakingly lifelike prerecorded music. Changes in physical production technologies have been important in other industries as well, but these changes often explain only a small part of the picture.

Of central importance in many instances has been the emergence of the so-called information revolution. In the global village, there is unprecedented market consensus on who the top players are in each arena, and unprecedented opportunity to deal with these players. A company that made the best refrigerator in the Midwest was once assured of being a player in at least its own regional appliance market. But today's sophisticated consumers increasingly purchase their appliances from only a handful of the best manufacturers worldwide. Armed with this insight more than a decade ago, GE's chairman Jack Welch instructed his managers to sell off any division whose product was not among the top three in its U.S. market, and the company's subsequent performance has provided no reason to question the wisdom of this strategy.

THE ERA OF GLOBAL FREE AGENCY

For top performers to earn multimillion-dollar salaries, it is not sufficient that they generate commensurate value for their employers. There must also be effective competition for their services. Yet, in many markets, a variety of formal and informal rules traditionally prevented such competition.

Most major sports leagues, for example, once maintained restrictive agreements that prevented team owners from bidding for one another's star players. These agreements were first challenged in the courts in the mid-1970s, and by now, players have won at least limited free-agency rights in all the major professional team sports. It was the erosion of these barriers that caused the explosion of professional athletes' salaries to begin in earnest.

Unlike the owners of professional sports teams, the owners of businesses were never subject to formal sanctions against bidding for one another's most talented employees. Informal norms, however, often seemed to have virtually the same effect. Under these norms, it was an almost universal practice to promote business executives from within, enabling companies to retain top executives for a small fraction of today's salaries.

The anti-raiding norms of business have been eroding rapidly. As recently as 1984, the business community arched its collective eyebrow when Apple Computer hired a new chief executive with a background in soft-drink marketing. But since then, company and industry borders have become increasingly open, with the result that business executives and other professionals are today little different from the free agents of professional sports. Thus no one expressed surprise in April of 1993 when Louis Gerstner left RJR Nabisco to head up IBM, whose stock has risen more than five-fold since then. Firms that fail to pay standout executives their due now stand to lose them to aggressive rivals. The number of leading U.S. corporations that brought in CEOs from the outside has grown almost 50 percent during the past 20 years.[22] Even those companies that continue to promote from within find themselves under steadily growing pressure to match salary standards established in the open market.

CEOs are not the only ones for whom free agency has increasingly become the norm. In earlier decades, most workers could reasonably expect that once they were hired and launched upon their respective career trajectories within large firms, their wages and other conditions of employment would be relatively insulated from the vicissitudes of the external marketplace. According to several recent studies, however, the wages of even manufacturing workers have become significantly more sensitive to external labor market conditions.[23]

A SPREADING PATTERN

Looking to the future, can we expect the recent growth in income inequality to diminish, or should we expect the trends that have been driving the current luxury consumption boom to continue? On the technology side, the forces that enable top performers to serve broader markets show no signs of abating. Despite all the media hype inspired by the information revolution, a majority of families in the United States are still not connected to the Internet—and this despite double-digit growth rates in the number of families connected for most of the past decade. As more and more people go on-line around the world, the ability of gifted producers to displace incumbents in distant markets will inexorably grow.

Such growth will be abetted by the continuing spread of free-trade agreements promising to eliminate the few remaining barriers to global competition. With ongoing improvements in transportation technology, the cost of shipping goods across long distances will continue to fall. This effect will be reinforced by continuing growth in the dollar value of goods per pound. A growing share of the value embodied in computers, for instance, resides not in the materials used to manufacture their hardware, but in the intellectual capital that lies behind that hardware and the software required to run them.

In some industries, successful new formulas have been discovered and proven out in many markets but have not yet spread fully to other markets. Starbucks, for example, has displaced thousands of local coffee retailers in major cities but has yet to open franchises in small communities like Ithaca, New York, which also does not yet have a Borders bookstore. Income disparities can be expected to grow further as these winning formulas continue to spread.

In still other cases, such as the automobile repair business, diffusion of the winning formula appears even less far along. Automobile repairs were traditionally performed almost start-to-finish by a single, jack-of-all-trades mechanic. The same man diagnosed the problem, retrieved the parts, and installed them on the car. This model will increasingly give way to an alternative structure in which a highly skilled and experienced master mechanic employs sophisticated electronic equipment to diagnose what needs to be done, then transmits orders to a battery of specialized assistants who, by comparison to traditional auto mechanics, are relatively unskilled. One does nothing but remove defective parts; another retrieves replacement parts from inventory; another bolts the new parts in; and still others specialize in fluid changes, wheel rotation, and other routine maintenance operations. As traditional auto repair businesses continue to be displaced by this new model, the distribution of earned income in the auto repair industry will evolve along the same lines we saw in the tax-advice industry, with similar implications for spending patterns.

The potential for even more dramatic change looms ahead in online retailing. Investors have wagered heavily that firms like Amazon.com will completely transform how books make their way from publishers to retail buyers. Many similar efforts are already underway in other industries, each with the potential to displace a host of small-scale retail enterprises. The issue is not whether these changes will lead to further skewness in the distribution of income but rather by how much.

Perhaps the most telling change of all, however, will be the continuing breakdown of barriers that limit competition for the services of the best performers. In the market for executive talent, for example, these barriers have largely disappeared in the United States but remain strong in many other industrial nations. This explains why chief executives in Germany and Japan, who are arguably just as productive as those in this country, currently earn considerably less. According to the estimates of compensation consultant Graef Crystal, German and Japanese CEOs earn not hundreds of times as much as the average worker, but less than 25 times as much.[24] There is simply no reason to expect that the promotion-from-within norms still prevailing in those countries will withstand competitive pressure indefinitely. Thus, as we move inexorably toward a single global market economy, the executive paychecks at Honda and Ford will continue to converge. The American pattern has already spread widely in the United Kingdom, where the richest 20 percent now earn more than seven times as much as the poorest 20 percent, up from four times as much in 1977.[25] And whereas the poorest 10th in Britain are 13 percent worse off in real terms than they were in 1979, the richest 10th are now 65 per cent better off.[26] The gap between males with the highest wage rates and those with the lowest wage rates is larger now in Britain than at any time since the 1880s, when statistics on wages were first gathered systematically.[27]

Yet despite the recent growth in earnings inequality in the United Kingdom, the income distribution there remains considerably more egalitarian than in the United States. And even within this country, there remains considerable room for earnings inequality to grow further. For example, a 1997 study by the Center on Budget and Policy Priorities, a Washington, D.C., research group, reported that the top 20 percent of earners in the bellwether state of New York took home almost 20 times as much as the bottom 20 percent in 1996, compared to the national average of less than 13.[28] (These figures do not include New Yorkers' considerable earnings from capital gains.) The corresponding ratio for egalitarian Utah was nearly the same as in the United Kingdom, just over 7.[29]

In sum, as the market forces unleashed in the United States and the United Kingdom continue to spread, the share of the economic pie captured by those near the top is likely to continue to grow rapidly,

even as those further down the ladder struggle to hold their own. And
with continued growth in the disparity of incomes, we can look forward to continued growth in the share of the world's resources spent
on luxury consumption goods.

Is this a problem? Many will respond that if people work hard and
play by the rules, why shouldn't they spend their money in whatever
ways they please? I hasten to emphasize that it is not my claim that the
current luxury consumption boom, by itself, has been a bad thing. Indeed, there is much to admire among the many fine products spawned
by this boom, and if historical patterns persist, we may expect that
much of the new technology embedded in these products will soon
find its way into the goods and services consumed by middle- and
lower-income families.

At the same time, luxury goods and services cost real resources to
produce, resources that we could have put to other uses. In the end, it
is a question of balance. If we stand back and consider all the possible
things we could have bought with our money, can we say that the recent changes in our spending patterns constitute an improvement? Do
we simply have more of everything now, or have we had to give up important things to pay our bills? To these questions, let us now turn.

CHAPTER 4

THE PRICE OF LUXURY

It is not just the rich who have gone on a spending spree. Middle- and lower-income earners have been spending more as well. The prime mover in this change may have been the increased spending of the superrich, but their higher spending level has set a new standard for the near-rich to emulate, and so on down the income ladder. But although middle- and lower-income families are spending much more than in the recent past, the incomes of these families have not been growing. The median earner in the United States has essentially the same income now, in real terms, as in 1979, and earnings of those in the bottom 20 percent of the income distribution have actually declined by more than 10 percent during the same time span. These consumers have thus been forced to finance their consumption increases largely by reduced savings and increased debt. The U.S personal savings rate, which now stands at roughly 5 percent, is down almost 40 percent since 1980.[1]

BURGEONING CONSUMER DEBT

Americans in the lower reaches of the income distribution never saved much to begin with, so for most of these people, every extra dollar of spending has meant an extra dollar of consumer debt. A disproportionate acceleration of credit-card debt has occurred among lower-income Americans, those with annual incomes less than $25,000.[2] According to David Wyss, research director of DRI/McGraw-Hill, 27 percent of families with household incomes less than $10,000 now have credit-card obligations that exceed 40 percent of their incomes. Fewer than 5 percent of families earning more than $50,000 are burdened to that extent by credit-card debt.[3]

Overall, credit-card debt as a percentage of household disposable income is up 60 percent since 1989.[4] Total household debt grew from 56 percent of disposable personal income in 1983 to 81 percent by the beginning of 1995, at which point home mortgage debt stood at $3.15 trillion and consumer installment credit was more than $900 billion.[5] At prevailing credit-card interest rates, that translates into more than $100 billion a year in credit-card interest alone.

Much of this increased consumer debt has been facilitated by a proliferation of bank credit offerings. Banks sent out 2.7 billion preapproved credit-card solicitations in 1995—an average of 17 to every American between 18 and 64.[6] *The Guinness Book of World Records* lists Walter Cavanaugh, a middle-aged California man, as having the largest number of active credit cards—1,262 as of 1995. Cavanaugh, whose total credit limit on these cards as of 1995 was $1.6 million, has had an application rejected only once.[7]

Indeed, the issuers of bank cards positively encourage consumers to carry unpaid balances. My own credit-card company cheerfully announces on my bill each month that, because of my excellent credit history, I am free to take a "payment holiday." (I am free, in other words, to pay them 17 percent interest on any balance I carry forward.) Another card company told me that I would receive triple frequent-flyer bonus miles for each month I failed to pay my entire balance. General Electric Company now levies a $25 annual penalty on GE Rewards MasterCard accounts that are paid in full.[8]

The incentives that generate these moves are clear: Credit-card issuers can borrow money at 4 to 5 percent and then charge 17 percent or more on unpaid balances, a point spread sufficient to generate profits of $12.5 billion in 1996.[9]

For those whose credit-card limits prevent them from charging their vacation expenses, Credit Bank MBNA now has a joint venture with Princess Cruise Lines in which consumers can enjoy seven-day, six-island tours financed by monthly payments spread out over four years.[10] And used-car lender Jayhawk Acceptance Corporation recently diversified its business by offering installment loans to finance breast augmentation and other cosmetic surgery.[11] The program has proved popular, and in early 1997 Jayhawk reported that it was adding 300 new surgeons per month to its group of participating doctors.[12] In a similar plan, MedCash LP, of Mission, Kansas, has issued elective-surgery credit cards to 35,000 potential patients. The MedCash card extends credit lines of up to $15,000 at an annual interest rate of almost 22 percent.[13]

There are broad indications, both anecdotal and systematic, that these offerings have led many consumers to spend beyond their means. Thus the amount of credit-card debt more than 90 days' overdue nearly doubled between 1994 and 1996.[14] Credit-card delinquency rates rose 44 percent between 1994 and 1995.[15] Debtors Anonymous groups now hold some 45 weekly meetings in the San Francisco Bay Area alone.[16] And a recent *Wall Street Journal* poll reported that 26 percent of respondents live paycheck to paycheck, up from 20 percent in 1989.[17]

Individual case histories suggest the flavor of the problem. Deborah Gross, a 26-year-old Fort Worth secretary, negotiated an agreement in 1994 whereby her creditors rescheduled $4,500 worth of overdue credit-card debt into a single, interest-free monthly payment. She then took on an additional $145 monthly payment in 1996 to cover her loan from Jayhawk for breast-implant surgery. "It sounded too good to be true," she said. "I hope they're still around to approve me again three or four years down the road if I decide to have something else done."[18]

THE BANKRUPTCY BOOM

Diane Curran, a teacher in Syracuse, New York, accumulated $27,452 of debt on a dozen credit cards and other loans. She continued to receive new solicitations even when her monthly payments equaled her take-home pay—payments she often met with the new credit available through an additional card. She was forced to file for bankruptcy when she was finally denied a new advance. "I wish somebody had cut me off 10 years earlier," she lamented.[19]

Even people who have just emerged from bankruptcy proceedings often have no difficulty securing credit. A recent *Wall Street Journal* article describes a former stockbroker who "declared bankruptcy in 1992 after charging up $90,000 in debt, including $25,000 on a single MBNA card. Now employed as a car salesman and earning $100,000 a year, he has a $125,000 mortgage, 15 new credit cards and a $15,000 line of available credit."[20]

Personal bankruptcy filings rose 23 percent between 1994 and 1995.[21] More than 1.1 million Americans filed for bankruptcy in 1996 alone—an all-time high and more than twice the number who filed in 1986. This means more than one U.S. family in 100 went through bankruptcy in 1996.[22] Filings again surged in 1997, hitting 1.4 million, or one for every 70 households.[23]

Bankruptcy was once primarily the province of formerly well-to-do people who had suffered heavy losses on business investments. But the average income of people filing for bankruptcy has been falling steadily.[24] In a study of personal bankruptcies in 13 cities, the Consumer Federation of America reported that the after-tax incomes of Chapter 7 bankruptcy filers averaged $19,800 in 1996, just slightly more than their average credit-card debt of $17,544.[25]

RECENT REDUCTIONS IN INCONSPICUOUS CONSUMPTION

Our increased consumption spending has come at the expense of not only lower savings and greater debt but also many other things we value. Foremost among these has been the amount of time we have away from work. The historical presumption was that steadily rising labor productivity would lead to ever shorter workweeks, and this was in fact the pattern for at least the century prior to 1950.[26] But this pattern was not to endure. In his 1970 book, *The Harried Leisure Class,* Staffan Linder was the first to call our attention to the paradox that growing affluence would make ever stronger demands on our time: "There will be an increasingly hectic tempo of life," he predicted, "marked by careful attempts to economize on increasingly scarce time."[27]

Linder's prediction was right on the money. Thus, as the economist Juliet Schor has argued in *The Overworked American,* the downward trajectory in the workweek stabilized shortly after World War II and has been trending steadily upward since the late 1960s. Schor estimates that the increases have been substantial for both men and women, but particularly for women, who worked an average of 22 percent more hours in 1987 than they had in 1969.[28]

Schor's findings were challenged in *Time for Life,* a widely discussed 1997 book by leisure-time analysts John Robinson and Geoffrey Godbey. Instead of relying on massive government surveys that ask subjects to recall how much they worked in the past weeks or months, Robinson and Godbey used detailed time-study diaries filled out each day by a much smaller number of subjects. On the basis of data drawn from these diaries, the authors claim that Americans were actually working slightly fewer hours in 1985 than they were two decades earlier. Part of the reason, they explain, is that subjects in 1985 were more likely than those in 1965 to take time during their normal workdays to make personal phone calls and perform other personal errands.

Robinson and Godbey have attracted critics of their own. Schor, for example, attributes their finding to the fact that their base-year sample contained an unrepresentatively large number of people who worked long hours. Thus, she explains, the time diaries show no decline in measured hours of work after a representative sample was adopted in 1975.[29] In a similar vein, Dale Dauten questions the wisdom of trying to generalize from the behavior of people with enough time to fill out time diaries in the first place: "The professors cite one survey that reported 32 percent of the respondents have done needlepoint in the past year. One out of three Americans, male and female? Hey, there isn't even a needlepoint cable channel."[30]

Despite their claims that the time we spend actually working has fallen slightly, Godbey and Robinson concede that people today feel considerably more time pressure than in the past. They also concede that time spent in the workplace is greater for most people now than in

1965, and that the same is true of the actual number of hours spent working in the case of several important groups—more educated workers, those with higher incomes, and those with families. The latter finding is consistent with Bureau of Labor Statistics data that show the proportion of professionals and managers working extremely long hours (49 or more each week) is up 37 percent since 1985.[31]

Although Godbey and Robinson were not the only ones to challenge Schor's findings,[32] the notion that we are spending more time at the office has also received support from a variety of other sources. The economist Paul Wallich, for example, reported in *Scientific American* that Americans' leisure time has declined steadily during the postwar era despite the fact that our productivity has more than doubled during that period.[33] In a 1992 survey by sociologist Robert Wuthnow, 66 percent of respondents reported working longer hours than they had five years earlier.[34] A 1991 Louis Harris Survey reported that Americans work nearly 8 hours a week more than in 1973 and have 37 percent fewer hours available for leisure time.[35] In a recent Gallup Poll, 39 percent of respondents reported working more than 45 hours a week, one in eight more than 60.[36] And Bureau of Labor Statistics data suggest that women are working 233 more hours a year now than in 1976, men 100 more hours.[37]

Controversy over the trends in time spent actually working will undoubtedly continue to simmer, but for our purposes the more important issue is time spent *at* work. And here, there is a broad consensus that the numbers are up. Thus, as Sue Schnellenbarger, the *Wall Street Journal's* resident expert on home and work issues, recently summed up the debate: "The Schor camp is probably for you if you think all time spent at work should be counted as 'work' (the more important measure to those concerned with work's effect on family and community life)."[38] Since it is precisely these issues that will be our focus in much of what follows, I shall take this position, although none of my substantive conclusions depends critically on it.

With the increase in time spent at the office and in other nonwork activities, it is no surprise that time-study researchers report a growing sleep gap.[39] In one national survey, 4 respondents in 10 reported sleeping an average of six hours a night or less.[40] It is good to keep busy, no doubt, but there is also troubling evidence that chronic sleep deprivation contributes to many serious illnesses.[41] And according to one estimate, some 100,000 traffic accidents involving approximately 1,500 deaths are caused each year in the United States by drivers who fall asleep at the wheel.[42]

In a 1996 Survey by the Families and Work Institute, 40 percent of workers reported that they felt unable to get personal chores done because of extended work commitments; 35 percent complained of having insufficient personal time; and 24 percent complained of lacking time for their children.[43] The case studies reported by the sociologist Arlie Hochschild in her recent book *The Time Bind* provide vivid illustrations of these trends.[44] Although Hochschild reported that many people appear to choose longer working hours to escape stresses at home, there is also evidence that many feel uneasy about their growing attachments to the workplace. For instance, in one national survey, 77 percent of respondents expressed concern about being workaholics.[45]

American workers must also work longer now to obtain a day of paid vacation time. For example, a study by Primark Decision Economics, a Boston research firm, estimated that American workers received one day of paid vacation time for each 23.9 days of work in 1996, as compared to one for every 22.4 days of work in 1987.[46] A recent study by Hewitt Associates reported that the 10 days of annual paid vacation received by the average entry-level worker in the United States ranked dead last among a sample of 13 industrial nations. Ten of the 13 nations offered at least 20 paid vacation days to entry-level workers, and Austria offered 30.[47] Adding to the discrepancy is the fact that European nations typically have many more national holidays than we have in this country.

There are signs that American workers could use a little more time off. In a recent Gallup Survey done for Accountants on Call, 25 percent of workers reported that they experience significant stress on the job almost every day, and fewer than 12 percent reported their jobs to be generally free of such stress.[48]

Companies are clearly concerned about the effects of worker stress. Thus nearly 40 percent of employers in a recent survey were found to offer some type of help for handling stress, up from 27 percent in 1985.[49] Yet it is the work environment that companies themselves provide that seems to account for much of the stress. An International Survey Research Corporation study found that 46 percent of workers described themselves in 1995 as being frequently worried about being laid off, up from 22 percent in 1988. The same study found that in 1995, only half felt their jobs were secure if they performed well, down from 73 percent in 1988; and that 44 percent found their workload excessive in 1995, up from 37 percent in 1988.[50] Still another survey found that balancing the demands of work and family was a leading source of pressure for 74 percent of men and 78 percent of women.[51]

Another new source of stress is that workplaces are growing significantly smaller. Whereas just a decade ago, newly constructed office buildings allowed an average of 250 square feet of space per worker (including a proportionate share of a building's lobby, corridors, and restrooms) the current figure is close to 200 square feet, and the rapidly growing ranks of telemarketing employees and customer-service phone operators typically receive 100 square feet or less.[52] In some locations, conditions are more crowded still. "You're literally getting guys into 60 or 70 square feet," complains Patrick Moultrup, president of a nationwide group of real-estate firms. These cuts are usually accomplished by relegating employees to space-saving cubicles and eliminating private offices.[53]

Along with smaller workspaces, American workers are having to make do with fewer and smaller parking spaces. Sharon Dunnam, a manager at AT&T's suburban Indianapolis office, has a reserved parking spot and thus has no difficulty parking when she arrives at work. But when she went out for lunch recently with a colleague who lacked a reserved spot, she experienced for the first time the stress that for many has become a routine element in arriving for work: "As they circled various AT&T parking lots, her 12-story office building receded into the distance. 'It took us forever,' she griped. AT&T employees who dare venture out, she discovered, 'could spend the better part of their lunch hour looking for parking.' "[54]

Such situations have grown increasingly common. As one sales agent complained, "Every one of their parking lots is busting at the seams. Sometimes when I go to see clients, it takes me 10 minutes to find a spot."[55] Some companies have responded by repainting the parking stripes closer together to create additional spots.[56] But whereas this obviously makes it easier for workers to find a spot, at least for the time being, it introduces stress of yet another form.

SACRIFICES IN THE PUBLIC SPHERE

As economists never tire of saying, there is no free lunch. To pay for larger and more elaborate consumption goods, we must devote fewer resources to other things. In many of the cases just considered, the trade-off was between one form of private consumption and another. For instance, one cost of having more luxurious cars has been having to spend more time at the office, less time with family and friends.

Paying for luxury consumption has also meant having to curtail spending in the public sphere. Apart from high rates of increase in public spending on medical care and income transfers for the elderly, the past two decades have been a time of across-the-board retrenchment in public goods and services of all sorts. Some of the programs that were cut probably never should have been implemented in the first place. But many others delivered good value for the money.

If a government program is to be cut, it should be for the right reason—namely, that it fails to deliver value commensurate with its price tag. There are surely many such government programs—subsidies to tobacco growers spring to mind. Yet, as even the staunchest critics of government freely concede, many other programs yield benefits that far exceed their costs. In today's sterile political discourse, however, this cost-benefit discussion seldom even makes the agenda.

Suppose that we were somehow able to slow the rate at which our expenditures on luxury goods have been growing. Would there be valuable uses in the public sphere for the money thus freed up? Some examples:

Clean Drinking Water

Most Americans draw their tap water from municipal water systems, many of which were constructed early in this century. Typical conduits in these systems were cast-iron fittings joined by lead solder. Gray cast iron normally contains 0.4 to 0.6 percent manganese, and as the conduits age and rust, lead, manganese, and other toxic metals leach into our drinking water. As the superintendent of one municipal water department in New England described a recent repair operation, "When we dismantled the standpipe, we found two and a half feet of a substance with the consistency of pudding."[57] According to one estimate, some 45 million Americans are served by water systems that deliver potentially dangerous levels of toxic metals, pesticides, and parasites.[58]

Children are especially sensitive to lead, which can cause brain damage, related behavioral and learning problems, hearing loss, and slow growth. Extremely high levels of lead produce severe clinical symptoms, but more subtle forms of damage are found even in children who present no clinical symptoms. Thus, in one large sample of such children, those with relatively high levels of lead in their bodies scored more than five points lower on a standard IQ test than those with relatively low levels of lead.[59] Another study found that "reducing the burden of lead in the child with chelating agents, usually penicillamine, brings about a substantial IQ increase (typically of 7 IQ points) in about two children out of three."[60] According to the U.S. Environmental Protection Agency (EPA), about 1.7 million American children currently have unsafe levels of lead in their blood.[61]

Although adults absorb only 8 percent of the lead they ingest, as compared to 50 percent for children, lead exposure can also cause serious health problems in adults.[62] These include infertility, high blood pressure, muscle and joint pain, digestive and nerve disorders, memory loss, and concentration problems.[63] Lead exposure in adults has also been linked with impulse-control problems and violent behavior.[64]

Compared with the toxic effects of lead, those of manganese have been less widely studied. It has long been known, however, that high levels of exposure can damage the central nervous system in ways that produce clinical symptoms similar to Parkinson's disease.[65] At lower levels of exposure, neuronal uptake of manganese reduces neuronal levels of the neurotransmitters dopamine and serotonin, and has been associated with impulsive violence and other impulse-control disorders.[66]

The serious consequences of exposure to toxic metals in our water supply are entirely preventable. Although it would not be cheap to replace the pipes and fittings in municipal water-supply systems, it is an investment well worth making. Yet many communities insist they cannot afford to make it.

Air-Quality Standards

Throughout the 1980s, Provo, Utah, had air quality that was, on average, roughly in compliance with existing EPA standards. Most of its air pollution came from cars and from a single steel mill that operated in the isolated mountain valley in which the city is located. In the late 1980s, a labor dispute shut the steel mill down for 13 months, providing a natural experiment for assessing the effect of air quality on human health. Professor C. Arden Pope, an environmental economist at Brigham Young University, used records from Provo's three hospitals to compare the number of admissions for respiratory illnesses before, during, and after the steel plant closure. His findings were striking. When the mill was in operation, admissions ran 40 percent higher for bronchitis and 17 percent higher for pneumonia than during the months it was closed. For preschool children, the differences were even larger—only half as many admissions for asthma and bronchitis during the plant shutdown.[67]

Epidemiologists estimate the annual toll from air pollution at roughly 50,000 deaths a year in the United States—more than the number that die each year in automobile accidents. Two of the most important contributors to these deaths are ozone and particulate matter (soot and other fine particles). Studies in nine major U.S. cities show that daily mortality rates increase with the concentration of ozone in the air, even when this concentration is well within legal limits.[68] And a six-city study found that residents of the city with the highest concentration of particulate matter (Steubenville, Ohio) had 25 percent higher mortality rates than those in the city with the lowest concentration (Portage, Wisconsin). Virtually all of the excess deaths were from lung cancer and cardiopulmonary disease.[69]

Spurred by these findings, the Environmental Protection Agency recently proposed a tightening of existing standards for concentrations of ozone and particulate matter in the air.[70] According to agency estimates, compliance with the tighter ozone standard would prevent millions of cases of diminished lung capacity and reduce the cases of acute respiratory distress by more than 140,000 a year; compliance with more stringent particulate standards would save more than 15,000 lives a year and avoid 8,000 hospitalizations. The EPA also estimated that the annual increase in total compliance costs resulting from the tighter standards would be approximately $9 billion.[71]

The EPA proposal drew intense and immediate political fire. Even Senator John Chafee (R, Rhode Island), normally a strong supporter of environmental legislation, was vocal in his opposition to it. Chafee did not question the evidence that existing concentrations of particulate matter and ozone cause serious health problems. Rather, his objections were based on cost. In times of budgetary stress, he seemed to be saying, we simply could not afford tougher air-quality standards.[72] And in July of 1997, Senators Jim Inhofe (R, Oklahoma) and John Breaux (D, Louisiana) introduced a bill to repeal the EPA's new standards.[73] A companion bill was introduced in the House.

Beef Inspection

Although the bacterial strain E-coli 0157 was first identified by scientists in 1982, few people had heard of it before 1993, when it was implicated in the illnesses of hundreds of people who had eaten hamburgers at Jack in the Box restaurants in four western states. Four children died in that episode. Other outbreaks have been traced to contaminated water and raw vegetables, but the primary source of infection is, as in the Jack in the Box case, ground beef. Found in the intestines of about 2 percent of all cattle, E-coli 0157 appear to cause the animals no difficulty. But if the bacteria are transmitted to humans when beef becomes contaminated by intestinal residues during the slaughtering process, they wreak havoc.

In humans, E-coli 0157 cause severe diarrhea, and often lead to intestinal bleeding. Among the most serious complications are intestinal perforation, heart attack, fluid in the lungs, seizures, strokes, coma, and death of organ tissue. Six percent of infections progress to a disease called hemolytic uremic syndrome (HUS), which causes damage to red blood cells, kidneys, and the brain.[74] The disease is fatal in more than 4 percent of cases, and many survivors suffer chronic kidney, heart, and neurological problems. Michael Osterholm, an epidemiologist at the Minnesota Department of Public Health, said "there is nothing in foodborne disease I fear more than HUS."[75]

Exposure to E-coli 0157 now causes an estimated 20,000 infections each year in the United States, and between 200 and 500 deaths.[76] If all beef were slaughtered and processed in strict accordance with Food and Drug Administration regulations, the risk of human exposure to E-coli 0157 in ground beef would be virtually eliminated. But enforcement of these regulations requires field teams to inspect the nation's meat-processing facilities, and in recent decades the number of federal inspectors not only has not grown, it has declined significantly.

For example, the Food and Drug Administration (FDA), which performed 21,000 inspections of food-processing plants in 1981, had the resources to inspect only 5,000 in 1997.[77] An important supplement to direct inspection of food at the processing stage are well-organized systems for reporting and tracking food-borne illnesses once they occur. And yet, as of September 1997, 12 states simply had no such systems in place.[78] Also lagging has been the ability of food inspectors to examine the dramatically higher levels of foodstuffs imported from other nations. Food imports into the United States have doubled since 1980s, but inspections of imports by the FDA have fallen by half during that same period.[79]

According to a recent study by a consumer watchdog group, the Washington-based Government Accountability Project, meat process-ing inspectors in Springfield, Illinois, recorded 17,577 instances in which they had not been able to perform expected inspection tasks in the fourth quarter of 1995, more than four times the number reported a year earlier.[80] Staff shortages recently resulted in one inspector's hav-ing to cover 19 Chicago-area processing plants in a single day. "That is totally unrealistic to cover a processing assignment," said David Carney, chairman of the National Joint Council of Food Inspection Locals.[81]

Given the seriousness of the illnesses caused by new strains of bac-teria, closer inspection of meatpacking and other food-processing plants is a good investment. But when budget cutbacks lead us to re-duce the number of inspections we perform, the clear message is that this is an investment we cannot afford.

Better Pay for Public School Teachers

People who choose public school teaching as a career seldom mention salary as an important motivating factor. Yet this does not mean that teacher pay is unimportant. After all, teachers have financial obliga-tions to meet, just like the rest of us. And as any public school adminis-trator can attest, qualified teachers become much more difficult to recruit whenever teachers' salaries fall too far behind the salaries that teachers could earn in other locations or occupations.

In relative terms, teachers have lost considerable salary ground over the last several decades. Thus the national average starting salary for primary and secondary school teachers fell from 118 percent of the average salary of college graduates in 1963 to only 97 percent in 1994.[82] And through much of this period, there has been a steady de-cline in the average SAT scores of people who choose public school teaching as a profession.[83]

Better quality teachers make an important difference in how well our children learn. In one recent study, for example, the economists Susanna Loeb and Marianne Page estimate that if teacher salaries had merely kept pace with the salaries available to comparably qualified professionals in other fields during the last three decades, then current school dropout rates would be 8.4 percent lower, and college enrollment rates about 4 percent higher, than their current levels.[84]

Children also learn more effectively in small classes than in larger ones. Researchers followed more than 6,000 elementary school students in Tennessee for four years, comparing the performance of students in small classes (13–17 students) with the performance of those in larger ones (22–25 students). Among second graders, for example, they found that 61 percent of students in small classes performed at or above the national average on the Stanford Achievement Test in reading, as compared with only 52 percent in larger classes. The corresponding figures for math were 76 percent and 68 percent.[85]

In September of 1996, the National Commission on Teaching and America's Future proposed "an audacious goal for America's future. Within a decade—by the year 2006—we will provide every student in America with what should be his or her educational birthright: access to competent, caring, qualified teaching in schools organized for success."[86] This is a worthy goal. To meet it, however, we will need to spend significantly more than we do now on teachers' salaries. And yet, in community after community, we say we cannot afford to.

Bridge and Highway Maintenance

Deferred maintenance is a pervasive problem on American roads and bridges. In McHenry County, Illinois, for example, fully one-third of the highways maintained by the state are "cracked, crumbled and overdue for repaving."[87] These roads are officially classified as being "in backlog," meaning that they should have been repaired long before reaching their current condition. Nationwide, according to one recent Federal Highway Administration estimate, more than 50 percent of our major roads and highways are in backlog.[88] And a recent U.S. Department of Transportation study reported an $84 billion backlog in the repair and replacement of the nation's bridges.[89]

When highway and bridge maintenance reaches the backlog stage, total costs begin to escalate sharply. Thus, according to Illinois Department of Transportation official William Yuskus, "you might get by for $125,000 to $150,000 per mile to patch and resurface a two-lane road" during the early stages of deterioration.[90] But postpone those repairs for two to three years and the cost of resurfacing goes up to $250,000 to $275,000 per mile. When maintenance is deferred still further, the underlying pavement quickly deteriorates to the point at which it has to be removed and completely replaced, an operation that costs $750,000 to $850,000 per mile, not counting the cost of restoring the landscaping that is damaged or destroyed in the process.[91]

Deferred maintenance imposes other costs. Potholes are destructive, as I discovered while driving on a freeway in Boston several years ago. When I failed to notice a huge pothole in time to avoid it, the impact destroyed a front tire and rim, which cost more than $200 to replace. Between blown tires and damaged wheels and axles, bent frames, misaligned front ends, destroyed mufflers, twisted suspension systems and other problems, potholes on U.S. roads cause an average of $120 worth of damage per vehicle each year.[92]

These are not the only, or even the most important, costs of deferred maintenance. Rutted roads and worn-out bridges are also dangerous. On April 5, 1987, for example, a 50-foot span of a bridge on the New York State Thruway suddenly collapsed, causing four cars and a tractor-trailer to plummet into raging Schoharie Creek below. In all, 10 lives were lost, and the state later settled wrongful death suits for damages ranging from $98,000 to $4.7 million each.[93] The bridge over Schoharie Creek was in backlog, as thousands of others were, and continue to be, throughout the country. No one knows how many serious accidents are caused by collapsed bridges and deep potholes, but the number surely is not small.

The nation's railroad crossings are also in a state of profound neglect. According to a recent study by the Federal Railroad Administration, for example, more than one-third of our 162,000 public highway-rail crossings have not been inspected in five or more years.[94] Frequent inspections save lives by helping to identify high-risk crossings in need of improved warning devices. Thus the state of Ohio, which recently mounted an intensive inspection campaign, saw its annual highway-rail crossing death toll fall from 45 to 13.[95] In most other states, however, inspections continue to lag.

Why don't we maintain our roads, bridges, and rail crossings any better? A drop in federal highway aid is partly to blame, according to Illinois Department of Transportation officials. And the problem figures to get worse. Thus, whereas federal highway funds to Illinois averaged $572 million annually from 1990 to 1997, they are projected to average only $482 million annually between 1997 and 2002.[96] Simply put, spending on highway and bridge maintenance is falling because of pressure to balance government budgets.

Yet timely maintenance of our bridges and highways is a good investment. Even if we ignore the savings that would result from reduced vehicle damage, injuries, and deaths, this investment would yield extremely high returns. The omnibus highway bill passed by Congress in 1998, although an important step, was simply too little, too late.

Drug Treatment and Prevention Programs

The crack cocaine epidemic that began in American cities in the 1980s has claimed literally hundreds of thousands of lives. Hundreds of thousands more have fallen to other hard drugs, such as heroin and methamphetamines, whose use rose steadily in the 1990s. The annual costs of drug abuse have been estimated in the hundreds of billions of dollars.[97] They include damages caused by the crimes that users and dealers are prone to commit; the incomes that many drug abusers forgo because they are unable, or unwilling, to work; the productivity lost because of drug use on the job; and the costs of apprehending, trying, and incarcerating the suppliers of illicit drugs—to say nothing of the pain and suffering experienced by most drug abusers and their families.

Most troubling of all, however, is the emotional and physical damage imposed on children born to drug-abusing parents. These problems afflicted our inner cities first, and they are occurring with growing frequency elsewhere. For example, a recent study revealed that 18 percent of a large sample of babies in Wichita, Kansas, tested positive for cocaine at birth.[98] Whereas the average hospital costs associated with a normal birthweight baby in Wichita were $3,700 at the time of this study, drug-exposed infants ran up hospital bills that averaged $150,000.[99] On top of these costs are the much more serious delayed costs incurred as these children develop attention-deficit disorders, behavioral disorders, and learning disabilities.

Yet the sad fact is that governments at every level have repeatedly cut back or refused to fund the drug counseling and treatment programs that have proven so effective in curbing this damage. In the scattered instances in which these programs have received adequate funding, they have been astonishingly successful investments. In Little Rock, Arkansas, for example, a comprehensive drug prevention program reduced drug-related low-birthweight births by more than 80 percent, and the number of drug-related crimes by 37 percent.[100] Project DREAM in Hattiesburg, Mississippi, which focused on teen drinking, resulted in a 45 percent decrease in the number of people under 21 arrested for drunk driving.[101]

Drug-prevention programs not only work but are also cheap, especially in relation to the enormous costs they prevent. A Rand Corporation study, for example, estimated that every $1 spent on cocaine prevention and treatment programs results in a $7 savings in law-enforcement and health-care expenses.[102] Yet consistently we say we cannot afford these programs.

The patterns we see in the United States are different in degree but not in kind from those that have begun to emerge in Europe and elsewhere. In each case, a growing share of national income is spent on consumption and, in each case, budget deficits increasingly threaten vital public services.

THE MOST SENSIBLE PATTERN?

Ever since the appearance of Adam Smith's *Wealth of Nations* in 1776, free-market economists have insisted that the self-seeking actions of consumers and firms produce, as if by an invisible hand, the best allocation of society's resources. But others can be forgiven for asking whether our current consumption patterns really satisfy this description.

The free-marketeer will invariably respond that if people would prefer to work fewer hours and buy fewer Patek Philippe wristwatches, they are free to do so. By the same token, people are free to vote for politicians who would spend more on clean air and water. Yet consistently people have chosen otherwise. Consumers know best what works for them, the free-marketeers say, and the fact that people have chosen the current mix is the strongest possible argument in its favor. This is a powerful claim—indeed, far more powerful than many critics of our current system seem to appreciate.

And perhaps it is even true, in the end, that the pleasure of having stoves with 15,000-BTU burners is more than enough to compensate for having to work weekends, for having to consume tainted food and water, for having to travel over unsafe highways and bridges. Yet we would be foolish to accept this conclusion as a simple matter of faith. The far more prudent course is to examine the best available evidence that bears on the relationship between consumption and human well-being.

CHAPTER 5

DOES MONEY BUY HAPPINESS?

Being a slave to money is a dead-end road, for money can
never bring us lasting happiness and peace.
            —Billy Graham

Those who say that money can't buy happiness don't know
where to shop.

            —Anonymous

In the preceding chapter, we saw numerous examples of seemingly
useful things we could have bought if we had been willing to settle
for slightly smaller houses and slightly less expensive automobiles.
Many social critics regard as self-evident that we would have done better to have spent our money differently. Yet the mere fact that there are
useful things we could have bought does not, by itself, imply that we
have chosen poorly. An alternative interpretation—the one strongly favored by defenders of the status quo—is that the pleasures of additional material goods are more than enough to compensate for the
sacrifices they make necessary in other areas. Life is full of trade-offs,
they say, and the people whose own money is at stake are in the best
possible position to resolve them.

Our goal in this chapter is to explore which of these competing interpretations is best supported by available evidence. If the defenders

of the status quo are correct, we should expect to find at least some indications that further accumulations of material goods continue to provide significant increments in satisfaction, even after countries achieve levels of affluence like those currently enjoyed in the United States. But as we shall see, the scientific literature provides no support at all for this position. Behavioral scientists find that once a threshold level of affluence is reached, the average level of human well-being in a country is almost completely independent of its stock of material consumption goods.

DOES HAPPINESS MATTER?

The sources of human satisfaction have been a subject of discussion and debate through the ages. Does happiness spring from wealth and power, romantic love, and steadily improving golf scores? Or do the sources of true and lasting happiness lie, as many insist, beyond the self—in helping others, or in religious devotion?

Philosophers have even questioned whether happiness, in and of itself, is an important human goal. Thus Robert Nozick asks us to imagine an opportunity to hook up to an "experience machine" capable of simulating any experience we might desire. This machine could "make you think and feel that you were writing a great novel, making a friend, or reading an interesting book. All the time you would be floating in a tank, with electrodes attached to your brain."[1] You could choose from a huge library of the experiences that have been found satisfying by people from all walks of life. You would even be free to program in intervals during which the machine would shut down, allowing you to reconsider and adjust your mix of experiences.

While the machine is in action, however, the experiences it delivers will constitute perfect virtual reality. Subjectively, you will experience them exactly as if they were actually happening. Given this opportunity, Nozick's question is, should you plug in?

He concedes the powerful attractions of doing so. Yet no matter how pleasurable the experiences you might imagine, he argues, there are even more compelling reasons for refusing the offer: "we want to *be* a certain way, to be a certain sort of person. Someone floating in a tank is an indeterminate blob. There is no answer to the question of what a person is like who has long been in the tank. Is he courageous, kind, intelligent, witty, loving? It's not merely that it's difficult to tell; there's no way he is. Plugging into the machine is a kind of suicide."[2]

Nozick's vivid thought experiment drives home the point that feeling happy is hardly the only important goal in life. And it reminds us that a society cannot be judged solely by how happy its citizens are. Perhaps most important, it underscores why freedom is such an important value. Given the multitude of competing conceptions of the good life, perhaps the most we can hope for in our social institutions is that they grant each of us the widest possible latitude to forge lives that suit us.

How are we to evaluate the extent to which an economy succeeds at this task? In the context of modern democracies in which fundamental political liberties have been assured, the approach most often taken by economists is simply to measure the aggregate value of the economy's goods and services. This sum is essentially the same as national income, and the presumption, explicit or implicit, is that the economy that serves up the largest per-capita national income is the one that best serves the interests of its citizens.

This is not as stupid as it sounds to many noneconomists. Critics lambaste national income as a measure of human welfare, noting that it is augmented by additional production of not only goods like food and shelter but also pollution-control equipment, burglar alarms, and drug counseling services.[3] Yet economists themselves are well aware that the composition of what we produce matters; they concede that the national income measure could be improved, in principle, by adjustments that take account of crime, pollution, diminished leisure, congestion, and other factors that affect the quality of life.

Another criticism of national income is that it ignores the value of work performed within the family. For instance, if a man marries his accountant, national income goes down even though the amount of accounting services she performs remains the same. To such complaints, economists respond that it would be perfectly acceptable to adjust national income to account for estimates of the value of work performed within the family.

Critics also complain that national income rises when sophisticated advertising campaigns manipulate us to buy goods and services we don't really need.[4] Yet economists are by no means oblivious to the fact that people often make foolish or ill-informed decisions about how to spend their money. It's an imperfect world, they concede. But does that mean we'd be better off if we entrusted government with the decision of what goods to produce? The unhappy experience of collectively managed economies provides little support for that alternative.

Despite the obvious shortcomings of using national income as a measure of national well-being, economists believe that it has one deeply attractive feature—namely, that the larger per-capita national income is, the more resources people will have for pursuing their respective visions of the good life.

The economist's belief that national income is a good measure of national well-being is not predicated on the view that happiness is the only thing that matters. Yet neither does it imply that happiness is unimportant. On the contrary, if happiness could actually be measured, most economists would predict that people in rich countries would be happier, on the average, than people in poor countries; and that, in an environment in which incomes are rising over time, people should be happier today, on the average, than they were in earlier times.

Unlike economists, psychologists and other behavioral scientists tend to have few preconceptions about the extent to which free-market transactions promote human satisfaction. Their approach is an empirical one that attempts to measure human satisfaction and identify the factors that influence it. Whereas economists simply *assume* that money buys satisfaction (because having more of it broadens one's options), psychologists try to measure individual differences in satisfaction and then investigate how these differences are related to differences in income and other factors.

Measuring Subjective Well-Being

In the economist's parlance, it is customary to speak not of happiness but of utility. The analogous construct in the psychological literature is *subjective well-being,* a composite measure of overall life satisfaction. For present purposes, little will be lost if we view both expressions as being roughly synonymous with *satisfaction.*

Other things being equal, people who experience a greater balance of positive over negative emotions will tend to experience higher levels of subjective well-being. Yet the relationship between the balance of emotions someone experiences and her overall level of subjective well-being is by no means simple and deterministic. Although it might seem natural to think that a person must be either in a good mood or in a bad mood at any moment in time, in fact it is possible for people to experience both strong positive and strong negative emotions simultaneously.[5] Indeed, neuroscientists now recognize that positive and negative feelings are governed by two largely independent sets of neural circuitry,[6] and that emotions in the two classes are not strongly correlated with one another.[7]

The stereotypically happy person is someone who experiences frequent and intense levels of positive affect, and infrequent and mild levels of negative affect. By contrast, the stereotypically unhappy person is someone for whom frequent and intense levels of negative affect are coupled with infrequent and mild levels of positive affect. People who experience high levels of both positive and negative affect are often described as volatile or highly emotional, while those with low levels on both scales are called phlegmatic. [8]

These stereotypes notwithstanding, an individual's overall level of happiness or life satisfaction is not perfectly correlated with the frequency and intensity of positive and negative affect. People who experience a preponderance of positive emotions are more likely than others to describe themselves as happy and to report high degrees of life satisfaction. Yet many such people describe their lives as unsatisfying, thereby confirming Nozick's skepticism about the quality of a life lived in an experience machine. Moreover, a significant proportion of people who do not experience a preponderance of positive emotions nonetheless report high levels of life satisfaction.

It thus appears that many factors other than the cumulative totals of positive and negative feelings enter into people's evaluations of their lives.[9] Even so, psychologists find that the overall balance between positive and negative affect is an important component of life satisfaction, and it hardly appears controversial to assume that most of us would prefer to feel happy rather than unhappy.

Psychologists measure life satisfaction in various ways. By far the most popular approach has been simply to ask people how happy or satisfied they are.[10] For example, people may be asked to respond, on a numerical scale, to a question like, "All things considered, how satisfied are you with your life as a whole these days?" Or, "Thinking of your life as a whole, would you consider yourself (*a*) very happy; (*b*) fairly happy; or (*c*) not happy."

Another approach measures the frequency and intensity of positive emotions by asking people the extent to which they agree with such statements as:

> When good things happen to me, it strongly affects me.
> I will often do things for no other reason than that they might be fun.
> When I get something I want, I feel excited and energized.
> When I'm doing well at something, I love to keep at it.[11]

Some find it difficult even to imagine that there are people who fail to agree strongly with such statements. Yet many individuals appear remarkably unresponsive to the kinds of circumstances that others find highly rewarding. The strength with which people agree with statements like the preceding ones turns out to be a consistent and reliable measure of high positive affect. High levels of negative affect are consistently associated with failure to agree with these statements.

More recently, neuroscientists have also used brainwave data to assess positive and negative affect. Subjects with relatively greater electrical activity in the left prefrontal region of the brain are likely to indicate strong agreement with statements like the previous ones, while those with relatively greater electrical activity in the right prefrontal region are much more likely to disagree with these statements.[12] The left prefrontal region of the brain is rich in receptors for the neurotransmitter dopamine, higher concentrations of which have been independently shown to be correlated with positive affect.[13]

High satisfaction levels as identified by any of these measures are predictive of a variety of observable behaviors that most of us take to be indicative of well-being. For example, people who call themselves happy, or who have relatively high levels of electrical activity in the left prefrontal region, are

> more likely to be rated as happy by friends;
> more likely to initiate social contacts with friends;
> more likely to respond to requests for help;
> less likely to be absent from work;
> less likely to be involved in disputes at work;
> less likely to die prematurely;
> less likely to attempt suicide; and
> less likely to seek psychological counseling.[14]

People who consider themselves happy are "less self-focused, less hostile and abusive. . . . They are also more loving, forgiving, trusting, energetic, decisive, creative."[15] And people who call themselves unhappy are more likely to experience a variety of symptoms of physical distress, such as frequent headaches, digestive disorders, rapid heartbeat, and dizziness.[16]

For any given individual, the various self-reported measures of subjective well-being tend to be strongly positively correlated over time.[17] In one pair of surveys taken eight months apart, for example, fewer than 2 percent of respondents switched between extreme categories— reporting "not happy" in one survey and "very happy" in the other.[18]

Observed consistency is, if anything, even more powerful for the brain-wave measures. In a sample consisting mostly of American college students, the neuropsychologist Richard Davidson found that people who registered high positive affect on one occasion (as measured by a high level of electrical activity in the left prefrontal regions of their brains) tended to register similarly high levels one month later. Davidson observed similar stability among subjects showing high levels of negative affect. (Davidson notes with interest that, on both occasions, the brain waves of one particular individual in his sample—a Tibetan monk who was in the United States for a brief visit—registered dramatically higher positive affect levels than any other subject.)

Ratings derived from interviews with mental-health professionals are highly correlated with self-reported subjective well-being.[19] People who describe themselves as happy are able to recall more positive events from recent experience, and fewer negative events.[20] And the various measures of subjective well-being also respond to good and bad life experiences, and to therapy, in the expected ways.[21] Someone who has experienced the recent death of a loved one, for example, is likely to exhibit sharply reduced subjective well-being, irrespective of the measure chosen.

In short, it seems that what the psychologists call subjective well-being is a real phenomenon. The various empirical measures of it have high consistency, reliability, and validity.[22] What is more, it seems clear that social arrangements that enhance subjective well-being should be counted as a good thing, provided they do not cause commensurate harm in the process. Again, I stress that this is not the same as saying that the only goal of a person or a society should be to achieve the highest possible subjective levels of well-being. (As philosophers are fond of asking, would you rather be Socrates dissatisfied or a pig satisfied?) The argument that unfolds over the coming chapters requires only that an increase in subjective well-being constitute an improvement if it is achieved without having to compromise other important values.

Let us turn now to the first substantive step in this argument, an assessment of the relationship between subjective well-being and income. Throughout the industrialized world, average incomes have been growing sharply for the past several hundred years, and the amount and quality of the goods and services we consume have increased accordingly. Are we significantly happier on that account?

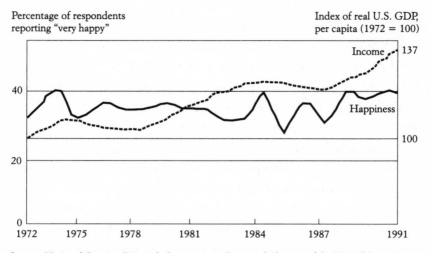

Percentage of respondents   Index of real U.S. GDP,
reporting "very happy"   per capita (1972 = 100)

Sources: National Opinion Research Center, 1991: Statistical Abstract of the United States, 1997.

Income and Subjective Well-Being

One of the central findings in the large scientific literature on subjective well-being is that once income levels surpass a minimal absolute threshold, average satisfaction levels within a given country tend to be highly stable over time, even in the face of significant economic growth. The diagram above, for example, plots the percentage of Americans surveyed who respond "very happy" when asked, "Taken all together, how would you say things are these days—would you say that you are very happy, pretty happy, or not too happy?" Although per-capita income was 39 percent higher in real terms at the end of the period shown than at the beginning, the proportion of people who considered themselves very happy actually declined slightly over the period.

Of course, other factors affect satisfaction levels besides income and the material goods it commands. Perhaps a large income effect on happiness during the period shown was offset by some other negative effects. Yet average satisfaction levels are also found to be unresponsive to changes in average income levels in other countries and during other time periods. As shown in the diagram below, for example, the average satisfaction level reported by survey respondents in Japan remained essentially unchanged between 1958 and 1986, a particularly striking finding in view of the fact that per-capita income rose more than five-fold during that period.

Average reported level of well-being   Index of Japanese GNP,
in surveys (10 = extremely happy)   per capita (1960 = 100)

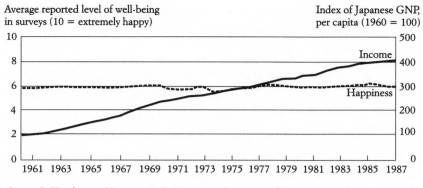

Source: R. Veenhoven, *Happiness in Nations,* 1993; International Monetary Fund.

In automobile and appliance ownership, Japan in the late 1950s was essentially no different from many developing countries today. Yet the pattern in the previous diagram cannot be extrapolated to conclude that people are equally satisfied no matter how poor they might be. On the contrary, most careful studies find a clear relationship over time between subjective well-being and absolute income at extremely low levels of absolute income. Thus, in a country in which most people lack minimally adequate shelter and nutrition, across-the-board increases in income appear, not surprisingly, to yield significant and lasting improvements in subjective well-being.[23] In the same vein, average satisfaction levels are significantly lower in extremely poor countries than in rich ones.[24]

Our concern here is with how differences in consumption affect citizens' well-being in countries that have already achieved a measure of affluence. And for such countries, average satisfaction levels are not significantly correlated over time with income.

INCOME REQUIRED FOR AN
"ACCEPTABLE" STANDARD OF LIVING

A second approach in the psychological literature has been to investigate the relationship between absolute income levels and the levels of income thought necessary for achieving an acceptable standard of living. The Gallup Poll, for example, has for many years asked its respondents the following question: "What is the smallest amount of money a family of four needs to get along in this community?" The median response rises steadily from year to year, in absolute terms, but when expressed as a percentage of per-capita disposable income, this trend largely vanishes.

The same pattern has also been found in numerous other surveys. For example, Eugene Smolensky reports that the median values of reported estimates of "minimum-comfort" budgets for workers in New York City have hovered around half of average per-capita national income since the beginning of the twentieth century.[25] Lee Rainwater reports that for surveys taken between 1950 and 1986, the "income necessary to get along" has grown at the same rate as per-capita national income.[26] And Bernard van Praag and Arie Kapteyn have found similar patterns in European data.[27]

———

Most people certainly *think* that having more money would make them happier. As John Kenneth Galbraith once put it, "Wealth is not without its advantages and the case to the contrary, although it has often been made, has never proved widely persuasive."[28] And yet the more we have, the more we seem to feel we need. Our real per-capita income is now almost two-and-a-half times as high as when Galbraith's *The Affluent Society* was published in 1958. Why didn't the actual experience of having more money live up to our expectations? One answer, as we shall presently see, is the speed with which we adapt to new standards.

CHAPTER 6

GAINS THAT ENDURE

Behavioral scientists have found persuasive evidence that once a threshold level of affluence is achieved, the average life-satisfaction level in any country is essentially independent of its per-capita income. Some social scientists who have pondered the significance of this finding have concluded that, at least for people in the world's richest countries, no useful purpose is served by further accumulations of wealth.[1]

On its face, this should be a surprising conclusion since, as we saw in chapter 4, there are so many seemingly useful things that having additional wealth would enable us to do. Would we really not be any happier if, say, the environment were a little cleaner, or if we could take a little more time off, or even just eliminate a few of the hassles of everyday life? In principle at least, people in wealthier countries have these additional options, and it should surprise us that this seems to have had no measurable effect on their overall well-being.

In this chapter, I will describe evidence that supports a rather different conclusion—namely, that having more wealth *would* be a good thing, provided we spent it in certain ways. The key insight is that even though we appear to adapt quickly to across-the-board increases in our stocks of most material goods, there are specific categories in which our capacity to adapt is more limited, and in which additional spending therefore appears to create significant and lasting improvements in well-being.

ADAPTATION

The human ability to adapt to changed circumstances is one of the most remarkable features of our species. It spans the range of biological functioning, all the way down to molecular changes at the cellular level. For example, autonomic changes in pupil dilation, photochemical changes in the retina, and neural changes in the visual cortex of the brain allow us to see, more or less normally, in environments whose actual physical luminosity varies by a factor of more than 1 million.[2]

Our power to adapt is no less impressive at the level of the entire organism. When asked to choose, most people state confidently that they would rather be killed in an automobile accident than to survive as a quadriplegic. And so we are not surprised to learn that severely disabled people experience a period of devastating depression and disorientation in the wake of their accidents. What we do not expect, however, are the speed and extent to which many of these victims accommodate to their new circumstances. Within a year's time, many quadriplegics report roughly the same mix of moods and emotions that able-bodied people do.[3] There is also evidence that the blind, the retarded, and the malformed are far better adapted to the limitations imposed by their conditions than most of us might imagine.[4]

We adapt swiftly not just to losses but also to gains. Ads for the New York State Lottery show participants fantasizing about how their lives would change if they won. ("I'd buy the company and fire my boss.") People who actually do win the lottery typically report the anticipated rush of euphoria in the weeks after their good fortune. Follow-up studies done after several years, however, indicate that these people are often no happier—and indeed, are in some ways less happy—than before.[5]

In short, our extraordinary powers of adaptation appear to help explain why absolute living standards simply may not matter much once we escape the physical deprivations of abject poverty. This interpretation is consistent with the impressions of people who have lived or traveled extensively abroad, who report that the struggle to get ahead seems to play out with much the same psychological effects in rich societies as in those with more modest levels of wealth.[6]

These observations provide grist for the mills of social critics who are offended by the apparent wastefulness of our recent consumption boom. What many of these critics typically overlook, however, is that the power to adapt is a two-edged sword. It may indeed explain why having bigger houses and faster cars doesn't make us any happier; but if we can also adapt fully to *not* having things that more money can buy, or if we can adapt fully to the seemingly unpleasant things we often have to go through to get more money, then what's the problem? Perhaps social critics are simply barking up the wrong tree.

It is a serious misreading of the evidence, however, to conclude that absolute living standards do not matter. What the data seem to say is that as national income grows, people do not spend their extra money in ways that yield significant and lasting increases in measured satisfaction. But this still leaves two possible ways that absolute income might matter. One is that people might have been able to spend their money in other ways that would have made them happier, yet for various reasons did not, or could not, do so. The evidence we are about to see strongly supports this possibility. (Let us postpone for the moment an attempt to answer the compelling question raised by this evidence: If people could have spent their money in ways that would have made them happier, why *didn't* they?)

A second possibility is that although measures of subjective well-being may do a reasonably good job of tracking our experiences as we are consciously aware of them, that may not be all that matters to us. For example, imagine two parallel universes, one just like the one we live in now and another in which everyone's income is twice what it is now. Suppose that in both universes you would be the median earner, with an annual income of $100,000 in one and $200,000 in the other. Suppose further that you would feel equally happy in the two universes (an assumption that is consistent with the evidence we have seen thus far). And suppose, finally, that you know that people in the richer universe would spend more to protect the environment from toxic waste, and that this would result in healthier and longer, even if not happier, lives for all. Can there be any question that it would be better to live in the second universe?

My point is that although the emerging science of subjective well-being has much to tell us about the factors that contribute to human satisfaction, not even its most ardent practitioners would insist that it offers the final word. Indeed, it is easy to envision ways in which across-the-board increases in incomes might facilitate changes for the better that would be unlikely to have much impact on subjective well-being as currently measured. Of course, we must not simply *assume* that across-the-board increases in incomes will automatically lead to such changes. But neither should we be blind to this possibility. Whether growth in national income is, or could be, a generally good thing is a question that must be settled by the evidence.

In fact, a rich body of evidence bears on this question. One clear message of this evidence is that beyond some point, across-the-board increases in spending on *many types* of material goods do not produce any lasting increment in subjective well-being. Sticking with the parallel-universes metaphor, let us imagine people from two societies that are identical in every respect save one: In society A, everyone lives in a house with 4,000 square feet of floor space, whereas in society B each house has only 3,000 square feet. If the two societies were completely isolated from one another, there is no evidence to suggest that psychologists and neuroscientists would be able to discern any significant difference in their respective average levels of subjective well-being. Rather, we would expect each society to have developed its own local norm for what constitutes adequate housing, and that people in each society would therefore be equally satisfied with their houses and other aspects of their lives.

Moreover, we have no reason to suppose that there would be other important reasons to prefer being a member of society A rather than society B. After all, the larger houses in society A would not contribute to longer lives, more freedom from illness, or indeed any other significant advantage over the members of society B. Within broad limits, it would appear that the human capacity to adapt to across-the-board changes in house size is virtually complete.

Of course, it takes real resources to build 4,000-square-foot houses instead of 3,000-square-foot houses. Put another way, a society that built a 4,000-square-foot house for everyone could instead have built 3,000-square-foot houses and had considerable resources left over with which to produce something else. Hence this central question: Are there alternative ways of spending these resources that could have produced a lasting increment in human welfare?

An affirmative answer would be logically impossible if our capacity to adapt to every other possible change were as great as our capacity to adapt to larger houses. As it turns out, however, our capacity to adapt varies considerably across domains. There are some stimuli, such as environmental noise, to which we may adapt relatively quickly at a conscious level, yet to which our bodies continue to respond in measurable ways even after many years of exposure. Indeed, there are even stimuli to which we not only do not adapt over time but actually become sensitized. Various biochemical allergens are examples, but we also see instances on a more macro scale. For instance, after several months' exposure, the office boor who initially took two weeks to annoy you can accomplish the same feat in only two seconds.

The observation that we adapt more fully to some stimuli than to others opens the door to the possibility that moving resources from one category to another might yield lasting changes in human well-being. The pages ahead summarize evidence that this is not merely an abstract possibility.

Spending Categories that Matter

A convenient way to examine this evidence is to consider a sequence of thought experiments in which you must choose between two hypothetical societies. The two societies have equal wealth levels but different spending patterns. Let us again suppose that residents of society A live in 4,000-square-foot houses while those in society B live in 3,000-square-foot houses. I use these figures because each is significantly larger than the current average house size in the United States. This means that most of you can contemplate a move from A to B without having to imagine moving to a smaller house than the one in which you now live. If your current house is larger than 3,000 square feet, simply replace 3,000 with the size of your current house and suppose that the houses in society A are 1,000 square feet larger than that. (For example, if you currently live in a 6,000-square-foot house, let the houses in society B be 6,000 square feet and those in A be 7,000.)

In each case, the residents of society B use the resources saved by building smaller houses to bring about some other specific change in their living conditions. And in each case we shall ask what the evidence says about how that change would affect the quality of their lives.

Which would you choose: society A, whose residents have 4,000-square-foot houses and a one-hour automobile commute to work through heavy traffic; or society B, whose residents have 3,000-square-foot houses and a 15-minute commute by rapid transit?

The only difference between these societies is that they have allocated their resources differently between housing and transportation. The residents of society B have used the same resources they could have employed to build larger housing to transform the nature of their commute to work. Let us also suppose that the savings from building smaller houses are sufficient not only to fund the construction of high-speed public transit but also to make the added flexibility of the automobile available on an as-needed basis. Thus, as a resident of society B, you need not give up your car. You can even drive it to work on those days when you need extra flexibility, or you can come and go when needed by taxi. The *only* thing you and others must sacrifice to achieve the shorter daily commute to work of society B is additional floor space in your houses.

A rational person faced with this choice will want to consider the available evidence on the benefits and costs of each alternative. Regarding the psychological cost of living in smaller houses, the evidence provides no reason to believe that if you *and all others* live in 3,000-square-foot houses, your subjective well-being will be any lower than if you and all others live in 4,000-square-foot houses. Of course, if you moved from society B to society A, you might be pleased, even excited, at first to experience the additional living space. But we can predict that in time you would adapt and simply consider the larger house the norm.

Someone who moved from society B to society A would also experience stress initially from the extended commute through heavy traffic. Over time, his consciousness of this stress might diminish. But there is an important distinction: Unlike his adaptation to the larger house, which will be essentially complete, his adaptation to his new commuting pattern will be only partial. Available evidence clearly shows that even after long periods of adjustment, most people experience the task of navigating through heavy commuter traffic as stressful.[7]

In this respect, the effect of exposure to heavy traffic is similar to the effect of exposure to noise and other irritants. Thus, even though a large increase in background noise at a constant, steady level is experienced as less intrusive as time passes, prolonged exposure nonetheless produces lasting elevations in blood pressure.[8] If the noise is not only loud but also intermittent, people remain conscious of their heightened irritability even after extended periods of adaptation, and their symptoms of central nervous system distress become more pronounced.[9] This pattern was seen, for example, in a study of people living next to a newly opened noisy highway. Whereas 21 percent of residents interviewed four months after the highway opened said they were not annoyed by the noise, that figure dropped to 16 percent when the same residents were interviewed a year later.[10]

Among the various types of noise exposure, worst of all is exposure to sounds that are not only loud and intermittent but also unpredictably so. In a laboratory, subjects exposed to loud, aperiodic noise experience not only physiological symptoms of stress but also behavioral symptoms. These subjects become less persistent in their attempts to cope with frustrating tasks and suffer measurable impairments in performing tasks requiring care and attention.[11]

It is plausible to suppose that unpredictable noise is particularly stressful because it confronts the subject with a loss of control. The psychologist David Glass and his collaborators confirmed this hypothesis in an ingenious experiment that exposed two groups of subjects to a recording of loud, unpredictable noises. Whereas subjects in one group had no control over the recording, subjects in the other group could stop the tape at any time by flipping a switch. These subjects were told, however, that the experimenters would prefer that they not stop the tape, and most of them honored this preference. Following exposure to the noise, subjects with access to the control switch made almost 60 percent fewer errors than other subjects on a proofreading task and made more than four times as many attempts to solve a difficult puzzle.[12]

Commuting through heavy traffic is in many ways more like exposure to loud, unpredictable noise than to constant background noise. Delays are difficult to predict, much less control, and one never quite gets used to being cut off by others who think their time is more valuable than anyone else's. A large scientific literature documents a multitude of stress symptoms that result from protracted driving through heavy traffic.

One strand in this literature focuses on the experience of urban bus drivers, whose exposure to the stresses of heavy traffic is higher than that of most commuters, but who have also had greater opportunity to adapt to those stresses. Compared to workers in other occupations, a disproportionate share of the absenteeism experienced by urban bus drivers stems from stress-related illnesses such as gastrointestinal problems, headaches, and anxiety.[13] Many studies have found sharply elevated rates of hypertension among bus drivers relative to a variety of control groups, including, in one instance, bus drivers themselves during their preemployment physicals.[14] Additional studies have found elevations of stress hormones such as adrenaline, noradrenaline, and cortisol in urban bus drivers.[15] And one study found elevations of adrenaline and noradrenaline to be strongly positively correlated with the density of the traffic with which urban bus drivers had to contend.[16] More than half of all urban bus drivers retire prematurely with some form of medical disability.[17]

A daily one-hour commute through heavy traffic is presumably less stressful than operating a bus all day in an urban area. Yet there is no question that this difference is one of degree rather than kind. Studies have shown that the demands of commuting through heavy traffic often result in emotional and behavioral deficits on arrival at home or at work.[18] Compared to drivers who commute through low-density traffic, those who commute through heavy traffic are more likely to report feelings of annoyance.[19] And higher levels of commuting distance, time, speed, and months of commuting are significantly positively correlated with increased systolic and diastolic blood pressure.[20]

The prolonged experience of commuting stress also suppresses immune function and shortens longevity.[21] Even spells in traffic as brief as 15 minutes have been linked to significant elevations of blood glucose and cholesterol, and to declines in blood coagulation time—all factors that are positively associated with cardiovascular disease. Commuting by automobile is also linked positively with the incidence of various cancers, especially cancer of the lung, possibly because of heavier exposure to exhaust fumes.[22] Among people who commute to work, the incidence of these and other illnesses rises with the length of commute,[23] and is significantly lower among those who commute by bus or rail,[24] and lower still among noncommuters.[25] Finally, the risk of death and injury from accidents varies positively with the length of commute and is higher for those who commute by car than for those who commute by public transport.

In sum, there appear to be persistent and significant costs associated with a long commute through heavy traffic. We can be confident that neurophysiologists would find higher levels of cortisol, norepinephrine, adrenaline, noradrenaline, and other stress hormones in the residents of society A. No one has done the experiment to discover whether people from society A would report lower levels of life satisfaction than people from society B. But because we know that drivers often report being consciously aware of the frustration and stress they experience during commuting, it is a plausible conjecture that subjective well-being, as conventionally measured, would be lower in society A. Even if the negative effects of commuting stress never broke through into conscious awareness, however, we would still have powerful reasons for wishing to escape them.

On the strength of the available evidence, then, it appears that a rational person would have powerful reasons to choose society B, and no reasons to avoid it. And yet, despite this evidence, America is moving steadily in the direction of society A. Even as our houses continue to grow larger, the average length of our commute to work continues to grow longer—a 7 percent increase between 1983 and 1990, according to a U.S. Department of Transportation survey.[26] The Federal Highway Administration predicts that delays during driving time will increase to 11.9 billion vehicle hours in 2005, compared to 2.7 billion in 1985.[27]

Several of the next thought experiments ask you to choose between societies that offer different combinations of material goods and free time to pursue other activities. Each case assumes a specific use of the free time and asks that you imagine it to be one that appeals to you. (If not, feel free to substitute some other activity that does.)

Which would you choose: society A, whose residents live in 4,000-square-foot houses and have no time to exercise each day; or society B, whose residents live in 3,000-square-foot houses and have 45-minutes available to exercise each day?

Again we have two societies that have different bundles from the same menu of opportunities. Residents of society B could have built larger houses, but instead they spent less time at work each day and devoted the time thus saved to exercise. As before, we assume there are no other relevant differences between the two societies. And imagine yourself to be someone who views exercise as neither more nor less intrinsically pleasurable than work.

From our earlier discussions, we can take as given that no reduction in well-being will result from the mere fact that everyone lives in a smaller house in society B. The only question, then, is whether the additional time available for exercise will result in a significant increase in well-being. And on this question, the evidence could hardly be more clear.

Numerous studies, for example, have documented a variety of positive physiological and psychological effects of regular aerobic exercise.[28] Exercisers report more frequent and intense positive feelings and tend to have better functioning immune systems.[29] Exercisers also have higher life expectancy and are less likely to suffer from heart disease, stroke, diabetes, hypertension, and a variety of other ailments.[30]

Evidence for the causal nature of these relationships is seen in the fact that subjects randomly assigned to exercise programs experience improved physical and psychological well-being.[31] For example, people diagnosed with moderate depression who were randomly assigned to an aerobic exercise program experienced recovery rates comparable to others being treated by psychotherapy, and both groups fared substantially better than controls.[32]

Some critics have expressed concern that the psychological benefits found in many studies may result not from exercise itself but from the break these subjects experienced in their normal routines. Some support for this possibility emerged in a study in which one group of volunteers was assigned to an aerobic exercise program and another group to a hobby class.[33] Both groups experienced measurable improvements in mood. But breaks in routine cannot be the entire explanation because the mood improvements were significantly larger for the exercise group. That group experienced improvements in each of six mood indicators, and all but two of these were large and statistically significant. Although the hobby-class group improved on five of the six indicators, their improvements were smaller and only two were statistically significant.

Even programs of relatively light exercise, such as walking, yield significant physiological and psychological benefits. One experiment, for example, showed that premenopausal women randomly assigned to a supervised walking group experienced significant reductions in heart rate and blood pressure, and significant improvements in self-esteem relative to nonwalkers.[34]

Despite the compelling evidence for the beneficial psychological and physical effects of regular exercise, and despite the evidence that no discernible increase in life satisfaction results when all have larger houses, it is difficult to insist that all rational persons would necessarily choose society B over society A. Indeed, many people are so averse to physical exercise that they would be willing to give up material goods to *escape* having to do it.

Many of these people might change their minds if they stuck with an exercise program for just a little while. For although people often report that exercise is an unpleasant experience at first, especially if they try to do too much too soon, most adapt to it quickly and come to think of it as pleasurable. In the end, however, even this knowledge may not tip the balance in favor of society B for some people. If you are in this group, just think of society B as providing a little more time for some other daily activity, or mix of activities, that you might like to pursue.

In any event, lack of time is the reason most frequently cited by people who say they wish they could get more exercise. Jon Robison, codirector of the Michigan Center for Preventive Medicine in Lansing, says that most exercise regimens are doomed from the start because people try to cram an hour of exercise into a daily schedule that is too busy to begin with, and end up quitting because they can't find the time.[35] Extra time is readily available, however, if we are willing to spend less time working to acquire goods. The evidence strongly suggests that our lives would be healthier, longer, and more satisfying if we all made that choice. Yet, as a nation, we are exercising less and spending more time at work.

Which would you choose: society A, whose residents have 4,000-square-foot houses and one evening each month to get together with friends; or society B, whose residents have 3,000-square-foot houses and get together with friends four evenings a month?

The question is again whether one use of time produces a larger impact on subjective well-being than another. Because the residents of society A work longer hours, they can build larger houses but have less time to socialize with friends. Here again, the evidence suggests that whereas the payoff when all have larger houses is small and fleeting, the pleasures that result from deeper social relationships are both profound and enduring. People with rich networks of active social relationships are much more likely to call themselves happy, and are much more likely to be described as happy by friends.[36] In the findings of one survey by the National Opinion Research Center, for example, persons who could name five or more friends with whom they discussed matters of personal importance were 60 percent more likely to feel "very happy" than others who listed no personal confidants.[37] Another survey of 800 college graduates found that subjects whose values emphasized high income and occupational prestige were twice as likely as others to describe themselves as "fairly unhappy" or "very unhappy."[38]

It might seem natural to wonder about the direction of causation in the link between social integration and subjective well-being. Does having close relationships make people happy, or is it just that happier people are more likely to enjoy close relationships? Without discounting the second possibility, I note that there is at least some evidence that social integration is an important causal factor. Thus one study found that soldiers assigned to small, stable, cohesive units scored significantly higher on several important measures of subjective well-being than did others assigned to large units with high turnover.[39]

Even more striking is the link between networks of close personal relationships and physical health. People who lack such networks tend to be less physically healthy, and confront a higher risk of dying at every age. For example, in a study of leukemia patients about to undergo bone marrow transplants, the two-year survival rate was 54 percent for those who experienced strong emotional support from family and friends, but only 20 percent for those who experienced little social support.[40]

A more broad-based study investigated whether the presence or absence of various kinds of social relationships—marriage, contact with friends, membership in churches and other organizations—predicted subsequent rates of death for a sample of 2,229 men and 2,496 women living in Alameda County, California. For both men and women across all age groups, people who were low or lacking in such relationships at the beginning of the study in 1965 were from 30 to 300 percent more likely to die during the subsequent nine years.[41]

Here, too, one might wonder about the causal link between mortality and social integration. Could the higher mortality of the less socially integrated subjects have reflected the fact that preexisting poor health caused them to be less socially integrated at the time of the ini-

tial interview? The results of a later study seem to rule out this interpretation. Based on a sample of 1,322 men and 1,432 women in
Tecumseh, Michigan, that study found essentially the same relationship between mortality and social integration even after controlling for
the results of a physical examination conducted at the outset.[42]

In sum, the evidence is clear that closer social ties promote both
physical health and subjective well-being. But close social ties cannot
be achieved by waving a magic wand. Relationships take time, and as
economists correctly insist, time is money. Is this money well spent?
The answer is almost surely yes, if the alternative is to use that money
to build larger houses for all. Here again, it appears that a rational person has compelling reasons for choosing society B, in which everyone
has a smaller house but more time to spend with friends. Yet, as a nation, we have been moving in precisely the opposite direction.

> *Which would you choose: society A, whose residents have 4,000-
> square-foot houses and one week of vacation each year; or society B,
> whose residents have 3,000-square-foot houses, and four weeks of
> vacation?*

If we all lived in smaller houses, or drove less expensive cars, we
could all take more weeks of vacation each year. The physical and psychological benefits of periodic breaks in routine have long been established.[43] Thus studies of people on vacation find that they are less tired,
irritable, and worried than at other times.[44] Vacationers also experience
reduced incidence of stress-related disorders such as indigestion, con-
stipation, headaches, and insomnia.[45]

Vacations offer the opportunity to see new places, visit with distant relatives and friends, take up a new sport, read books, lie on a
beach, hike in the wilderness, or do whatever the spirit moves you to
do. Provided they are of sufficient duration, vacations have also been
found to have restorative effects that persist long after people return
to work. Citing evidence of these effects, German legislation encourages a vacation to be taken "as a single, uninterrupted period unless
pressing requirements of the establishment or of the employee make
it necessary to split leave into parts."[46] The German legislation goes

on to say that if the statutory minimum of 24 vacation days is split into parts, "one of the parts . . . shall comprise at least twelve consecutive working days."[47]

Despite the many clear advantages of longer vacations, few entry-level jobs in the United States offer more than 10 days of paid vacation a year, and many offer less. There appears little doubt that a package with a lower annual salary and a longer vacation allotment would increase subjective well-being by much more than enough to offset an across-the-board move to slightly smaller houses. And yet Americans must work longer now than in the recent past to earn each day of paid vacation.

Which would you choose: society A, whose residents have 4,000-square-foot houses and a relatively low level of autonomy in the workplace; or society B, whose residents have 3,000-square-foot houses and a relatively high level of autonomy?

Because most of us spend the majority, or at least a large proportion, of our waking hours on the job, our satisfaction with our lives as a whole depends importantly on how satisfied we are with our jobs. A consistent finding in the industrial psychology literature is that job satisfaction increases with the degree to which workers enjoy autonomy and choice with respect to which tasks they do and the manner in which they perform them.[48] In laboratory experiments, for example, subjects allowed to choose their own activities spent significantly longer times on a task than did those to whom activities were assigned arbitrarily.[49]

Autonomy is, of course, not the only factor that influences job satisfaction. For example, workers tend to find greater satisfaction in jobs that provide greater opportunities to make use of their skills.[50] And numerous studies have found that job satisfaction increases with the variety of tasks workers are called on to perform.[51] The list is endless. For instance, if pay were the same, people would choose safe jobs over risky ones; quiet jobs over noisy ones; jobs with convenient parking over those without; jobs with security over those without; and so on.

Giving workers more autonomy sometimes results in greater productivity, sometimes not. When it does, it will of course be in the interests of profit-seeking employers to grant additional autonomy. But beyond some point, greater autonomy usually comes at the expense of profits. And once this point is reached, workers can enjoy increased autonomy only by accepting lower salaries. The same holds true for other valued job characteristics. To the extent that workers become more productive the more they specialize, pay cuts will be necessary if workers are to enjoy more variety and the opportunity to utilize more fully the various skills they possess. Likewise, additional safety equipment, employment security, parking spaces, office privacy, and other amenities inevitably mean lower paychecks.

For the purposes of this thought experiment, we assume that the only consequence of gaining these desirable working conditions is an across-the-board reduction from 4,000 to 3,000 square feet of housing space, which, as we have seen, entails no sacrifice in subjective well-being. Yet there is a lasting gain in well-being when everyone gains additional autonomy on the job—or when all gain additional variety or safety. Here again, the available evidence strongly favors the choice of society B. Yet the combination of alternatives in society B is just what we seem to be moving away from.

Inconspicuous Consumption

The choice in each of the thought experiments considered thus far has been between conspicuous consumption (in the form of larger houses) and what, for want of a better term, I call "inconspicuous consumption"—freedom from traffic congestion, time with family and friends, vacation time, and a variety of favorable job characteristics. In each of the examples discussed, the evidence suggests that subjective well-being will be higher in the society with a greater balance of inconspicuous consumption.

The list of inconspicuous consumption items could be extended considerably. For instance, we could ask whether all living in slightly smaller houses would be a reasonable price to pay for higher air quality, for more urban parkland, for cleaner drinking water, for a reduction in violent crime; or for medical research that would reduce premature death. And in each case the answer would be the same as in the examples we have considered thus far.

Although many forms of inconspicuous consumption—the use of rapid transit systems to alleviate traffic congestion, for example—entail expenditures in the public domain, many others—such as spending additional time with family and friends—do not. Many private goods, such as automobiles, embody elements of both conspicuous and inconspicuous consumption.

If we fix the total amount spent on such goods, we confront a trade-off between conspicuous and inconspicuous consumption. For example, a given sum can be spent to make a car faster and more luxurious, or to make it safer and more reliable. If we all buy faster or more luxuriously appointed cars (conspicuous consumption), the evidence suggests that we will experience little lasting improvement in subjective well-being. But the outcome will be different if we all buy safer, more reliable cars (inconspicuous consumption). With increased safety, the distribution of the increase in well-being will be highly uneven: Most people won't be affected directly, but a small proportion of us will escape the pain and suffering that follows a serious injury or the loss of a loved one. With increased reliability, a large majority of us will escape the stress of repeated mechanical breakdowns.

My point in the thought experiments is not that inconspicuous consumption is always and everywhere preferable to conspicuous consumption. Indeed, in each of the individual thought experiments, we might envision a minority of rational individuals who might choose society A over society B. Some people may simply dislike autonomy on the job, or dislike exercise, or dislike spending time with family and friends.

But if we accept at face value the evidence that there is little sacrifice in subjective well-being when all move to slightly smaller houses, the real question is whether a rational person could find *some* more productive use for the resources thus saved. Given the absolute sizes of the houses involved in the thought experiments, the answer to this question is almost certainly yes.

And this suggests that the answer to the question posed in the title of the preceding chapter (Does Money Buy Happiness?) is that it depends. Considerable evidence suggests that if we all work longer hours to buy bigger houses and more expensive cars, we do not end up any happier than before. As for whether money *could* buy happiness, however, the evidence paints a very different picture. The less we spend on conspicuous consumption goods, the better we can afford to alleviate congestion; the more time we can devote to family and friends, to exercise, sleep, travel, and other restorative activities; and the better we can afford to maintain a clean and safe environment. On the best available evidence, reallocating our time and money in these ways would result in healthier, longer, and more satisfying lives.

SO WHY HASN'T SUBJECTIVE WELL-BEING BEEN RISING?

It might seem natural to suppose that when per-capita income rises sharply, as it has in most countries since at least the end of World War II, most people would spend more on both conspicuous and inconspicuous consumption. In many instances, this is what seems to have happened. Thus the cars we buy today are not only faster and more luxuriously equipped but also safer and more reliable. If both forms of consumption have been rising, however, and if inconspicuous consumption boosts subjective well-being, then why has subjective well-being not increased during the last several decades? (Recall from the previous chapter the study showing that Japan's average subjective well-being remained essentially unchanged during a period of more than five-fold growth in per-capita income.)

A plausible answer is that whereas some forms of inconspicuous consumption have been rising, others have been declining, often sharply, during the period in question. For example, as we saw earlier, there have been increases in the annual number of hours spent at work in the United States during the last two decades. Traffic has grown considerably more congested; savings rates have fallen precipitously; personal bankruptcy filings are at an all-time high; and there is at least a widespread perception that employment security has fallen sharply.

Declines in these and other forms of inconspicuous consumption might easily have offset the effects of increases in others.

The much more troubling question is *why* have we not used our resources more wisely? If we could all live healthier, longer, and more satisfying lives by simply changing our spending patterns, why haven't we done that? This is the central question, and it will occupy much of our attention in the pages to come.

CHAPTER 7

OUR FORGOTTEN FUTURE

On the best available scientific evidence, we seem not to be spending our money in the ways that would most promote our own interests. We should be buying smaller houses and less expensive cars, the evidence seems to say, and spending more on a variety of less conspicuous forms of consumption. Defenders of the status quo may respond by questioning the validity of the evidence—saying, in effect, that we must value material goods far more than the scientific studies suggest.

For the sake of discussion, let us grant the possibility that increasing our stocks of material goods is a highly effective way to promote our well-being. If so, then we ought to be willing to consume a little less today if that would mean being able to consume a great deal more in the near future. The evidence we will see in this chapter, however, provides no support at all for this prediction. On the contrary, it provides an even more compelling reason than the ones we have already seen for questioning the wisdom of our current spending patterns. To see why, we must examine how postponing consumption today gives rise to much more favorable consumption opportunities in the future.

THE MIRACLE OF COMPOUND INTEREST

The paramecium is a single-celled animal about the size of the period at the end of this sentence. It is found in bodies of fresh water everywhere, but especially in quiet ponds that contain the decaying organic matter on which it feeds. Many species reproduce asexually, with each mature cell dividing into two identical daughter cells every day, in some cases twice a day.

In elementary schools around the world, this particular aspect of the paramecium's behavior has made it a favorite tool for illustrating the miracle of compound interest. I recall my third-grade teacher asking us to imagine that we started with one paramecium on the lower-left square of a checkerboard, then put its two daughters on the next square, the four daughters of those two on the square after that, and so on all the way to the 64th square. How many paramecia, she asked with a twinkle in her eye, did we think would be on that last square?

The answer, of course, is an incomprehensibly big number—something like 9,223,400,000,000,000,000. If we figure that 125 paramecia lined up elbow-to-elbow would span a distance of about an inch, this means that if the reproduction of a single paramecium were left unchecked for a mere 64 days, the result would be a string of paramecia spanning more than 1,164,600,000,000 miles—over 6,000 round trips between the earth and the sun.

Needless to say, the miracle of compound interest plays out less dramatically when the relevant growth rate is substantially smaller than the paramecium's. Even so, the results can be impressive with even relatively small growth rates. For example, money invested at an annual interest rate of 7 percent will more than double itself in only 10 years, which means that a $1,000 deposit left in trust at that rate by Benjamin Franklin in the late eighteenth century would be worth more than $1 trillion today. Money invested in the U.S. stock market has grown at an after-tax average annual rate of more than 13 percent since World War II, and many individual investors have managed to do considerably better. Shares in Warren Buffett's Berkshire Hathaway, for instance, have appreciated at an average annual rate of almost 30 percent for more than four decades. Someone who invested only $10,000 in Berkshire Hathaway stock when Buffett started out in 1956 would be worth more than $100 million today.[1]

An Opportunity Wasted

Given the miracle of compound interest, our ability to invest money at even modest rates of return represents an extraordinary opportunity. It is a chance, so to speak, to create new wealth out of thin air. The sad fact, however, is that as a direct result of our spending spree in recent decades, we in the United States have largely squandered this opportunity. Our savings rate, always low by international standards, has fallen precipitously relative to the rates in other major industrial nations. The table below, for example, shows the net savings rates for the five largest OECD countries for the 1970s, 1980s, and early 1990s.[2] Note that the United States ranked dead last in this group in each period, and that the disparity between the United States and the others has been growing sharply. Thus, whereas the net savings rate in Japan was less than three times as high as ours in the 1970s, it is now more than nine times as high. Similarly, Germany's net savings rate, once less than twice ours, is now almost five times as high.

Even more troubling is the large proportion of Americans who save virtually nothing. For example, half of respondents in one national survey reported life savings of less than $3,000. And another 40 percent said that it would be a "big problem" if they had to deal with an unexpected bill for $1,000.[3]

The U.S. savings rate may have begun to recover slightly in the late

NET SAVINGS AS A PERCENTAGE OF NET NATIONAL
INCOME IN THE FIVE LARGEST OECD COUNTRIES

	1970s	1980s	1990–92
Japan	25.6	20.9	23.0
Germany	15.1	11.2	12.4
France	17.1	9.0	8.7
Italy	16.4	11.2	7.6
United States	9.1	5.2	2.5
All OECD	13.8	9.7	8.7

Source: Laurence Seidman, *The USA Tax: A Progressive Consumption Tax,* Cambridge: MIT Press, 1997, p. 19.

1990s, a change that many have attributed to demographic shifts. The baby-boom generation has entered its prime earnings years, when people tend to save more, and many in this generation are also prodded by their fears about the fiscal future of the Social Security system. Many analysts remain skeptical, however, that the behavior of baby boomers will have an enduring effect on American savings rates, which, even with the recent small upturn, remain extremely low.[4]

The fact that we save at such a low rate does not mean that there are simply fewer dollars languishing in some musty bank vault. It means that our companies invest less in new technology, plant, and equipment. Our productivity depends in large part on the amount of capital we have to work with. Each additional computer, lathe, or optical-scanning device increases the amount we can produce each day. Money that is not spent on consumption can instead be deposited into a savings account, and then loaned to a business that will use it to buy new capital equipment that will enhance the productivity of its workers—typically by much more than enough to repay the full principal of the loan plus interest.

Irrespective of our views about the high consumption levels that characterize the United States and other modern industrial societies, we must recognize that becoming more productive is a good thing, if only because it gives us more options. It enables us to earn more and buy more if we choose to, but it also enables us to earn the same amount by working fewer hours, or to spend more on environmental cleanup. Other things being equal, the more productive a society is, the greater is each citizen's ability to pursue his vision of the good life.

The investment financed by savings is of course not the only source of growth in productivity. Even without new capital equipment, for example, productivity would grow as we gain experience and develop new knowledge and ideas. Yet investment remains a major source of productivity growth. And the low United States savings rate of recent decades is an important reason that American productivity growth in the last quarter of the twentieth century has been less than half what it was in the third quarter (see chapter 3).

From an American perspective, it is a matter of additional concern that a growing share of the investment that has taken place in this country has been financed by savings from abroad. Indeed, so reliant have we become on foreign savings that in the span of less than two decades we have gone from being the world's largest creditor nation to being the world's largest debtor.[5] Of course, it is better for Americans that foreign-financed investments are made on U.S. shores than not at all. But the future wealth of Americans would be much higher if we financed a larger proportion of our investment out of our own savings. In 1994, for example, the foreign holders of U.S debt collected more than $100 billion in interest payments from American citizens.[6] Had we saved more, much of this interest income would have been ours instead.

An Illustrative Example

In short, our failure to save has been extremely costly. If there is a bright side to our current savings picture, however, it is that we have the potential to generate dramatic improvements in our future living standards by simply increasing the rate at which we save. To appreciate how truly striking this opportunity is, we need only compare the consumption trajectories of two otherwise identical baby-boom families, one with a high savings rate, and the other with a low savings rate. To simplify matters, suppose that the salary income of both families has been constant at $40,000 per year in current dollars since each family started out in 1980. But whereas one family—call them the Thrifts—saves 20 percent of its income each year, the other—the Spends—saves only 5 percent. This means that in their first year (1980), the Thrifts will save $8,000 and the Spends will save only $2,000. And since a family's consumption is equal to its income minus what it saves, the Spends will consume $38,000 in 1980 and the Thrifts will consume only $32,000.

Suppose both families put their savings in a mutual fund that performed somewhat below the historical average return for such funds in the years since 1980—let us say, conservatively, a return of 10 percent per year. The Thrifts' income in 1981 would then have grown by $800 (the 10 percent return on their $8,000 savings) over the previous year, compared to growth of only $200 for the Spends. With an income of

$40,800, the Thrifts will consume $32,640 in 1981 (80 percent of $40,800), compared to $38,190 (95 percent of $40,200) for the Spends. The consumption gap between the two families, which started out at $6,000, will be only $5,550 after one year. And that's just the beginning.

Each year the Thrifts' income grows faster than the Spends' income, and each year the Thrifts continue to save 20 percent of their higher incomes, compared to only 5 percent for the Spends. By 1985 (only five years after starting out), the consumption gap has shrunk to $4,000, and by 1993, the Thrifts have actually overtaken the Spends. From that point onward, the amount by which the Thrifts outspend the Spends keeps growing with each passing year. Even though the Spends continue to consume 95 percent of their income each year, their income grows so slowly that by 1998, they are consuming $3,000 a year less than the Thrifts ($41,802 a year vs. $44,808). And by the time the two families retire, in 2020, the Thrifts are consuming more than $20,000 per year more than the Spends ($69,272 vs. $49, 065). Even more striking is the difference between the retirement nest eggs of the two families. Whereas the Spends will enter retirement with total accumulated savings of less than $121,000, the Thrifts will have more than $483,000.

When we step back and compare the spending and savings histories of these two families, it is hard not to conclude that the Spends have simply made an egregious blunder by not saving more. In return for a small and quickly shrinking consumption advantage in their early years, they have consigned themselves to a standard of living that steadily worsens, in relative terms, for the rest of their lives. The disturbing fact is that the typical American household saves even less than the 5 percent rate assumed for the Spends in this example.

Is this example plausible? The assumed rate of return of 10 percent is a generous one by many standards, yet it is not unrealistically high. For example, funds invested in the U.S. stock market have earned about that much since 1926. And in an important sense, this is a misleadingly low figure because it is net of the corporate income tax, whose nominal rate has averaged more than 30 percent in the postwar

years. (Society's gain from additional investment is the before-tax rate
of return, not the after-tax rate. Thus, if everyone saved and invested
more, corporate earnings and tax payments would be higher, which
would mean that the government would need to collect less tax money
from private citizens.) In any case, I use 10 percent merely for the sake
of illustration. If the true return were lower, the difference between the
two consumption profiles would be smaller; and if the true return were
higher, the difference would be larger.

With the end of the cold war and market reforms in full swing in
countries across the globe, many investors believe that the decades to
come offer investment possibilities with much higher rates of return
than we have experienced in the past. Whether or not that is so, one
thing remains clear: Given *any* reasonable assumptions about the rate
of return on new investment, the *only* cost of moving from our current
low-growth trajectory to a high-growth trajectory would be a brief—
incredibly brief, on the grand scale of human history—interval of postponed growth of consumption. With this in mind, even those who regard the continued accumulation of material goods as the best
yardstick of social progress must rethink the wisdom of the consumption boom of recent decades.

IS GROWTH REALLY A GOOD THING?

Many might wonder whether achieving higher growth rates would be
such a good thing in the end, since, after all, people do tend to adapt
quickly to higher material living standards. One might also worry that
more consumption would mean more garbage, acid rain, greenhouse
gases, and other noxious side effects.

On the first point, the evidence suggests that although we adjust
rather quickly to any *stable* standard of living, we seem to derive continuing satisfaction from an ongoing increase in our standard of living.[7]
It is a plain fact of human nature that a person who earns $50,000 this
year is more likely to be satisfied with her standard of living if she
earned $45,000 last year than if she earned $55,000. The faster the
economy is growing, the greater the proportion of individuals whose

current standard of living constitutes a significant improvement over their recent past experience.

What is more, growth in productivity frees up additional resources to spend on a variety of less conspicuous forms of consumption that would promote enduring gains in the quality of life. As we have seen, for example, most people would lead longer and more satisfying lives if they had more time to spend with family and friends, or if they had shorter and less stressful commutes to work. The more productive our economy is, the better we are able to afford such changes.

As for the relationship between growth rates and environmental pollution, the popular perception is that since industrialization is what led to environmental degradation in the first place, higher growth rates must be threatening to the environment. In keeping with this perception, societies at extremely primitive levels of economic development seldom suffer serious pollution problems. Indeed, the languages of early hunter-gatherer societies didn't even have expressions for smog or acid rain.

Yet the relationship between wealth and pollution is not a simple linear one. Rather, it takes an inverted U shape, much like the one between wealth and population growth rates: The societies with the most serious pollution and population problems are neither the richest nor the poorest, but those with intermediate levels of wealth.

In nations that are extremely poor, population growth rates are low because infant mortality is high, and pollution is low because there is little industrial activity. Countries with intermediate levels of wealth have high population growth rates because of public health measures that limit infant mortality; and they also have enough industrial activity to generate high levels of pollution, but not enough wealth to finance meaningful cleanup efforts. Countries that have achieved very high levels of wealth, finally, typically have low levels of environmental pollution and low rates of population growth. Thus, as the *New York Times* writer John Tierney recently wrote, "Technology helps to conserve natural resources and diminish pollution. Today's farmers are so efficient that unneeded cropland is reverting to forests and parks; the most high-tech countries have the cleanest air and water."[8]

History has taught that tax and regulatory policy can provide strong incentives to clean up the pollution that accompanies some forms of consumption. There is less smog today in most American cities than there was 20 years ago, even though the number of vehicle-miles driven has roughly doubled during the same period.[9] If certain forms of consumption generate harmful effects—noise, garbage, toxic waste, congestion, greenhouse gases, whatever—we can simply tax them more heavily. Such taxes would encourage not only the development of cleaner technologies but also a shift to cleaner forms of consumption. Taking clarinet lessons doesn't pollute; nor does planting flowers in one's garden.

The important point is that *all* opportunities are greater in a rich society than in a poor one. The former Soviet Union generated more pollution than any other nation on earth not because of its high rate of economic growth, but because its productivity lagged so far behind that of its rivals. A richer society has more resources for medical research, more resources for rapid transit, more time for family and friends, more time for study and exercise—and more resources for better insulated houses and cleaner, more fuel-efficient automobiles. Contrary to popular impressions, the path toward environmental progress lies not in policies that curtail economic growth but in those that stimulate it.

SAVINGS AND RETIREMENT

Another important advantage of a higher private savings rate is that it would enable families to enter retirement in a much more financially secure position than the typical retiree enjoys today. Most people in the United States rely on two principal sources of income during retirement: withdrawals from their own personal savings (including employer-provided pension accounts) and payments from the Social Security system. For most middle- and low-income families, these sources of retirement income fall considerably short of family earnings just prior to retirement, often necessitating painful retrenchments in living standards.

Private savings is an especially advantageous way to provide for retirement because it takes full advantage of the miracle of compound interest discussed earlier. For example, a thousand dollars deposited in any decent mutual fund by a young worker 40 years ago would pay for more than $50,000 worth of goods and services during that person's retirement this year. The Social Security system, by contrast, takes no advantage whatsoever of the miracle of compound interest.

Strictly speaking, Social Security is not a retirement savings program at all, but rather a tax-and-transfer program. A payroll tax is levied on the incomes of those currently employed and the proceeds of this tax are deposited in accounts on which Social Security checks are written to retirees that same year. Under this system, if a retiree is to receive checks this year totaling $40,000, then $40,000 in tax payments must be collected this year from people who are still working. Unlike private savings, our Social Security tax payments are spent almost immediately, and therefore do not draw interest over a period of many years. And this simple fact makes Social Security vastly more expensive than private savings as a means for financing retirement.

This is an especially important consideration as we approach the retirement of the baby-boom generation. During times of demographic stability, there are approximately three workers for every person who is retired. This means that if everyone were to rely exclusively on Social Security during retirement, workers would need to pay roughly 25 percent of their incomes as Social Security taxes (in addition to all other income, sales, and other taxes) to enable retirees to maintain their preretirement living standards. With the upcoming retirements of the large baby-boom generation, there will soon be fewer than two workers per retiree, thereby placing an even heavier tax burden on workers. The consequences of this simple arithmetic would be less daunting if we were all to raise our savings rates substantially.

ECONOMIC GROWTH ALSO PROMOTES CIVILITY

There are still other reasons to favor higher rates of saving and the higher rates of economic growth to which they inevitably give rise. In a forthcoming book, for example, the economist Benjamin Friedman argues persuasively that higher growth rates promote a more open, democratic, and civil society. As he puts it, "a society that experiences a rising *material* standard of living over time is, on that account, the more likely to exhibit such positive *moral* characteristics as openness of opportunity, tolerance of diversity, social mobility, commitment to fairness and dedication to democracy itself."[10]

Friedman begins with the observation that most people's fundamental economic goal is to have more, an aspiration that can be satisfied in either of two ways: by having more than they themselves had in the recent past, or by having more than others currently have. When incomes are stagnant, as they have been for a majority of Americans during the last two decades, the first source of having more is simply not available to most people. Their aspirations thus focus on the second source—the zero-sum contest to outpace their neighbors. The problem, of course, is that although any one person can move forward in relative terms, society as a whole cannot. A stagnant economy, Friedman observes, is therefore an almost fail-safe recipe for widespread frustration.

Friedman argues that this simple fact has important consequences for people's attitudes toward institutions and public policies that support mobility and equality of opportunity. A more open society, he notes, is necessarily one in which it is easier for some people to move forward relative to others. By the same token, however, greater openness also increases the likelihood that people will move backwards. In a rapidly growing economy, it is possible to move backwards slightly in relative terms and yet still have more than one had in the past. In a stagnant economy, however, this cannot happen. For each person who wins, someone else must lose. In the context of a stagnant economy, greater openness thus means a significant possibility of ending up a loser.

If the value people assign to winning such a gamble were on a par with the value they assign to losing, they might nonetheless be inclined to roll the dice. For most people, however, these values are highly discrepant. As a burgeoning literature in psychology and economics has amply demonstrated, people assign much greater weight to losses than to gains of the same magnitude.[11]

The economist Richard Thaler coined the term *loss aversion* to describe this tendency. Loss aversion means not just that the pain of losing, say, $1,000, is larger, for most of us, than the pleasure from winning that same amount. It means that it is *much* larger. Thaler illustrates the asymmetry in our reactions to gains and losses by asking his students to consider the following hypothetical questions:

1. By attending class today, you have been exposed to a rare, fatal disease. The probability that you have the disease is one in a thousand. If you have the disease you will die a quick and painless death in one week. There is a cure for the disease that always works, but it has to be taken now. We do not know how much it will cost. You must say now the most you would be willing to pay for this cure. If the cure ends up costing more you won't get it. If it costs less, you will pay the stated price, not the maximum you stated. How much will you pay?

2. We are conducting experiments on the same disease for which we need subjects. A subject will just have to expose him or herself to the disease and risk a one-in-a-thousand chance of death. What is the minimum fee you would accept to become such a subject?[12]

Think about how you would answer these same questions yourself. In each scenario, you are asked, in effect, to reveal how strongly you feel about a one-in-a-thousand chance of death. But whereas the first scenario asks how much you would pay to eliminate a risk of death to which you have already been exposed, the second asks you how much you would have to be paid before exposing yourself to a similar risk voluntarily. Thaler reports that the median responses from his students are approximately $800 for the first question and $100,000 for the second.[13] "In general," Thaler explains, "people seem willing to pay more to keep something already in their possession than to acquire the same item had they not already owned it [in these examples, their good health]."[14] Loss aversion also helps us understand why workers expend vastly more effort to avoid a 10 percent cut in pay than to win a 10 percent increase.

One important consequence of loss aversion, Friedman argues, is
that the overriding goal for a majority of citizens in a stagnant economy
becomes the protection of their current positions. In such environments, proposals to reduce employment barriers almost invariably fall
on deaf ears. As Friedman observes, however, the picture is markedly
different in a quickly growing economy, where

> The asymmetry between "more" and "less" takes a reduced impor-
> tance because for most people downward mobility, should that be their
> lot, would be not a matter of "less" but merely a question of not as
> much "more." Over a much broader range of the existing income distri-
> bution, therefore, in a growing economy people will be willing to accept
> enhanced mobility, and they will support measures like anti-discrimina-
> tion laws, or special education programs for disadvantaged children,
> designed to make actual mobility greater.[15]

The concept of loss aversion also enriches our understanding of
the relationship between wealth and the amounts people are willing to
spend for environmental cleanup and other public goods. In particular,
it suggests that the rate of *change* of wealth is likely to be important. In
a rapidly growing economy, the cost of having a cleaner environment is
a slight reduction in the rate of growth of private consumption. But in
a stagnant economy, additional expenditures on the environment mean
having to retreat from private spending patterns that people have already grown accustomed to. Because of loss aversion, environmental
cleanup may thus be more easily achieved in a society with rapidly
growing incomes than in a wealthier society with stagnant incomes.
The general psychological principle is that it is much easier to pay for
something with forgone gains than with out-of-pocket losses. This
principle provides yet another reason to favor the more rapid economic growth that can be achieved by higher savings rates, and yet another reason to question the wisdom of our current spending patterns.

CHAPTER 8

EXCELLENT, RELATIVELY SPEAKING

By scaling back on the rate at which luxury consumption has been growing, we could drink safer water, breathe cleaner air, and eat food that is less likely to make us seriously ill. We could have more autonomy, variety, and safety in the workplace. We could fill the potholes in our streets, fix our crumbling bridges, and provide more help for people with serious drug problems. We could save enough to retire with complete financial security.

Credible scientific evidence suggests that making these and other changes would, on balance, enhance our physical and psychological well-being. Our current consumption patterns are thus all the more puzzling when we consider that the higher income growth rates that would result from higher savings would finance every one of these changes and more. The only required sacrifice, as we have seen, would be a *very* brief reduction in the rate of increase in our spending on material goods. After a short time, we could buy even larger houses, and even more luxuriously appointed cars and appliances if we chose to.

And yet we do not appear poised to make any of these changes. On the contrary, we appear to be straying even further from the more balanced consumption mix that the evidence suggests would be best. If we take the existing evidence on the determinants of human health and well-being at face value, we seem forced to reject the claim that the invisible hand leads to the greatest good for all.

Defenders of the status quo may concede that although our choices may not be the ones that make us happiest, there is still much to be said for letting people choose for themselves. Happiness, after all, isn't the only important human goal. If the people vote with their dollars that they want gilded private goods—not later, but now—and are willing to tolerate harried schedules, diminished future opportunities, and a host of other costs to get them, then so be it, the free-marketeers say. Their claim is not that market incentives will necessarily lead us to choose what is objectively best for us, but rather that we should simply be left to choose whatever we want.

Fair enough. Despite the possible attractions of a different mix of goods and services, there are indeed good reasons to fear living in a world in which self-appointed experts might be empowered to tell us how best to spend our money. As experience has taught, regulatory cures all too often turn out to be far worse than the diseases they were meant to heal. So even granting that our spending decisions may be far from perfect, it is by no means clear that there is anything we could, or should, do about it.

Let us set aside, for the moment, the question of whether there is any practical way to change our current consumption patterns for the better. For now, the far more pressing question is *why* we spend our time and money in the ways we do. If in fact we could all live better lives by simply changing our spending patterns, why haven't we done that? Could it be that the experts are simply wrong about what makes us healthier and happier? Or is it that we just don't *care* about being healthier and happier? Or perhaps we do care, but for some reason are simply incapable of acting in our own interests. In that case, is it just a matter of lacking the discipline to do what needs to be done? Or is it that powerful corporate interests manipulate our desires and constrain our choices?

Although each of these possibilities may be important in some settings, none holds the key to understanding why we fall short so often. For example, although we are by no means the perfect rational satisfaction maximizers assumed in orthodox economic models, we are surprisingly good, for the most part, at rooting out the information we need to get ahead. And although many of us are lazy and undisciplined at times, most of us can muster considerable energy when there are important tasks to be done. We may suspect, moreover, that most of us could summon the willpower to resist the temptations of Madison Avenue if we felt that doing so would substantially improve the quality of our lives.

Perhaps our difficulty is not that we fail to perceive our interests clearly, but rather that we perceive them only too well. Many people are fully aware, at some level, that we might be better off if *all* saved more and *all* spent less on houses and cars. But that choice is simply not an item on any individual family's menu. A family can choose the amount it spends on its own house, but it cannot choose the amounts that others spend. If it buys a smaller house, it inescapably alters its position in the overall size distribution of houses. And the consequence of having a *relatively* small house—or, perhaps more important, a house in a weaker school district—is vastly different from the effect of *all* having smaller houses.

In this observation lies an important key to understanding why the things we buy are so often not the things that best promote our own interests. Our conflict is rooted in the fact that human nature is simply not what economic orthodoxy assumes it to be. The orthodox models that underlie Adam Smith's invisible hand take the primary economic determinant of a person's sense of well-being to be his absolute standard of living. But as virtually everyone else has long been aware, it is relative living standards that often prove far more important. And as we shall see, when satisfaction depends importantly on relative living standards, all bets regarding the efficacy of the invisible hand are off.

CONCERNS ABOUT RELATIVE POSITION

Having been raised as an only child, I have always observed the sibling rivalries among my own children with great interest. On returning from a friend's house, my 8-year-old son immediately asks "Where's Chris?" if his 11-year-old brother is nowhere in sight. When Chris is at his violin lesson, or at the orthodontist's office, we have no problem. But let him be at a movie, or just visiting a friend, and the next thing we'll hear is Hayden's angry shout of "That's not fair!"—the inevitable prelude to an anguished outburst about the injustice of life. "He *always* gets to do fun stuff and I *never* do!"

No matter that Hayden may have seen the same movie a day earlier, and no matter that it may not even have been one he particularly enjoyed; and never mind that he himself just returned from visiting a friend; his reaction is always exasperatingly, tediously the same. If there were a dial we could turn to attenuate this reaction, my wife and I would pay a lot for it.

There is no such dial, of course, and so, like most parents, we try to teach our children to tend to their own business and not worry so much about what others have. There will always be somebody with a better deal, we tell them, and if you can't learn to live with that, you'll always be unhappy. When these admonitions fail, as they usually do, we manipulate the reward structure to deflect their concerns: "Stop complaining that Chris is at a movie; you got to see one yesterday, but if you keep whining, you won't get to go to another one any time soon."

As children grow older, their complaints become more muted, but it is clear that their concerns about unequal outcomes never truly disappear. And even if we could, would we really want to stifle these concerns completely? Sorely tempting though it might be, our carefully considered response would surely be no. For despite all the pain and suffering that spring from concerns about unequal outcomes, real or imagined, it is hard to see how someone stripped of these concerns could function effectively in the world as we know it.

Even in wealthy societies, after all, rivalry for important resources is a fact of life. Most of us want interesting jobs, caring and intelligent mates, safe neighborhoods, good schools for our children. Yet not all jobs are equally interesting, and not all potential mates are equally attractive; some neighborhoods are far safer than others; and no matter how many institutions aspire to do so, only 20 universities make the *U.S. News and World Report*'s annual top-20 list. A child who didn't care at all how her own serving of ice cream compared with her brother's would be unlikely to achieve the station in life that her talents and abilities might otherwise command.

SUBJECTIVE WELL-BEING AND RELATIVE INCOME

Study after careful study appears to show that, beyond some point, the average happiness level within a country is almost completely unaffected by increases in its average income level. Thus, as we have seen, average satisfaction levels register virtually no change even when average incomes grow many-fold, as they have in the industrialized countries in the years since World War II. Yet despite the strength and consistency of this finding, the notion that income has only negligible effects on happiness stands in sharp conflict with what most of us seem to believe.

Both in what we say and what we do, we give every indication that our incomes are a matter of enormous personal concern. As noted earlier, for example, when psychologists ask what change in our circumstances would most improve the quality of our lives, our most frequent response is "more money."[1] And indeed, if this were not so, why would we go to such lengths to increase our incomes? Why would first-year associates work 80-hour weeks in New York law firms? Why would oil-field firemen risk their lives and health? Why would the Tobacco Institute's expert witnesses humiliate themselves by making preposterous claims on the witness stand? If getting ahead doesn't make people significantly happier, why not simply avoid these experiences? The short answer seems to be that getting more money *does* make people happier, if by getting more money we mean moving forward in *relative* terms.

When psychologists examine how subjective well-being varies with income within a country at a single moment in time, the consistent finding is that richer people are, on the average, more satisfied with their lives than their poorer contemporaries. This relationship is illustrated in the diagram on page 112, which plots reported satisfaction levels against annual income for a U.S. sample of 4,942 persons surveyed between 1981 and 1984. Each point in this diagram represents

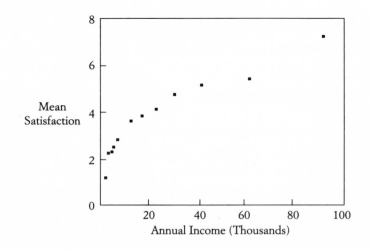

INCOME VERSUS SATISFACTION IN THE UNITED STATES, 1981–84

Source: Diener, Sandvik, Seidlitz, and Diener, 1993.

the average satisfaction level reported by a large number of sample members with essentially the same income. The relationship shown is typical of income-satisfaction relationships observed in other times and places.

In virtually every such study, the rich report significantly higher levels of life satisfaction than the poor. Note the striking contrast between this relationship and the one we saw earlier in which average satisfaction levels remained constant as average per-capita incomes rose many-fold over time within a country.

Notwithstanding the consistency of findings like the one summarized in the diagram, however, the actual numerical correlation between income and subjective well-being across individuals is relatively small. Thus, according to one typical study, the partial correlation coefficient between income and subjective well-being for Americans at a single moment in time was only 0.13.[2] (This means that, after controlling for the influence of other factors, variations in income explain less than 2 percent of the observed individual variance in subjective well-being.)

Numbers like these have inspired many psychologists to assert that income is not, in fact, an important determinant of individual differences in subjective well-being. As the late Richard Kammann wrote, for example, "Objective life circumstances have a negligible role to play in a theory of happiness."[3]

Adding to this impression are results from several recent studies purporting to show that as much as 80 percent of the individual differences in subjective well-being may be the result of heritable differences in temperament.[4] For example, the long-run average subjective well-being levels of identical twins reared apart are far more strongly correlated with each other than are the corresponding levels for fraternal twins reared together.[5] Some of us are born with sunny dispositions and seem to take great pleasure in our lives almost without reference to the nature of our objective circumstances. Yet others seem burdened by discontent even when, by all external measures, things are going exceptionally well.

These observations, however, simply do not imply that income has only a negligible effect on well-being. To see why, suppose we take as given that factors other than income explain the vast majority of individual differences in subjective well-being. In the statistician's parlance, this means that if we were to plot the actual individual data on happiness versus income, the scatter diagram would be much less orderly than the plot of group averages shown in the earlier diagram. Thus we would see a diagram more like the one below, which is simply a reproduction of the earlier diagram in which the smaller dots represent individual data points (in contrast to the large dots, each of which, again, represents the average satisfaction value for a large group of people with the same income).

When statisticians say that the relationship between the individual data points is less orderly—or "noisier"—than the corresponding relationship between the group averages, they mean simply that there is significant variation in satisfaction levels among individuals with any given income level. For example, among people earning $20,000 a year, there will be some individuals—such as the one denoted by point A—who are much more satisfied than average, and others—such as the one denoted by point B—who are much less satisfied than average. The same will be true of individuals earning $80,000 a year (see the in-

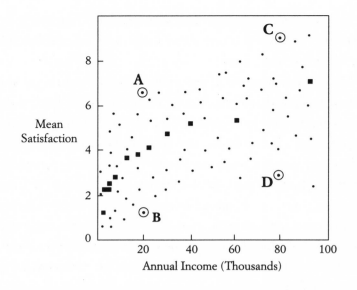

Mean
Satisfaction

Annual Income (Thousands)

THE RELATIONSHIP BETWEEN INDIVIDUAL INCOME AND
SUBJECTIVE WELL-BEING IS "NOISY."

dividuals denoted C and D). Psychologists are therefore correct to
conclude that the noisiness in the relationship means that knowing a
specific person's income does not enable a confident prediction of
what her level of subjective well-being will be.

Note, however, that even though temperament may be the most important single determinant of well-being, the individual denoted B can
still expect her subjective well-being to rise significantly if her income
rises. Thus, if B's temperament were essentially like D's, and if B's income were to rise from $20,000 to $80,000, then B's subjective well-
being would rise to the level currently experienced by D. Relative to
people in her new income group, B would still have low subjective well-
being, just as before. But the clear message in the data is that such moves
are likely to make people significantly happier than they were initially.

This point is important. To think about it in yet another way, note
that even though most differences in height are the result of genetic
differences, diet and medical care remain significant determinants of
height. Thus the average height of 15-year-old American boys has increased some five inches since the nineteenth century, a difference at-

tributable almost entirely to changes in what we eat and to better neonatal and pediatric medical care.[6] Indeed, if behavior is our primary concern, diet and medical care are more important than genes. After all, a teenager worried about his height can alter what he eats, or seek medical care when he is ill, but he cannot change his genetic inheritance.

By analogy, even though most individual differences in subjective well-being may be the result of factors other than income, income nonetheless remains an important contributor to subjective well-being. And like diet and medical care in the height example, it is perhaps the most important factor over which we have at least some control.

Behavioral Evidence

Measures of subjective well-being are not the only evidence that people care strongly about relative income. Unlike psychologists, who often rely on survey evidence, economists prefer behavioral evidence when attempting to make inferences about what people care about. The relevant literature is not extensive, but several studies shed light on the strength of concerns about relative income.

In one recent paper, for example, David Neumark and Andrew Postlewaite investigate how individual labor supply decisions depend on the incomes of important reference group members.[7] The idea here is that if someone cares strongly about how her income compares with the incomes of others, an increase in others' incomes will cause her to become more likely to seek employment, or more likely to work longer hours if she is already employed. The difficulty in testing such predictions has always been that it is hard to know whose incomes really matter to the decision maker. Most people presumably care most about the incomes of people with whom they associate most closely. Unfortunately, researchers seldom have reliable data about who knows whom, much less about which specific individuals people care most about.

Neumark and Postlewaite cleverly finesse this problem by examining the behavior of sisters. Perhaps inspired by Mencken's definition of wealth, the specific question they pose is this: Does a woman's decision about whether to work outside the home depend on her sister's economic circumstances? According to economic orthodoxy, which holds that only her own absolute income matters to her, it would not. But Neumark and Postlewaite find differently for a large sample of women whose sisters are not employed. Specifically, they find that such a woman is 16 to 25 percent more likely to work outside the home if her sister's husband earns more than her own husband.[8]

Additional evidence for the strength of concerns about relative position comes from an elegant experiment known as the "ultimatum bargaining game."[9] The game is played by two players, Proposer and Responder. It begins with Proposer being given a sum of money (say, $100) that he must then propose how to divide between himself and Responder. Responder then has two options: (1) he can accept, whereupon each party gets the amount proposed; or (2) he can refuse whereupon each party gets zero, and the $100 goes back to the experimenter.

If both players cared only about their own absolute incomes, as assumed by economic orthodoxy, Proposer should propose $99 for himself and $1 for Responder (only whole-dollar amounts are allowed). And Responder should then accept this one-sided offer because getting $1 is better than getting nothing.

Yet in scores of experiments performed in many different countries, this almost never happens. Thus, in one typical study in which the total amount to be divided was $10, the average amount offered by Proposer was $4.71, and in more than 80 percent of all cases Proposer offered exactly $5, a fifty-fifty split.[10] When Responders in this same study were asked to report the minimum amounts they would accept, their average response was $2.59. These experiments suggest clearly that laboratory subjects care not only about how much money they get but also about how it is apportioned in relative terms.[11] Most people seem predisposed to reject offers whose terms they find sufficiently "unfair." A large literature has emerged in recent years, much of it based on laboratory experiments, showing that concerns about fairness influence numerous similar economic choices.[12]

As in the laboratory, so in life. Believing their current contracts to be unfair, workers are often willing to go on strike, even when they know it may cost them their jobs. Customers often refuse to patronize merchants whose terms they believe to be inequitable, even when it will be more costly or less convenient to buy from alternative suppliers.

Concerns about relative position also appear to account for a long-standing anomaly in the distribution of pay among workers within any given firm. According to economic orthodoxy, workers evaluate their paychecks purely by the absolute amount of goods and services they buy, and standard theory predicts that workers will be paid in strict accordance with the value of what they produce. The wage structure within most private firms, however, seems far more egalitarian than that. Many firms, for example, follow strict salary formulas based on experience, education, and length of tenure within the firm, despite large and visible differences in the productivity of workers paid the same amounts under these formulas. Indeed, pay patterns of the sort predicted by orthodox models are virtually never observed in practice.

Here is a simple thought experiment that illustrates how strikingly the pay distributions we observe in practice depart from the ones predicted by economic orthodoxy. Among your co-workers of roughly similar rank, job title, and seniority, try to envision the two most productive individuals and also the three who are least productive. Now suppose that either the top two or the bottom three were to suddenly disappear. Which group's absence would most reduce the total value of what gets produced in your group? Most people answer without hesitation that the disappearance of the top two would hurt most. On the basis of this answer, economic orthodoxy would predict that the combined salaries of the top two individuals would be greater than the combined salaries of the bottom three. Yet in most groups the reverse is true.

The apparent anomaly can be resolved if we amend the orthodox position by simply assuming that in addition to whatever other concerns they may have, workers care about how their pay compares with the pay received by their co-workers.[13] Other factors being the same, workers with this concern naturally prefer to work in firms in which they do not earn less than most of their co-workers. By the laws of simple arithmetic, however, not everyone's preference to avoid low rank in the wage distribution of his firm can be satisfied. After all, only 50 percent of the members of any group can be in the top half. But if people are free to associate with whomever they please, why are the lesser-ranked members of groups content to remain? Why don't they all leave to form new groups of their own in which they would no longer be near the bottom?

Some workers undoubtedly do precisely that. And yet we also observe many stable, heterogeneous groups. Not all accountants at General Motors are equally talented; and in every law firm, some partners attract much more new business than others. If everyone prefers to avoid being near the bottom of her group of co-workers, what holds these heterogeneous groups together?

The apparent answer is that their low-ranked members receive extra compensation. If they were to leave, they would gain by no longer having to endure low status. By the same token, however, the top-ranked members would lose. They would no longer enjoy high status. If their gains from having high relative pay are larger than the costs borne by members with low relative pay, it does not make sense for the group to disband. Everyone can do better if the top-ranked workers induce their lesser-ranked colleagues to remain by sharing some of their pay with them.

Of course, not everyone assigns the same value to having high rank. Those who care relatively less about it will do best to join firms in which most workers are more productive than themselves. As lesser-ranked members in these firms, they will receive extra compensation. People who care most strongly about rank, by contrast, will want to join firms in which most other workers are less productive than themselves. For the privilege of occupying top-ranked positions in those firms, they will have to work for less than the value of what they produce.

Workers thus appear to sort themselves among firms in accordance with their demands for within-group status. The resulting wage distributions within each firm, although far more compressed than the ones predicted by economic orthodoxy, are perfectly consistent with the incentives confronting both firms and workers. The extra compensation received by each firm's low-ranked workers is exactly offset by the shortfall in pay of its high-ranked workers, which means that the employer remains whole. And workers within each firm find it mutually advantageous to be, in effect, either purchasers or suppliers of high rank. The resulting distributions of wages and salaries within firms are inconsistent with the view that workers care only about absolute income, yet are precisely the expected pattern if workers care also about relative income.

Sheryl Ball and her co-authors have shown that even simple laboratory manipulations of relative position can have profound implications for market exchange.[14] In one experiment, for example, they awarded half of their subjects stars on the basis of their performance on a transparently meaningless quiz. Following these awards, subjects were given objects of known value and allowed to exchange these objects with one another for cash. The subjects who received stars consistently received better terms—that is, they bought at lower prices and sold at higher prices—when they exchanged goods with subjects who did not receive stars.

Further evidence that interpersonal comparisons are important comes from studies of markets for collectibles. Economic orthodoxy holds that the value of a good to one consumer will typically not depend on how many other consumers own essentially similar goods. There are exceptions, of course, as when the actual usefulness of a good depends on the number of others who have it. (E-mail accounts and fax machines are examples.) But where such functional linkages do not exist, the amount that a consumer is willing to pay for a good is assumed independent of the number of others who own it. In purely functional terms, a coin with a slight flaw is a perfect substitute for one that comes from the mint in perfect condition. And because both provide equivalent legal tender, orthodox economic models say that both should be valued equally. As the market for rare coins attests, however, this is manifestly not the case. The economists Kenneth Koford and Adrian Tshoegl, for example, show that the prices of flawed coins are often literally millions of times higher than those for otherwise identical coins that were minted in large quantities.[15]

This finding is not merely the same as having documented the orthodox demand relationship in which the price people are willing to pay for a good is inversely related to the quantity of it they consume. In every respect save rarity, a flawed coin is a perfect substitute for a normal one, and economic theory says that if one good is a perfect substitute for another, it should sell for the same price. If rarity per se truly didn't matter, the observed premium for flawed coins would be akin to finding that color-blind people are willing to pay much more for red toasters than for green ones.

Participants in the market for rare coins are numerous. For example, Jacob Zahavi reports that the Franklin Mint, a private issuer of collectibles, had over 3 million active customers and sales of more than $600 million in 1992.[16] And rare coins are obviously just the tip of the collectibles iceberg. For example, people pay more than twice as much for the Lamborghini Diablo than for the Porsche 911 Turbo not because the Lamborghini has better functional attributes, but because it is so rare. It is actually both slower and less reliable than the Porsche, and more difficult to obtain parts for when it breaks down. Its price premium, like the rare coin's, stems only from its exclusivity.

I also note in passing a variety of other economic behaviors that contradict the traditional assumption that satisfaction depends on absolute but not relative income. For example, the incidence of piece-rate pay schemes is much lower, and the frequency with which workers go on strike is much higher, than we would expect if relative income did not matter.[17] In addition, the observed structural differences between the compensation packages of unionized firms and nonunionized firms—for instance, the fact that unionized workers tend to receive a much larger share of total compensation in the form of nonmonetary fringe benefits—are difficult to explain without reference to concerns about relative position.[18] And the fact that the rich save significantly higher proportions of their permanent incomes than do the poor[19] is inconsistent with orthodox economic models,[20] but is the predicted pattern when satisfaction depends on relative consumption.[21]

Evidence from the large scientific literature on the determinants of subjective well-being consistently suggests that we have strong concerns about relative position. There is also evidence that a variety of important behaviors spring from these concerns. Whatever positive consequences may flow from our concerns about relative position, it is clear that they are also the source of a great deal of misery in the world.

Some societies have attempted to avoid the unhappiness that results from unequal outcomes by trying to prevent unequal outcomes. Hence the Marxian distributional maxim: From each according to his ability, to each according to his need. Yet, as the collapse of the economies of the former Soviet Union has shown, preventing unequal outcomes to assuage concerns about relative position is a sure recipe for economic failure. Why take risks and work long hours if you know that your success will not be tolerated?

The explosive progress of the industrial economies of the West has been in no small measure the result of a generally shared cultural understanding that concerns about relative standing are simply not legitimate. This is not to say that people in the capitalist economies never experience a twinge of envy or resentment when an acquaintance succeeds on a spectacular scale. It is just that such feelings have never been seen as a legitimate basis for restricting the options of others.

Setting aside the question of whether it was ever *sensible* to stifle innovation in the name of equality, as the socialist economies tried to do, most observers recognize that this is no longer feasible in any event. In the increasingly competitive global economy, those who are not rewarded will not take the necessary steps to innovate, and those who fail to innovate simply will not survive. What is not generally recognized, however, is that the other extreme position—complete intolerance of concerns about relative position—has itself proved a costly error, and not just in social terms, but in economic terms as well.

CHAPTER 9

WHY CONTEXT AND POSITION ARE SO IMPORTANT

A house may be large or small; as long as the surrounding houses are equally small, it satisfies all social demands for a dwelling. But if a palace rises beside the little house, the little house shrinks into a hut.

—Karl Marx

Concerns about relative position do not go away no matter how intolerant we are of them. On the contrary, despite our concerted efforts to stifle these concerns, they continue to express themselves in extremely costly ways. It is largely these concerns, we shall see, that tilt our spending patterns so strongly in favor of conspicuous consumption. My claim is that although we cannot eliminate concerns about relative position, we can rearrange our incentives in ways that will make them far less costly. But we are unlikely to take this step unless we first understand more clearly the origins of our concerns about relative position and the manifold ways in which they shape not only our perceptions of events but also our interactions with one another. We must learn to view these concerns not as a contemptible human shortcoming, but rather as an important practical barrier to achieving specific goals. Only then can we take the steps necessary to move forward.

UNDERSTANDING HUMAN NATURE

Different people care about different things. And although neuro-science has made great progress in recent decades, the sources of many of these differences may never really be known. Differences in genetic endowments and early childhood experiences may explain why some like Rachmaninoff while others prefer the Rolling Stones. Yet similar differences are sometimes observed even for identical twins reared together.

Despite the conspicuous variation in human psychology, there is also much that is strikingly the same across people from diverse genetic and cultural backgrounds. Recalling a scene at the international arrivals gate at Heathrow Airport, the British novelist Ian McEwan describes "the same joy, the same uncontrollable smile, in the faces of a Nigerian earth mama, a thin-lipped Scottish granny, and a pale, correct Japanese businessman as they wheeled their trolleys in and recognized a figure in the expectant crowd."[1] What drives this common response?

The evolutionary psychologist's approach to such questions begins with Charles Darwin's theory of evolution by natural selection, which holds that we like certain things because liking them helps us to survive and leave offspring—or at least had that effect during most of our evolutionary history.[2] The evolutionary psychologist's immediate reaction to the scene at Heathrow Airport is thus to focus on the survival value of extended kinship and friendship ties. The expressions of delight on renewal of close relationships are immediately intelligible in this light. Someone with both the desire and capacity for becoming deeply attached to other people is likely to weather life's storms much more effectively than others who cannot, or choose not, to form close relationships.

Yet not all appetites are so clearly adaptive. For example, in addition to our taste for close personal relationships, most of us also have in common a taste for sweet foods and foods with high fat content. Indulged without conscious restraint, this taste draws us to a diet that is harmful: The more sweets and fats we eat, the more our weight soars and the more clogged our arteries become.

Evolutionary psychologists explain the apparent paradox by noting that the principal threat to survival during the period in which humans evolved was not heart disease but starvation. Famine was a constant threat, and the best protection against it was to get as fat as you could when food was available. Someone who really *liked* sugars and fats would have been willing to expend extra effort to acquire these calorie-rich nutrients, and hence more likely to build up protective stores of body fat.

With most traits and desires, there is variation across individuals. Some are tall, others short; some dark-skinned, others light-skinned; and some have relatively more intense appetites for highly caloric foods. During an era of frequent famines, those with the strongest appetites for such foods would be more likely than others to survive, and hence more likely to pass the genes for those appetites on to their offspring.

As it happens, famine is no longer a serious threat to survival, at least not in most of the developed world. But natural selection works slowly. Although some of the appetites that served us so well in the Pleistocene era are not well adapted to modern conditions, we are stuck with them for the time being. We can of course try to develop strategies for overcoming costly appetites. But these strategies may themselves be costly, and in the end, many of us will surely die prematurely because of the simple fact we are driven by appetites for foods that are not good for us.

The evolutionary psychologist thus has an elegant theory to explain why many people pay hefty sums to attend camps that will put them through rigorous training regimens and restrict their food intake. In orthodox economic models of the purposeful rational actor, such behavior is completely unintelligible. But it is not at all surprising once we understand the environmental circumstances under which natural selection molded our appetites for food.

Drives and Emotions Complement Rational Calculation

If an appetite that is useful in one environment proves harmful in another, how did human food intake come to be driven by persistent, hard-wired appetites in the first place? Why didn't natural selection instead favor the more flexible alternative of regulating food intake on the basis of a dispassionate, cognitive assessment of caloric needs? It might seem, after all, that once people became intelligent enough to discover whether famines were a major threat, they could have adjusted their food intake accordingly. If the local environment were one plagued by frequent famines, people would realize that it was strongly in their interest to fatten up whenever they could. Conversely, people living in a time and place in which famines were not a threat could eat a healthful diet without constantly having to battle self-destructive appetites.

The flexibility issue also arises in the context of behaviors driven by extreme thirst. A shipwreck survivor may be a trained scientist who *knows* that drinking sea water will not only fail to quench his thirst but actually hasten his death. And yet such is the power of thirst that at some point even this person will drink sea water if no other water is available. Again, why didn't natural selection favor greater flexibility in the regulation of fluid intake?

The simple answer is that greater flexibility is not always advantageous. After all, the kinds of cost-benefit calculations envisioned by rational choice theory take time, and in many situations time is of the essence. Thus, as the evolutionary psychologists Leda Cosmides and John Tooby ask, "When a tiger bounds toward you, what should your response be? Do a cartwheel? Sing a song? Is this the moment to run an uncountable number of randomly generated response possibilities through the decision rule?"[3] The individual who simply flees in a burst of panic usually does better than the person who stops to consider all the options. She may not be able to outrun the tiger, but her odds of survival go up sharply if she can outrun at least some of the others the tiger is chasing.

This doesn't mean that considering relevant options is unimportant. But neuroscientists now understand that emotions actually assist, rather than hinder, in this task.[4] This is so in part because of the critical role played by emotion in learning. The human brain is agile and capacious by comparison with the brains of almost all other animals. But

even we can process only a small fraction of the information that bom-
bards us every instant. We need some means of focusing our attention
selectively. Inborn drives and emotional reactions to stimuli are the
brain's rough and ready way of telling us what counts.

Emotions are mediated by neural circuitry in the limbic structures
of the prefrontal region of the brain. Neuroscientists have discovered
that although patients with lesions in these structures typically have all
the cognitive power needed to perform complex cost-benefit calculations, they are often woefully unable to make even the simplest decisions. In his recent book, the neuropsychiatrist Antonio Damasio
describes his experience of trying to schedule his next visit with a pa-
tient whose limbic damage had robbed him of much of his capacity to
experience emotion:

> I suggested two alternative dates, both in the coming month and
> just a few days apart from each other. The patient pulled out his ap-
> pointment book and began consulting the calendar. The behavior that
> ensued, which was witnessed by several investigators, was remarkable.
> For the better part of a half-hour, the patient enumerated reasons for
> and against each of the two dates: previous engagements, possible me-
> teorological conditions, virtually anything that one could reasonably
> think about concerning a simple date . . . an endless outlining and fruit-
> less comparison of options and possible consequences. It took enor-
> mous discipline to listen to all of this without pounding on the table and
> telling him to stop, but we finally did tell him, quietly, that he should
> come on the second of the alternative dates. His response was equally
> calm and prompt. He simply said: "That's fine." Back the appointment
> book went into his pocket, and then he was off.[5]

Another important function of drives and emotions is that they
provide the impetus to confront formidable obstacles when the stakes
are sufficiently high. For example, we hear of a mother weighing only
100 pounds who rips a locked door from its hinges in a frantic effort
to rescue her toddler from a burning house. Likewise, under famine
conditions, those without food can obtain it only through extreme
measures—arduous, unpleasant actions that may themselves entail

significant risk of death. Under these conditions, it is important that a person not only *know* that he needs food, but also that he *care*, lest he be unwilling to risk what needs to be done.

It thus appears that natural selection was led to forge a painful compromise. On balance, the person who is desperately driven to achieve the goals most critical to survival enjoys an advantage over others who pursue their objectives dispassionately. Yet despite this advantage, there remain many situations in which intense appetites can work against us.

Emotions and the Commitment Problem

Suppose, for the sake of argument, that it were possible to construct a brain with infinite capacity to absorb information, perform complex cost-benefit analyses, and mobilize available bodily resources for action. There would *still* be circumstances in which even a person equipped with such an all-powerful and flexible brain would fare worse than someone driven by the normal mix of emotion and imperfect reason.[6]

For example, imagine yourself at a business conference in a distant city. A fellow conferee notices your elegant, hand-tooled leather briefcase and decides he would like to have it. If he steals it, you must decide whether to press charges. If you do, you will have to stay for an interview with a local police investigator, causing you to miss your flight home. Then, after some weeks or months pass, you will need to return to testify against the thief, whose lawyer will try to make it appear that you are somehow responsible for the theft. Conservatively, you estimate that the costs of pressing charges, including travel expenses and forgone earnings, will come to more than $5,000. Under the circumstances, if the potential thief believes that you are a perfectly rational, self-interested person, he will know that he is free to steal your briefcase with impunity. He knows, after all, that you are smart enough to realize that the cost of pressing charges would far exceed the value of the briefcase you stand to recover.

A natural response might be to attempt to deter the thief by *threatening* to press charges if he steals your briefcase. If you could somehow *commit* yourself to act on your threat, this tactic might be effective. But if the thief believes you to be a narrowly rational actor, your threat will simply not be credible. Because he can anticipate that it will not be in your interest to follow through when the time comes, he is free, in effect, to ignore it.

Suppose, however, that you are not like the narrowly rational actor who populates orthodox economic models but are instead a person driven by the normal mix of reason and emotion. And suppose that this aspect of your nature has become apparent to all during the course of your interactions at the conference. If the thief steals your briefcase, which was a gift from your spouse, you will be outraged. And even though it would cost you more than the value of the briefcase to press charges, you will feel impelled to do so. After all, your alternative would be to experience years of anger and frustration at the memory of having let the thief simply get away with it.

The irony is that if the thief perceives there is a good chance that this is the kind of person you are, he will be much less tempted to steal your briefcase in the first place. The mere fact that he realizes you might be *willing* to make an "irrational" investment in seeing justice done may provide all the deterrence you need.

In this and other ways, the evolutionary psychologist's portrait of the human decision maker is profoundly different from the orthodox economist's. The cool, cognitive strategy of the rational choice model has "far more to do with the way patients with prefrontal damage go about deciding than with how normals usually operate."[7] And as we shall see, social institutions designed with brain-damaged people in mind inevitably fail to make the most of available opportunities.

OTHER ADVANTAGES INHERENT IN CONCERNS
ABOUT RELATIVE POSITION

Our economic and social institutions are designed on the basis of the economist's model of the narrow rational actor. *Homo economicus,* as he is called, cares about his absolute income (more of it being clearly better than less), but does not care how his income compares with what others earn. Given a choice between two hypothetical worlds, one in which he would earn $100,000 a year in perpetuity while others earned only $90,000, and another in which he would earn $110,000 while others earned $200,000, he would immediately opt for the latter. After all, he will have $10,000 a year more to spend in the second world and, by assumption, he doesn't mind having low relative income.

From survey evidence, however, we know that a substantial proportion of people confronted with such a choice would opt for the first world.[8] I do not claim that theirs is necessarily the better choice. Indeed, it is evident that many feel sheepish about opting for high relative income, apparently feeling that they *should* choose the situation in which all incomes are higher. But although we need not endorse either choice, it is critical that we see clearly why, from the evolutionary psychologist's perspective, the attraction of high relative income is so powerful.

Context, Perception, and Evaluation

In his pioneering book, *Adaptation-Level Theory,* the psychologist Harry Helson explains that, within broad limits, the human nervous system responds less to the absolute level of any stimulus than to deviations between it and some relevant norm or reference level encountered in the local environment.[9] Thus a resident of Havana feels cold on a 60-degree day in November, while a resident of Montreal finds a 60-degree day in March pleasantly warm. Similarly, a light of given intensity may seem either bright or dim according to conditions in the local visual field. And so on.

These response patterns do not imply that absolute stimulus levels never matter. Let the temperature fall sufficiently far, for instance, and a person will feel cold no matter what conditions she is accustomed to. Helson's point is simply that local conditions are important; and that within the relatively broad environmental limits to which people are able to adapt, context is often decisive.

The influence of context on visual perception is captured by the simple estimation problem posed in the diagram below. Which of the two short vertical lines is longer? In psychology experiments around

WHICH VERTICAL LINE IS LONGER?

the world, most subjects confidently respond that the one on the right is longer, yet in fact the two have exactly the same length. The illusion stems from the fact that the line on the right bridges a larger fraction of the gap between the two longer lines.

Although it is easy to contrive illusions that dupe the normal brain mechanisms that rely on contextual cues, these mechanisms function with remarkable swiftness and effectiveness in most natural environments. When a dog and his rival each want the same bone, each must make a strategic decision in which contextual cues prove crucial. Should he fight for the bone, or defer to his rival and go off in search of another? The typical dog follows a simple decision rule: If his rival is considerably bigger than he is, he defers; if they are roughly the same size, he may fight, depending on how hungry he is; and if his rival is smaller, he will almost certainly fight, or at least make it clear that he intends to. It is therefore important that a dog be able to reach a quick and accurate judgment about how large his rival is.

An important factor in this judgment is the size of the rival's image that forms on the dog's retina. But the size of that image alone is not very informative, for a dog 10 meters away will cast an image only half as high as when it is just 5 meters away. Dogs whose ancestors survived the rigorous competition of evolutionary history are well aware of this relationship between distance and apparent size. The well-adapted animal thus judges a rival to be large or small not just according to the absolute size of the rival's visual image on his retina, but also according to how that image compares with other objects of known size in the same visual field.

Contextual cues are similarly important in our evaluations of most goods and services. Suppose, for example, that you are asked to evaluate the "adequacy" of the living space in the floor plan of a 500-square-foot house. The mental process triggered by this question is to compare that floor plan with other floor plans that you can summon easily from memory. Typically, mental images of the floor plan of your own house will be most readily accessible, followed by those of houses in which close friends and relatives live. If you are a middle-income professional living with your family in a contemporary American suburb, your likely judgment will be that the floor plan of this house is "too small." And if a sudden reversal in your economic fortunes were to force you to live in a house that size, your subjective experience would almost surely confirm that judgment.

Now suppose that you are asked to evaluate a floor plan depicting the 500-square-foot living quarters of a yacht. Unless you happen to be one of the world's wealthiest individuals, things will now look radically different. Although the living space is precisely the same as the earlier floor plan, 500 square feet of usable floor space amidships *seems* enormous. And this impression would almost certainly be confirmed by your subjective experience if you were actually to spend an extended vacation living on a boat that large.

I emphasize that these different evaluations need have nothing to do with the dreaded emotions of envy or pride. They are driven by brain mechanisms similar to the ones that explain why a Montreal resident's evaluation of a 60-degree day in March is more favorable than a Havana resident's evaluation of a 60-degree day in November.

Contextual forces of a similar sort influence almost every conceivable dimension of product quality evaluation. One need not care about owning nicer things than one's neighbors to take pleasure in owning an object that is handsome and carefully crafted. The man who takes pleasure in the striking appearance and solid, well-constructed feel of his new Lexus need not be seen as gloating that his car turns more heads than his neighbor's. Nor can we infer that he had been ashamed of the Pontiac sedan he previously drove.

Yet modifiers like *handsome* and *carefully crafted* are inherently contextual. If a time machine could transport today's Pontiac sedan to an earlier year—say, 1938—we can be sure it would attract at least the same attention and admiration that current luxury cars do. The sound that the Pontiac's doors make on closing, which to the ear of today's discerning buyer signals the suspect manufacturing standards of General Motors, would have been heard by that same person in 1938 as the unmistakable "thunk" of quality. And whereas today's auto enthusiast is likely to be disappointed by the Pontiac's performance and reliability, drivers in that earlier year would have been thrilled by the car's agile handling and powerful acceleration, and astonished by how infrequently it needed maintenance.

Similarly, the middle-class professional who lives in Manhattan is unlikely to be burdened by dissatisfaction that her apartment has no room for a Ping-Pong table or wine cellar, and she almost surely entertains no expectation of having a swimming pool. Yet that same woman living in a Westchester County suburb might not even consider a house that lacked these amenities.

The evolved human brain is hard-wired to employ contextual cues when making evaluative judgments. The cues on which we rely need not be drawn from the immediate context. For instance, a woman may reject a string of suitors because none measures up to her first love, who was killed in an accident 20 years earlier. Yet, to a considerable extent, the cues on which we rely are distinctively local in time and place. The psychologist Fritz Strack and his collaborators have found, for example, that people's assessments of their own lives go up if a disabled person is present in the room when the question is put to them. [10]

To earn a good evaluation, something must typically compare favorably with other things in its class in the immediate context. An inevitable consequence is that our evaluation of the things we have depends on how they compare with the things that others in the local environment have. If our children are endowed with normal human brains, there is little prospect that they will be able to heed our admonitions to see the world any differently.

The Dependence of Reward on Rank

The natural history of concerns about relative position is also surely rooted in the fact that so many important resources are distributed in accordance with relative rather than absolute capabilities. For example, as the economist Amartya Sen has emphasized, there is always *some* food available, even in the most severe famines, and the question of who gets it is settled largely by relative wealth holdings.[11] So it is not at all strange that someone might choose a world in which he earned $100,000 while others earned $90,000 rather than one in which he earned $110,000 while others earned $200,000. In particular, we need not assume that someone with that preference takes any pleasure in the knowledge that the needs of others have not been met.

If price were no object, most of us would be pleased to live in a house overlooking the water, city lights, or some other pleasing vista. Yet in most areas only a small fraction of homesites have commanding views. Whether a family gets one of these choice sites will depend much more on its relative income than on its absolute income. The average family income in a community may be $10,000 or it may be $10 million. But if only 10 percent of the homesites have views, and all families have the same preferences, then only families in the top tenth of the income distribution will end up with views. Here again, a family's enjoyment of its view might not be lessened in any way if it were somehow possible for all homesites to have views. But typically that will not be possible, and hence one more reason to care about relative income.

Relative income would be important for a variety of other practical reasons even in a world in which people really cared only about absolute income. For instance, because the clothing required to appear presentably dressed depends strongly on the clothing worn by others, one cannot compete effectively for jobs, or even, as Adam Smith himself once put it, appear in public without shame, without first having achieved a threshold level of relative income.[12] By the same token, whereas residents of many villages in developing countries have no need for an automobile, a resident of Los Angeles cannot meet even the most minimal demands of social existence without one.[13] And as the economist Richard Layard once wrote, "In a poor society a man proves to his wife that he loves her by giving her a rose, but in a rich society he must give a dozen roses."[14]

In purely biological terms, relative resource holdings are nowhere more consistently and decisively important than in the struggle between individuals for access to mates. For both humans and other animals, the most intense of these struggles typically involve males. The reason lies in an asymmetry in the reproductive strategies of the two sexes. Females, who in most species invest heavily in the gestation and care of offspring, have limited reproductive capacity relative to males, whose only contribution in many instances consists of cheaply manufactured sperm cells. This asymmetry means that any single male is capable, in principle, of siring an almost unlimited number of offspring. The result for males is a genetic tournament with enormously high stakes. In one species of seals, for example, 4 percent of the breeding-age males sire almost 90 percent of all surviving offspring.[15]

The variability of male reproductive success in humans, although smaller than in many other animal species, is nonetheless substantial. More than 85 percent of past and present human societies for which data are available were polygynous.[16] In such societies, high-ranking males often take numerous wives, and the biggest winners enjoy prodigious reproductive success. For example, Moulay Ismail, the last sharifian Emperor of Morocco, fathered more than a thousand children in the late seventeenth and early eighteenth centuries.[17] Even people who would be delighted if *everyone* had lots of grandchildren would thus have ample reason to want high relative incomes.

In modern industrial societies, of course, there is no longer a strong link between relative income and the number of grandchildren one expects to have. Even so, there is evidence that relative earning power continues to be an important factor in mate selection. Thus, according to one recent survey, women consider earning power the most important single characteristic when evaluating potential mates. And in apparent recognition of the growing importance of two-earner families, men in that same survey ranked earning power second behind only physical attractiveness.[18]

Over the course of human evolution, if individuals differed in the intensity of their respective desires to achieve high rank, and if those with more intense desires were more likely than others to achieve it, then it would be strange indeed if the relentless forces of natural selection had not honed a human brain that strongly motivated its bearer to seek high rank.

The Allocation and Regulation of Effort

It might seem natural to ask why a brain molded by natural selection would urge us to seek relative rather than absolute wealth since, in most cases, a person who maximizes her absolute wealth turns out to have maximized her relative wealth as well. We might also ask why our inner voices don't simply urge "do the best you can," rather than "try to achieve high rank." After all, most of us are destined to be outranked by at least *some* people in virtually every domain of life, making a relentless focus on relative position seem more like a recipe for unhappiness than a useful motivational tool.

As evolutionary psychologists stress, however, the purpose of human motivation is not to make us happy but to make us more likely to succeed against the competition. Someone who is unhappy about her low relative position in one arena may be motivated to compete in a different arena. For instance, a talented lawyer who is not willing to put in 80-hour workweeks will have a better chance of becoming an influential member of the local bar in a small city than in Manhattan.

There is also the problem that a command like "do the best you can" is hopelessly vague. Each of us has a unique mix of talent, experience, and ability. In most cases, doing the best we can will not yield much fruit unless we first discover just what it is we're good at. Once you've chosen to become a piano player, it may be good to try to become the best piano player you can; but how did you know that becoming a piano player was the right choice in the first place?

Much of human learning takes place as a result of the positive or negative reinforcement we receive from different actions. Slowly, often by trial and error, we purge our repertoires of behaviors that don't work and replace them with ones that do. If you are tone deaf, your relatively poor performance in grade school music classes will have spared you the trouble of seeking a career on the concert stage. If you are a slow runner, your poor performance in early footraces will have steered you away from training for the Olympics. And with any luck, your strong early performance in some other arenas will have helped guide you toward a career that provided more fertile ground for your talents. When it comes to finding the right arena in which to compete, an inner voice urging "try to achieve high rank" is likely to be far more informative than an inner voice urging "do the best you can."

There is yet another important reason for being concerned about rank per se. It is that rank serves as a convenient benchmark for use in regulating the amount of effort we expend. As wartime experience has vividly illustrated, human beings under duress can accomplish extremely demanding physical tasks with little sleep for weeks at a time. Even when faced with imminent threats of death, however, there are limits. Because each person's struggle for survival typically plays out over many decades, the expenditure of maximum possible effort at every moment is almost sure to be a losing strategy. To avoid burning out, we must also set aside time to reflect, to restore ourselves.

A far more prudent general strategy is thus to conserve our energy for the occasions when threats to survival are greatest. Here, too, an intrinsic concern about relative position appears almost tailor-made for the task at hand. As a general rule, the farther an individual fell in his local pecking order, the more serious were the threats to his survival. A decline in rank typically provokes distress and anxiety, and these feelings often spur the additional effort it takes to recover lost ground.

This is not to say that anxiety vanishes once someone achieves a threshold level of high rank. On the contrary, we all know people whose drive to advance remains unsated no matter how much they may have achieved. This may be explained in part by the fact that individuals differ in their respective drives to succeed, and those with the highest drives are more likely than others to have made it near the top.

But the evolutionary psychologist's perspective suggests the additional possibility that we ought not to have expected the relationship between subjective well-being and relative income to have been a simple, static one in the first place. From an evolutionary design standpoint, the most successful organisms will be concerned not just with their relative position but with *changes* therein. In competitive environments, after all, complacency with high rank often results in losing it.

Psychological well-being thus seems attuned to relative income in roughly the following way: Increases in relative income increase well-being, and reductions in relative income reduce well being, but both effects tend to decay at least partially over time.[19] Once people become adapted to their new circumstances, these constitute a new norm against which further changes are reckoned. (Hence the folk wisdom that "life is a journey, not a destination.")

The evolutionary psychologist's framework also calls attention to the fact that the relevant reproductive battles were typically decided by competitive balance in highly local environments. For instance, an ape's reproductive success depended not on how strong he was relative to the entire population of apes on the African continent, but on his strength relative to rivals in his immediate vicinity. Similarly, the economic and psychological rewards of today's tennis player depend not on his performance vis-à-vis all other athletes, but on how well he performs relative to other tennis players in the particular arena in which he competes. Achieving high or improving rank in this "local hierarchy" will make him feel good, and the reverse will be true for low rank or downward movements.

This may help to explain why the satisfaction levels reported by some who earn $200,000 a year are no larger than those of others earning half that amount. People in each category are involved in their own competitions to move forward in local hierarchies. And in each case, only half of the contestants can rank in the top half.

Commitment Problems in Bargaining

Human beings are quintessentially trading animals. From the evolutionary dawn of our lineage, our survival has depended on our ability to exchange goods and favors with one another. Concern about relative position also proves adaptive as we bargain with one another about how to divide the fruits of these exchanges.

To see how, imagine that you and an acquaintance are invited to write an article for a weekly newsmagazine describing events you have witnessed at a political rally at which several bystanders were injured by police. You are the only ones who can write the article, and neither of you has sufficient information to be able to do the job alone. The magazine offers a total of $10,000 for writing the article, and leaves it up to the two of you to decide how to divide this sum. Since contributing to the article is a task that you personally would have been willing to do for free, any money you get is a pure windfall.

Or so it would appear. Before you have a chance to discuss how to share the money with your partner, he shows you a copy of a binding legal agreement he has just signed that calls for him to donate $20,000 to the National Rifle Association (NRA) in the event that his share of the $10,000 turns out to be less than $9,990. Since you know your partner is a gun-control advocate, you both realize that this contract means that unless you agree to accept $10 or less as payment for writing your half of the article, the deal is off. (If he lets you have any more, he will have to donate $20,000 to the NRA, something you're sure he wouldn't be willing to do.)

Note that this contract puts you in the same position as that of the Responder in the ultimatum bargaining game discussed in the preceding chapter. You must either accept $10 as payment for your half of the article, or turn down the deal from the magazine, in which case each of you will receive nothing. If you cared only about absolute income, you would accept, since getting $10 would be better than nothing. But suppose your partner had known all along that you care also about how the total is divided. He would then have foreseen the likelihood that you would have refused a one-sided offer, and he would never have dared make such an offer in the first place. By virtue of your concern about relative income, you have become, in effect, a much more effective bargainer.

The willingness of workers to go on strike rather than submit to the terms of a contract they believe to be unfair sometimes places their jobs in jeopardy, but it may also protect them against unfair contracts in the first place. Likewise, the fact that merchants know that many customers will turn elsewhere if offered terms they find inequitable often restrains merchants from offering inequitable terms at the outset. Someone with no concern about how the gains from exchange were shared would be singularly ill-equipped as a bargainer.

Ability Signaling

Suppose that you have been unjustly accused of a serious crime and are looking for an attorney to represent you. And suppose your choice is between two lawyers who, so far as you know, are identical in all respects, except for their standard of consumption. One wears a threadbare polyester suit off the rack and arrives at the courthouse in a 15-year-old, rust-eaten Chevy Citation. The other wears an impeccably tailored sharkskin suit and drives a new BMW 740i. Which one would you hire? Remember, you are not looking for a friend, but for a competent attorney.

The odds suggest that the latter attorney is a better bet. The reason is that a lawyer's ability level in a competitive market is likely to be mirrored closely by his income, which in turn will be positively correlated with his consumption. There is obviously no guarantee that the lawyer who spends more on consumption will have higher ability. But as in other situations involving risk, it makes sense to be guided by the laws of probability. And these laws say unequivocally to choose the better-dressed lawyer.

Where important decisions involving people we do not know well are involved, even weak signals of ability are often decisive. Close employment decisions are an obvious example. First impressions count for a lot during job interviews, and as apparel manufacturers are fond of reminding us, we never get a second chance to make a first impression. Placement counselors have always stressed the importance of quality attire and a good address in the job search process. Even when the employer *knows* how good an applicant is, she may still care a great deal about how that person will come across to others. This will be es-

pecially true in jobs that involve extensive contact with outsiders who
do *not* know how good the employee is.

"It's all about who has what," said William Unger, a Madison Avenue retailer, as he described a conversation he had overheard between two men, each wearing a five-figure wristwatch. "The friend sees
his friend has a [Patek Philippe] Pagoda, and these are people who
have a certain intuitiveness; they know how much things cost. They as-
certain what a guy's capability or monetary status is by looking at his
watch. They know if he's a player. Or they think they know."[20]

From the perspective of the individual buyer, many lavish consumption expenditures may thus be considerably less frivolous than
they seem. To the extent that wearing the right watch, driving the right
car, wearing the right suit, or living in the right neighborhood may help
someone land the right job or a big contract, these expenditures are
more like investments than like true consumption. And this suggests
yet another reason that people often feel uneasy when in the presence
of others who have conspicuously more.

BIOCHEMICAL MARKERS OF CONCERN
ABOUT RELATIVE POSITION

If concerns about relative position are indeed part of the evolved circuitry of the human brain and not just a cultural artifact, then biologists ought to have found footprints of the actual physical processes
that give rise to these concerns. In this section I briefly mention
two recent lines of investigation that bear on this issue—one that
links relative position to the brain's internal regulators of emotion
and behavior, and another that links relative position to mortality and
morbidity.

The Serotonin and Testosterone Studies

UCLA neuroscientist Michael McGuire and his collaborators have
shown that relative position in local primate groups appears to affect,
and be affected by, concentrations of the neurotransmitter serotonin,
which regulates moods and behavior.[21] For example, in one study in-

volving 19 groups of adult vervet monkeys, McGuire et al. found that concentrations of serotonin metabolites in cerebrospinal fluid samples taken from the dominant member in each group were approximately 50 percent higher than the corresponding concentrations in samples taken from subordinate animals.

Is this difference the effect, or the cause, of high status? To investigate this question, McGuire and his colleagues removed the initially dominant animal from each group and placed him in an isolation cage. Shortly thereafter, a new individual established dominance within each group, and after roughly 72 hours passed, serotonin concentrations in the newly dominant animal rose to the levels seen in the formerly dominant animal. At the same time, the serotonin concentrations in the formerly dominant animal fell to the level associated with subordinate status. When the initially dominant animal was returned to the group, he reasserted dominance, and serotonin concentrations in both the originally dominant and interim-dominant animals responded accordingly.[22] These patterns suggest that changes in rank cause changes in serotonin levels.

In a subsequent study, Michael Raleigh and his collaborators found that higher serotonin concentrations also appear to facilitate the acquisition of higher status.[23] Their experiment involved administration of a drug that boosted available serotonin concentrations in the brain. Animals treated with this drug were more likely to ascend in the social hierarchy than others treated with a placebo.

The serotonin-status relationship is less clearly understood in humans than in nonhuman primates. But there are indications that the patterns found in the primate studies are apparently also present in at least some human groups. McGuire and his colleagues, for example, have found elevated serotonin levels in the leaders of college fraternities and athletic teams.[24] In another study, Douglas Madsen finds that the status-serotonin relationship is positive for some groups of male college students.[25]

Like dopamine, norepinephrine, and other neurotransmitters, serotonin affects mood and behavior in a variety of ways. It is especially important for transmitting impulses between nerve cells in the limbic, or prefrontal, structures of the brain. Within limits, having elevated serotonin concentrations is associated with enhanced feelings of well-being. Serotonin deficiencies are associated with a variety of affective disorders, including irritability, sleep disorders, mania, and depression.[26] Recent work suggests that serotonin deficiencies are also strongly linked with impulsive aggression and suicide attempts.[27] The drug Prozac, widely prescribed for depression and other mood disorders, is a serotonin uptake inhibitor, which means that it increases the effective concentrations of serotonin in the brain.

In males, concentrations of the sex hormone testosterone appear to have a relationship with status similar to the one seen for serotonin. Reductions in status thus tend to be followed by reductions in plasma testosterone levels, whereas these levels tend to rise following increases in status.[28] A player who wins a tennis match decisively, for example, experiences a post-match elevation in plasma testosterone, and his vanquished opponent experiences a post-match reduction. And as with serotonin, there is some evidence from primate studies that elevated concentrations of testosterone facilitate behaviors that help achieve or maintain high status.[29]

Relative Income and Health

It is no surprise that the wealthiest individuals in society also tend to be the healthiest and longest lived. After all, these people have more and better food than their poorer countrymen, and also better access to medical care and other important resources. What researchers did not expect to find, however, was that in developed economies these material advantages seem to have little to do with the better health outcomes of high-ranked individuals. Rather, it appears that low relative position—by itself, or in combination with other factors that go with it—is an important causal factor in a variety of diseases.

If differences in material living standards were the explanation for why the wealthier live longer, we should expect life expectancy to be significantly higher in rich countries than in poor countries. This is in fact the case, but only up to a point. As the British medical researcher Richard Wilkinson has shown, gains in absolute wealth affect human health with sharply diminishing returns: Once per-capita income reaches about $5,000 a year, additional income growth produces little, if any, gain in life expectancy. For example, there is no correlation between changes in life expectancy and changes in income between 1970 and 1990 across the 23 European nations in the OECD.[30]

Many scientists were reluctant to accept that low relative income could be an important cause of illness and premature death. Perhaps, they speculated, the true direction of causation might run the other way. Thus people born with the weakest constitutions might have low relative income largely *because* of their poor health and lack of energy. This hypothesis proved unpersuasive, however, in the light of evidence that death rates go down in response to increases in relative income.[31]

A related possibility is that the poorest individuals in every society also may happen to be least informed and well disciplined in maintaining their health. If this explanation were correct, it should be especially important for disorders like heart disease, which are heavily influenced by people's choices. Yet here, too, the evidence provides little support. Thus the major known environmental and behavioral risk factors can account for only about 20 percent of the observed relationship between relative income and death from heart disease.[32] Further indirect evidence that relative deprivation is a cause of illness comes from recent studies that have found an association between the degree of income inequality within a country and its incidence of disease.[33]

Perhaps the most vivid and persuasive demonstration of the link between relative income and disease comes from two landmark studies of the health of British civil servants carried out by epidemiologist Michael Marmot and several collaborators.[34] These studies have come to be known as the Whitehall Studies, after the London street along which are located the government buildings that house many of these civil servants. The striking feature of the Whitehall Studies is that they are based on subjects for whom poor health cannot reasonably be attributed to ignorance or absolute material deprivation. British civil servants are well educated, have ready access to the excellent British National Health Service, and are reasonably well paid.

Like governmental bureaucracies in most countries, the British

Civil Service constitutes a well-ordered social and income hierarchy. In both Whitehall studies, Marmot and his colleagues classified their subjects according to their grade of employment, which corresponds closely to both salary and position on the bureaucratic totem pole. In their first study (Whitehall I), which involved some 18,000 males between the ages of 40 and 69 in 1967–69, they found that the risk of death from coronary heart disease and other causes was strongly inversely related to employment grade among males between 40 and 64 years of age: The higher one's rank on the employment ladder the lower one's risk of death.[35] For example, the risk of death from coronary heart disease was less than one-third as high for men in the highest employment grade than for those in the lowest grade. The corresponding relationship between employment status and deaths from other causes was essentially the same.

The second study (Whitehall II) was carried out two decades later and was based on a sample of more than 10,000 male and female civil servants aged 35–55 in 1985–88.[36] The focus in Whitehall II expanded to include not only mortality from various diseases, but also the frequency with which civil servants experienced long spells of illness (defined as those resulting in at least a one-week absence from work, for which a doctor's certification is required). Here the patterns they found were essentially the same as in Whitehall I. The rates at which both men and women experienced long illnesses were again strongly inversely related to employment grade. For example, the incidence of long illnesses among women in the lowest employment grade was almost four times as high as for women in the highest grade. Strikingly, the gap in mortality and morbidity between the highest and lowest employment grades did not shrink at all despite the two decades of economic growth between the two studies.

The details of exactly how relative position influences health are not well understood. Since it is known that stress can compromise the human immune system in various ways, perhaps the simplest possibility is that health suffers because low relative position is experienced by many people as stressful. In his recent book, Richard Wilkinson argues for this explanation, citing evidence that greater income equality alleviates stress by promoting greater social cohesion.[37] One recent study suggests that it may not be low status per se that causes problems, but rather the reductions in autonomy and control that so often accompany low status.[38]

Researchers also do not yet understand the precise details of the relationships between relative position and concentrations of serotonin and testosterone. But for present purposes, it is not critical that we know these details. Suffice to say that no matter how the relevant mechanisms work, there is compelling evidence that concern about relative position is a deep-rooted and ineradicable element of human nature.

The conventional wisdom holds that concerns about relative position amount to no more than vicious envy and are therefore not to be given any weight in public policy decisions. But although positional concerns may often entail envy, we have seen that they would be strong even in envy's absence. They can be mitigated, but not eliminated, by cultural conditioning. Pharmaceutical research might someday deliver a drug that could completely eliminate concerns about relative position, but no one who took such a drug would be able to function effectively in the world as we know it.

Our task in the coming chapters will be to explore why, despite their clear adaptive significance for individuals, concerns about relative position also lead to many undesirable outcomes—including, but by no means limited to, the wasteful spending patterns that have been our focus.

CHAPTER 10

SMART FOR ONE, DUMB FOR ALL

Despite abundant evidence that across-the-board increases in our stocks of material goods have little impact on life satisfaction, we continue to spend more time at work to buy larger houses and more expensive cars. Much has been written about our failure to achieve better balance in our lives, which authors almost invariably attribute to dark forces of one kind or another—some rooted within us, such as greed, impatience, or stupidity, and others that work on us from the outside, such as exploitation by powerful corporate interests. Yet these forces could be swept aside entirely and the fundamental problem would remain, for its primary source lies not in individual or corporate imperfection, but in the cold, impersonal logic of competition.

Although recorded human history spans many millennia, our modern understanding of competition derives almost entirely from the writings of only two men: Adam Smith and Charles Darwin. Smith's view was by far the more optimistic, but Darwin's more hard-edged analysis holds the key to understanding our current situation.

SMITH AND DARWIN ON COMPETITION

Writing more than two centuries ago, Adam Smith introduced his concept of the invisible hand, which went on to become one of the most celebrated and influential ideas of all time. His insight was that individuals seeking to promote only their own interests in the marketplace would be driven, "as if by an invisible hand," to promote the greatest good for all. Thus producers seeking to steal market share from their rivals would develop cost-reducing innovations, which would be mimicked by others, and which in time would lead to lower prices for all. Farmers rush to adopt higher yielding varieties of hybrid corn; cattlemen rush to adopt faster growing breeds of cattle; and long-distance truckers rush to install fuel-saving air foils atop their cabs. In each case the early adopters enjoy lower costs than their rivals and hence reap higher profits. But as the superior methods spread, increasing supplies drive prices down, causing profits to return to levels that prevail in other sectors. The ultimate beneficiaries of this process are the consumers who pay lower prices.

The invisible hand not only applies relentless pressure to reduce costs but it also rewards those who are first to enter markets that were previously underserved. By the same token, it is quick to punish those who stay on in markets that are overserved. For instance, if there were too many carriage makers and not enough automobile assembly workers, wage adjustments in these and other labor markets would quickly restore the proper balance—all without government bureaucrats ever having to lift a finger.

Eighty-three years after publication of *The Wealth of Nations,* Charles Darwin launched a series of books that analyzed competition not among human traders but among animals in the wild. Darwin was much influenced by the British economist Thomas Malthus, an intellectual descendant of Smith's. It is therefore no surprise that Darwin's view of competition was in many ways similar to Smith's. For example, in Darwin's scheme, the beneficial mutation played the role of Smith's cost-saving innovation, and transmission was accomplished not by emulation but by relative reproductive success. Thus a mutant shark born with a keener sense of smell than its rivals would find more prey, and therefore tend to pass along its advantage to more surviving offspring. In a process spanning millions of generations, incremental refinements led to the exquisitely crafted modern shark, perhaps the most effective predator that ever lived.

Yet Darwin's view of competition was by no means as broadly optimistic as Smith's. Indeed, he identified numerous cases in which natural selection appeared to favor traits that helped individuals and yet proved deeply harmful to larger groups. The common feature of these traits is that they actually impose costs on the individual organism, but compensate by making it a more effective competitor against rivals in its own species.

Modern economists now recognize similar patterns in human rivalry. For example, reckless tackling in football may increase the likelihood of injury on the defensive team, yet will nonetheless tend to proliferate if it imposes even larger costs on the offense. In these situations, Smith's invisible hand simply breaks down. Competition among individuals does not promote the greatest good for all. But whereas economists recognize that such cases exist, they tend to view them as isolated and rare. They condemn industrial sabotage and kindred behaviors, but do not think them much of a problem in practical terms.

On careful examination, however, it becomes clear that rivalry undermines the interests of larger groups as often among humans as among any other animal species. And in this fact lies the most plausible explanation for our failure to achieve more balance in our lives.

The explanation I propose is neither complicated nor new. If there is any novelty to my claim, it is that the conflict between individual and group is far more widespread than commonly believed. It permeates virtually all animal species and has been a central concern in human societies ever since our ancestors first climbed down from the trees. What is more, it is a stubborn problem, one that simply cannot be attacked at the individual level.

CONFLICTS BETWEEN INDIVIDUAL AND SPECIES

Darwin recognized clearly that the interests of individuals are often in harmony with the interests of larger groups, just as Adam Smith had claimed. Consider, for example, the keen eyesight of the red-tailed hawk. At a distance of a quarter of a mile, this bird can spot a motionless brown mouse in a pile of dry leaves. This is fortunate, for visual acuity is of paramount importance to hawks, who make their living by cruising at hundreds or even thousands of feet above ground level in search of rodents and other small prey. But that hawks see so well is hardly an accident. The bird's magnificent complex of optical hardware and neural software evolved over millions of generations in which those with the keenest eyesight caught more prey, and hence left more offspring, than their more nearsighted conspecifics. The ability to see clearly at long distances is a trait that is advantageous not only to individual hawks but also to hawks as a species. If all hawks had keener eyesight, the species would fare better. For hawks, keen eyesight is smart for one, smart for all.

The same is true of many other traits and abilities. Thus, if all cheetahs could run a little faster, cheetahs as a species would fare better; if all chimps were a little smarter, chimps as a species would fare better; if all sharks had a keener sense of smell, sharks as a species would fare better; and so on.

There are many other traits and abilities, however, for which this pattern does not hold.[1] Consider, for instance, the antlers of the male elk. Natural selection favored individual males with larger antlers because the broader an individual male's rack of antlers, the more likely he was to prevail against his rivals for reproductive access to females. Over millions of generations, this advantage led to a gradual increase in the size of elk antlers, and today the antlers on some males span almost five feet. But whereas larger antlers help any given male gain advantage over others, they confer no similar advantage for male elks as a group. On the contrary, they are positively harmful.

The reason is that broader antlers make it more difficult to escape from predators. Once a pack of wolves chases a male elk with a 5-foot rack of antlers into the woods, the elk is trouble. Twist and turn though he might, he simply cannot transport these appendages quickly through the trees. This is a *serious* disadvantage, and it might seem that natural selection could not possibly have favored elks who were thus encumbered.

Weighing against this disadvantage, however, was the fact that elks with the broadest antlers had access to more females and, despite their briefer lives, therefore left more offspring. As long as this advantage was more than sufficient to compensate for the increased risk of death from predators, natural selection continued to favor bigger antlers. Eventually, however, the advantage from further increases in size no longer outweighed this risk, and from that point antlers grew no further.

The important message of this story is that even though all elks would clearly do better if every animal's rack of antlers were trimmed by half, it would not be advantageous for any single animal to trim his antlers. Thus, if a mutant male were born with half-sized antlers, he would be at a hopeless disadvantage in the competition for mates. He might survive to a ripe old age, but in evolution what counts is not how long he lives but the number of grandchildren he leaves. And a mutant with stubby antlers simply will not leave many grandchildren. Big antlers are smart for one, dumb for all.

Similar forces appear to explain the exuberant plumage of the peacock. Peahens, for reasons best known to them, favor males with the longest and brightest tailfeathers.[2] Experimenters have shown that males with artificially augmented tailfeathers are almost invariably much more successful than other males in attracting females. One hypothesis is that a vibrant display is a credible signal that the male is in robust health, a view that is supported by findings that plumage deteriorates sharply in animals with heavy parasite loads.[3] The logic is that females are likely to have more grandchildren if they mate with males with genes for parasite resistance.

In any event, once peahens came to favor peacocks with longer tailfeathers, natural selection relentlessly began culling males with the shortest displays in each generation, leaving us with modern peacocks whose tails reach five feet or more. But like larger antlers on male elks, longer tailfeathers entail costs. They make males not only less able to escape predators but also more likely to attract their attention in the first place. Peacocks as a group would fare much better if each bird's tail display were shorter by half. Yet any lone mutant with a shorter tail display would be at a hopeless disadvantage.

Sexual dimorphism—significant sex differences in size within a species—provides another vivid illustration of the conflict between individual and group. Many bull elephant seals, for example, weigh as much as a fully equipped Chevrolet sedan, and more than twice as much as their female counterparts. This enormous difference in size was driven by the advantage enjoyed by slightly larger males in their battles with one another for access to females. The victorious males typically command large harems, thereby eliminating a majority of their rivals from the reproductive sweepstakes.

But whereas size is advantageous in the contest for reproductive access, it is disadvantageous in several other ways. For one thing, it increases caloric requirements, with mature bulls needing to eat hundreds of pounds of fish each day to sustain themselves. A second disadvantage is that the victorious breeding males are so large that they sometimes crush their females to death in the act of mounting them. Larger animals may also be more prone to a variety of orthopedic maladies.

As with the evolution of antlers and tailfeathers, the disadvantages of becoming slightly larger eventually came into balance with the advantages, and the weight of surviving males stabilized. As before, however, there is nothing attractive about this outcome from the perspective of male elephant seals as a group. Each animal would fare much better if all were considerably smaller. The most able fighting males would still gain access to the most females, but most of the disadvantages of excessive size would be avoided. Yet here, too, the problem cannot be solved at the individual level. A smaller mutant would gain the advantages of not needing so much food and not crushing any female he mounted; but these advantages would be swamped by the fact that he would be unlikely to gain access to any females in the first place.

These examples illustrate Darwin's central insight that natural selection can, and often does, favor traits that increase the reproductive fitness of individuals at the expense of larger groups. If a trait serves the interests of both individuals and the groups to which they belong, so much the better. But when conflicts arise, individual interests often prevail.

Armed with this insight, modern behavioral biologists have begun to make sense of a long list of animal behaviors that are clearly counterproductive at the species level. Thus, in many polygynous species, such as lions, a successor's first act on defeating a dominant male is to kill all young offspring left behind. This practice accelerates the fertility cycle of the lactating females, and thus serves the genetic interests of the conquering male. Yet it is utterly wasteful from the perspective of lions as a group.

Baby birds in the nest must scream themselves hoarse because their parents make the reasonable assumption that the one who screams loudest must be most in need of food. In the end, of course, there are only so many worms to go around, and nestlings as a group would fare better if all screeched more softly. Yet any individual chick who showed restraint would be much more likely than his siblings to starve.

Dogs must devote scarce neurological capacity to the support of an elaborate mechanism that raises the hackles on their backs whenever they face off against rivals. Hackle raising makes the animal appear larger and thus more likely to dissuade his rival from fighting. Even though all dogs raise their hackles, however, only one dog in any pair can be larger than his rival. Dogs as a group would fare better if the neurological capacity that supports hackle-raising were instead used to support better hearing or a keener sense of smell. In these and countless other cases, we see behavior and traits that are smart for one, dumb for all.

INDIVIDUAL-GROUP CONFLICT IN HUMAN AFFAIRS

The Darwinian theme of conflict between the interests of individuals and groups plays out in human affairs in countless ways, both trivial and profound. Some examples:

STANDING TO GET A BETTER VIEW. When my wife and I went with friends to hear Diana Ross sing in a large auditorium a few years ago, we bought good seats, some 20 rows from the stage. Before Ross had finished her first song, several people in front of us rose to their feet, presumably to get a better view. This blocked the line of sight for others behind them, which led those people to stand to see better. Before long, the entire crowd was standing.

Presently, a few people in front climbed atop their seats, again blocking the views of others behind and leading others to stand on their own seats to restore their view. The auditorium seats had fold-up bottoms, and from time to time someone would stand too close to the pivot point and—whump!—take a tumble when the seat popped into its vertical position.

From the perspective of concert goers as a whole, this behavior was clearly self-defeating because standing involves costs but does not end up improving anyone's view. From each individual's perspective, however, it is easy to appreciate the incentives to stand. After all, no matter what others do, an individual sees better by standing than by sitting. Our problem was not that we didn't *understand* the folly of all having to stand on our seats for several hours. Nor were we greedy, impatient, or the victims of powerful special interests. Rather, our problem was that as individuals the only alternative available to us was to sit down, which would have made matters worse.

SHOUTING AT COCKTAIL PARTIES. Whenever large numbers of people gather for conversation in a closed space, the ambient noise level rises sharply. After attending such gatherings, people often complain of sore throats and hoarse voices from having had to speak so loudly to be heard. If guests spoke at normal voice levels at cocktail parties, they would avoid these symptoms. And because the overall noise level would be lower, they would hear just as well as when they all shout at one another.

So why shout? The problem again stems from the difference between the incentives seen by individuals and those seen by the larger group. Everyone starts by speaking at normal levels, but because of the crowded conditions, it is difficult for conversation partners to hear one another. The natural solution from the point of view of you and your conversation partner is to simply raise your voices a bit. But that is also the natural solution for all other conversation pairs. And when all raise their voices, the ambient noise level rises, so that no one hears any better than before.

This is wasteful, sure enough. But here again there is precious little that individuals acting alone can do about it, for if any one conversation pair were to lower their voices while others didn't, they wouldn't be able to hear at all. No one wants to go home with raw vocal cords, but we apparently prefer that cost to the alternative of not being able to engage in conversation.

ANABOLIC STEROID CONSUMPTION. The offensive linemen of the 1996 SuperBowl champion Dallas Cowboys averaged 333 pounds per man, and 300-pounders on the front lines of other teams have become the rule rather than the exception. In the 1970s, by contrast, offensive linemen in the National Football League averaged barely 280 pounds, and the all-decade linemen of the 1940s averaged only 229.[4] One reason that football players of today are so much heavier is that players' salaries have escalated sharply over the last two decades, which has led to much more intense competition for the positions. Size and strength are the two cardinal virtues of an offensive lineman and, other things being equal, the job will always go to the larger and stronger of two rivals. Because size and strength, in turn, can be enhanced by the consumption of anabolic steroids, individual players confront compelling incentives to consume these drugs.

Yet if all players take steroids, the rank ordering of players by size and strength—and hence the question of who lands the jobs—will be largely unaffected. And since the consumption of anabolic steroids entails risk of serious long-term health consequences—heightened aggressiveness, severe psychosis, circulatory disorders, testicular atrophy, abnormal sperm morphology, and possibly a variety of cancers[5]—football players as a group are clearly worse off if they consume these drugs.

REDSHIRTS, OLD AND YOUNG. The term *redshirt* was coined to describe a college athlete who is held out of competition during his freshman year, thereby making him eligible to compete during his fifth year, when he will be bigger, stronger, and more experienced. The term is also used as a verb, and each team has a strong incentive to redshirt freshman athletes, even though the competitive balance is essentially the same when all teams follow this practice as when none of them does. From the collective vantage point, therefore, redshirting is wasteful.

Yet the practice has spread widely and indeed is no longer confined to college athletes. For example, parents in some parts of the country have begun to hold their eighth-grade sons out of school for a year to increase their chances of making varsity athletic teams in high school. And redshirting has even filtered down to preschoolers. A child who is a year or so older than most of his kindergarten classmates is likely to perform better, in relative terms, than if he had entered with children his own age. And since most parents are aware that admission to prestigious universities and eligibility for top jobs on graduation depend largely on *relative* academic performance, a growing number of families are holding their children out of kindergarten a year longer. There are obvious costs to this practice. And surely there is little social advantage in holding *all* children back an extra year, since relative performance would then be essentially unaffected. Redshirting at every level is smart for one, dumb for all.

SAT CRAM COURSES. As more and more of the nation's best and brightest high school students have sought admission to a small list of our most prestigious universities, admissions standards have risen accordingly.[6] Stanford University, for example, regularly has more high-school valedictorians in its applicant pool each year than slots in its freshman class. Because performance on the Scholastic Assessment Test (SAT) receives high weight in the admissions decisions at many leading schools, it is no surprise that thousands of students each year enroll in SAT cram courses offered by Stanley Kaplan and other companies. There is little question that these courses improve performance on the SATs. Yet it is also clear that they generate virtually no other benefit. The courses are costly, both in time and money, and the number of students who take them has no effect whatever on the number of students who are admitted to elite universities.

ADVERTISING WARS. In 1994 American cigarette manufacturers spent almost $5 billion advertising their products.[7] One of the key features of the proposed government settlement with the tobacco industry in 1997 was to prohibit the industry from advertising its products at all. Attorneys for the tobacco industry bitterly opposed the ad ban. But because the main effect of each company's advertisements is to offset its rivals' ads, their opposition was much like Br'er Rabbit's plea not to be thrown into the briar patch. From each individual company's perspective, failure to advertise vigorously is a recipe for disaster. Yet full-scale advertising campaigns have little effect on the overall demand for tobacco, as evidenced by widespread smoking even in societies in which commercial advertising is largely nonexistent. The irony of the proposed tobacco agreement is that, although companies would never have dared to curtail their advertising unilaterally, each can maintain its market share quite easily when all stop advertising.

MILITARY ARMS RACES. The feverish efforts of nations to acquire more weapons than their rivals is one of the most costly instances of the conflict between individual and collective interests. From each individual nation's point of view, the worst outcome is not to buy armaments while its rivals do. Yet when *all* spend more on weapons, no one is more secure than before.

Most nations recognize the importance of maintaining military parity, and the result all too often has been a wasteful escalation of expenditures on arms. Nations would spend much less on weapons if they could make their military spending decisions collectively. And with the money thus saved, each side could then spend more on things that promote, rather than threaten, human well-being.

ENVIRONMENTAL POLLUTION. Nowhere is the conflict between individual and group interests more clearly recognized by modern economists than in the case of environmental pollution. Left to his own devices, the rational, self-interested motorist in Los Angeles would never install a catalytic converter on the exhaust system of his car. The device costs money, after all, and will have no measurable impact on air quality in the Los Angeles basin. From the collective vantage point, however, the costs and benefits of installing catalytic converters are markedly different. When *every* car has one, the quality of the air will improve dramatically, a benefit that far outweighs the modest cost. Yet if most other motorists had catalytic converters, any individual motorist could refrain from installing one and enjoy the benefits of clean air for free. It is this simple incentive gap, not stupidity or corporate avarice, that has led to so much environmental degradation.

OVERHARVESTING. Modern economists also recognize that disparities between individual and group incentives have led to overfishing of coastal waters, overgrazing of common pasturelands, and overcutting of public forests. The problem is not that individual fishermen don't know that their activities threaten the viability of coastal fisheries; or that individual hunters don't recognize that rhinos are in danger of extinction; or that individual loggers don't know that valuable ecosystems are often destroyed by clearcutting. In each case, individuals know all too well what the collective consequences of their actions will be. Yet when property rights in the use of valuable resources are not clearly defined and enforced, no individual is in a position to take effective action. If a rhino isn't killed by one hunter, he will simply be killed by another; fish not taken by one boat will be taken by another; and logs left standing by one company will be quickly claimed by another. In its various forms, the overharvesting problem has been called "the tragedy of the commons."[8] It is yet another example of behavior that is smart for one, dumb for all.

HIGH HEELS AND COSMETIC SURGERY. In species in which males invest little in the care of offspring—which is to say, in the vast majority of mammals—males typically battle furiously with one another for access to females. But in a small number of species—including our own and a handful of other monogamous species in which males invest heavily in the care of offspring—the pattern is somewhat different. In these species, competition among males is still common, but we also see competition among females for males. And here again, the Darwinian logic is simple: Whereas females in most species can expect males to contribute no more than their genes and can therefore afford to sit back and let males fight it out, females in monogamous species stand to gain a great deal if they can monopolize the services of a relatively able caregiver. And hence their incentive to compete.

The competition among females plays out in different ways in different cultures, but invariably at least some aspects of it are wasteful. In cultures in which height is viewed as attractive, for example, it is common for women to wear high-heeled shoes. In cultures in which large eyes are valued, most women wear makeup that makes their eyes look larger. In cultures in which youth is considered attractive, most women use makeup to conceal the lines of time. In cultures in which body hair is considered unattractive, many women submit to electrolysis treatments. And in cultures that place a premium on large breasts, many women undergo surgical breast augmentation.

All these steps involve costs, sometimes very high costs. Even apparently innocuous actions like wearing high heels can cause foot, ankle, and back injuries, tendon shrinkage, and misalignment of internal organs. In a small but nonnegligible proportion of cases, cosmetic surgery leads to serious infection, disfigurement, and even death. And yet in each case the advantages that people seek are, to a considerable extent, mutually offsetting. Thus the height advantage someone gains by wearing high-heeled shoes is neutralized once high heels become the norm. Yet, as with concert goers standing on their seats, these costs often cannot be avoided without incurring even greater ones. Those who complain that women are foolish or vain to give in to the demands of fashion have simply failed to grasp the conflict between individual and group interests.

The alert reader will have long since discerned the common thread running through the preceding examples. Competitive forces hone exquisite physical and behavioral adaptations, both in the animal kingdom and in human societies. In the animal kingdom, these adaptations typically serve the interests of individual organisms and may either help or hinder the interests of larger groups. And the same is true in human societies.

Economic orthodoxy recognizes the existence of situations in which individual and group interests conflict, but views these situations as isolated exceptions. They are not. My claim, reduced to its essence, is that the conflict between individual and group is the single most important explanation of the imbalance in our current consumption patterns.

CHAPTER 11

UNDERSTANDING CONSPICUOUS CONSUMPTION

Do some people save too little because they are foolish and undisciplined? Without question. Recall from chapter 7 how, in the span of just over a decade, the high-saving Thrift family's standard of living began to dominate the low-saving Spend family's. So striking are the apparent advantages of the high-savings trajectory that it is tempting to conclude that families like the Spends are simply weak-willed and shortsighted for not having saved at a much higher rate.

Maybe so. But the problem of insufficient savings would still plague us even in the absence of such human frailties. Parents want to save for retirement, but they also have other important goals. For instance, they want to make sure that their children receive an education that qualifies them for the best jobs. For the typical American family, that means buying a house in the best school district it can afford. Most of us thus confront an almost irresistible opportunity to do more for our children: By saving a little less for retirement, we can purchase houses in better school districts.

From the collective vantage point, however, such moves are futile in the same way that military arms races are. When each family saves less to buy a house in a better school district, the net effect is merely to bid up the prices of those houses. Students end up at the same schools they would have attended if all families had spent less. But in the process, an important goal—being able to maintain an adequate living standard in retirement—is sacrificed for essentially no gain. Yet no family, acting alone, can solve this problem, just as no nation can uni-laterally stop a military arms race. The Spend family might have been well aware of how much better things would be if all saved more. Yet had they alone followed a high-savings path, they might have been un-able to provide important advantages for their children at crucial stages of development.

Housing is of course not the only expenditure driven by forces similar to those that govern military arms races. Spending on cars fits the same pattern, as does spending on clothing, furniture, wine, jew-elry, sports equipment, and a host of other goods. It is human nature to take pleasure in nice things. But as we have seen, it is also human na-ture that favorable evaluations are inherently context dependent. Many wines costing less than $10 today are superior, in absolute terms, to the wines drunk by the kings of France in centuries past. Yet in many social circles today, a $10 bottle of wine is simply not an acceptable way to mark a special occasion.

It is not because we are foolish or ill-informed that the things we feel we need depend on the kinds of things that others have. Nor must we invoke human frailties to explain why our needs tend to grow when we find ourselves in the presence of others who have more than we do. Yet when *all* of us spend more, the new, higher spending level simply becomes the norm. In the current environment, Bill Gates needs a $100 million estate to signal that he is the captain among captains of industry. If all executive mansions were to shrink by half, Gates could send essentially the same signal by spending only $50 million.

Regarding the imbalance in our consumption patterns, another im-portant conflict between individual and group would persist even if people were not concerned about relative position for its own sake. It lies in the fact that promotion decisions on the job often depend heav-ily on the *relative* number of hours someone works. For instance, an as-sociate in a law firm who goes home at 5 P.M. each day instead of 8 P.M. not only earns less in relative terms but is also less likely to be pro-moted to partner. If *all* the associates left the office a little earlier, of course, no one's promotion prospects would be affected. But each in-dividual has control over only the hours that she herself works. She cannot unilaterally decree that *everyone* scale back. The economists Renee Landers, James Rebitzer, and Lowell Taylor report in a recent paper that associates in large law firms voice a strong preference for having all work fewer hours, even if that means lower pay, and yet few dare take that step unilaterally.[1]

By the same token, most of us aspire to hold interesting jobs, yet how often do we hear of jobs thus described that are less than full time or, indeed, that require fewer than 50 hours a week? Many of us would be delighted to own a house with a view, but these too are generally not available to part-time workers. If everyone worked fewer hours each year, the distribution of interesting jobs and houses with views would not be much affected. Yet the cost of working fewer hours, as seen by the individual, will often be prohibitive.

As these observations suggest, to the extent that the imbalance in our current spending patterns stems from the fact that many activities are more attractive to individuals than to society as a whole, the potential for improvement through unilateral action will be sharply limited.

A PLAUSIBLE EXPLANATION?

That the conflict between individual and group *could* lie behind our seemingly wasteful spending patterns follows logically from the existence of other situations in which the rational pursuit of individual interest produces unattractive results. But we must go further if we are to establish the plausibility of an important causal link.

It would be helpful, for example, to establish that the incentives confronting individuals as they choose among competing consumption activities are structurally similar to the ones found in other choices that are smart for one, dumb for all. Consider again the individual nation's decision about how much to spend on military arms as opposed to nonmilitary goods and services. What, exactly, is the specific feature of this problem that leads us to conclude that countries as a whole spend too much on armaments?

What must be true is that each nation's payoff from spending on armaments must depend on how its spending compares with that of rival nations. But although this is surely so, it is not enough. Suppose, for example, that each nation's payoff from spending on nonmilitary goods also depended, and to the same extent as for military goods, on the amounts spent on nonmilitary goods by other nations. The tendency of military spending to siphon off resources from other spending categories would then be offset by an equal tendency in the opposite direction. That is, if each nation had a fixed amount of national income to allocate between military and nonmilitary goods, and if the payoffs in each category were equally context sensitive, then we would expect no imbalance across the categories.

For an imbalance to occur in favor of armaments, the reward from armaments spending must be *more* context sensitive than the reward from nonmilitary spending. And since this is precisely the case, the generally assumed imbalance occurs. After all, to be second-best in a military arms race often means a loss of political autonomy, clearly a much higher cost than the discomfort of having less elaborate outdoor cooking appliances.

In brief, we expect an imbalance in the choice between two activities if the individual rewards from one are more context sensitive than the individual rewards from the other. Does this rule fit the imbalance said to describe spending patterns in modern industrial societies? For simplicity, suppose we characterize this imbalance as being one of spending too much time earning money to buy material goods and too little time with family and friends. In earlier chapters we saw that the satisfaction provided by many types of material goods is indeed highly dependent on context. Is there any reason to believe that the satisfaction provided by time spent with family and friends is any less context dependent?

Precisely this question was posed by the economists Sara Solnick and David Hemenway in a recent survey of graduate students in the public health program at Harvard University.[2] Solnick and Hemenway actually asked a series of questions designed to probe the extent to which satisfaction in different domains is sensitive to context. In one question, for example, each subject was asked to choose between living in a world in which she earned $50,000 a year while others earned

$25,000, and another in which she earned $100,000 while others earned $250,000. In response, 56 percent of subjects chose the first world, which we may take as a rough measure of the extent to which these subjects believe that relative consumption is more important than absolute consumption.

Solnick and Hemenway then asked each subject to choose between a world in which he had two weeks of vacation a year while others had one, and another in which he had four weeks while others had eight. This time only 20 percent chose the first world, less than half as many as in the first question. On its face, this suggests that the satisfaction people receive from consuming material goods is indeed much more strongly context dependent than the satisfaction they take from having more free time. Put another way, it suggests that an across-the-board increase in free time would have much more impact on satisfaction than an across-the-board increase in material goods. And this means that the condition that gives rise to conflict between individual and collective incentives is met—in particular, that we may expect individuals to devote too much time working to buy goods and too little time with family and friends.

We may also note that precisely the same pattern of context sensitivity would be expected on evolutionary grounds. As noted in chapter 9, the evolutionary function of the brain's reward centers is not to make us happy but to guide us to those activities that are most likely to enhance our reproductive fitness. From a competitive standpoint, the most secure situation of all would be to have both more material resources and more free time than one's rivals. But if one or the other advantage had to be sacrificed, free time would be the logical choice, since survival prospects in most settings depend much more heavily on material resource holdings than on free time. The Darwinian perspective thus helps explain why many parents do not hesitate to work longer hours when that means being able to buy a house in a better school district.

Free time is of course not the only thing that gets short shrift in modern industrial life. As social critics endlessly remind us, we also suffer from growing traffic congestion, increasingly regimented and specialized jobs, dwindling savings, and a host of other ills. Are these categories also less sensitive than material-goods consumption to interpersonal comparisons? Consider first the case of traffic congestion, and recall from our earlier discussion that the effect of prolonged exposure to heavy traffic congestion is in many ways like exposure to loud, unpredictable noise. The effect of such noise on subjects in the laboratory occurs independently of the amount of noise to which other subjects are exposed (since each subject knows only the amount of noise to which he himself was exposed). Thus, if one subject experiences reduced exposure to noise, the benefits he enjoys are more or less the same as those he enjoys when noise is reduced for all subjects. In this sense, the effects of reduced exposure to noise and, by analogy, reduced exposure to traffic congestion, are strikingly less dependent on interpersonal comparisons than the effects of larger houses and faster cars.

Interpersonal comparisons are also unlikely to be important for savings, at least in the short run. After all, whereas most of us know what kinds of houses our friends live in and what kinds of cars they drive, we are much less likely to know how large their savings accounts are. But even if everyone's savings balance were on public display, the individual rewards from current consumption would still depend more on context than those from saving. As noted earlier, many parents might gladly settle for a diminished standard of living in retirement if by saving less they could scrape together enough to buy a house in a better school district. And the same incentives would lead many parents to accept more regimented and less satisfying, but better paying, jobs.

Some object that a desire for high consumption rank cannot really explain low savings rates, because those who save too little now simply consign themselves to having low consumption ranks in the future. As just discussed, however, having a lower consumption rank in the future may be an acceptable price to pay for the ability to have a higher rank with respect to some forms of current consumption. What is more, to the extent that driving the right cars and wearing the right clothes function as signals of ability (see chapter 9) and thereby help people land better jobs or more lucrative contracts, low savings now may not even entail reduced consumption rank in the future. But whereas this may be true from the perspective of each individual, it surely is not true for society as a whole. For when all of us spend more to signal our abilities, the relative strength of each signal remains unchanged.

For brevity, I again use the expression *inconspicuous consumption* to describe those consumption activities that appear to get short shrift in modern industrial life. The defining characteristic of inconspicuous consumption is this: By comparison to the satisfaction provided by conspicuous consumption, the rewards from inconspicuous consumption depend less heavily on context. This is all that separates the two categories. So, although it may appear that across-the-board increases in many forms of conspicuous consumption yield no measurable increase in satisfaction, this need not always be the case. Nor is it necessary that the rewards from all forms of inconspicuous consumption be completely independent of context. We get a surfeit of conspicuous consumption and a deficit of inconspicuous consumption simply because context matters *more* for conspicuous consumption.

ANOTHER TEST

There is yet another way to assess the plausibility of my claim that individual-group conflict is an important explanation for our current spending patterns. It rests on the observation that, whereas animals are largely stuck with the costs of wasteful competition, humans can often avoid them. Because we have far more powerful cognitive and communication skills than other animals, we often manage to recognize, and craft solutions to, the various conflicts between individual and group. If these conflicts lie behind our unbalanced consumption patterns, we should expect to see widespread evidence of attempts to resolve them. As the following examples suggest, such attempts permeate virtually every nook and cranny of human social life.

MANDATORY STARTING DATES FOR KINDERGARTEN. In most jurisdictions, the law requires children who reach their fifth birthday before a specific date—often December 1st—of a given year to start kindergarten that same year. With the stroke of a pen, legislators in these jurisdictions have thus managed to sharply curtail the wasteful practice of kindergarten redshirting.

POLITICAL CAMPAIGN SPENDING LIMITS. During election season, presidential candidates in the United States now routinely spend more than $100 million on campaign advertising. Yet when each side doubles its spending on ads, the candidates' respective odds of winning remain essentially the same. Recognition of this wasteful pattern led Congress to adopt strict spending limits for presidential candidates. Whether Congress can come up with effective ways to enforce these limits remains to be seen. But that the intent of the law was to resolve an individual-group conflict seems beyond question.

ZONING LAWS. A merchant's goal in erecting a sign is to call her business to the attention of potential customers. How well her sign accomplishes that goal depends in part on its absolute size, position, luminosity, and other features. But more important, it depends on how those features compare with the corresponding features of neighboring merchants' signs. If hers is larger or brighter, or if it extends farther than theirs, it will probably succeed. Otherwise, it may not be noticed. And hence the tendency for signs to grow ever larger and more garish as competition intensifies. This tendency has led many communities to enact zoning laws that sharply restrict the size and other characteristics of signs. That these laws solve an individual-group conflict is evidenced by the fact that the very merchants most constrained by them are often among their most enthusiastic supporters.

ROSTER LIMITS ON SPORTS TEAMS. Major league baseball permits each franchise to have only 25 players on its roster during the regular season. The National Football League sets roster limits at 49, the National Basketball Association at 12, and so on. In the absence of these limits, any team could increase its chances of winning by adding players. But other teams would inevitably follow suit, and teams taken as a whole would continue to win exactly 50 percent of all games played. On the plausible view that, beyond some point, larger rosters do not add appreciably to the entertainment value delivered to fans, roster limits are a sensible way to deliver this entertainment at a more reasonable cost.

HOCKEY HELMET RULES. Left to their own devices, hockey players invariably skate without helmets, in the apparently rational belief that being able to see and hear a little better will improve their team's chances of winning. Yet the competitive balance among teams is essentially unaffected when all players skate without helmets. Helmetless skaters thus confront the risk of serious injury largely for naught. And hence the almost universal attraction of helmet rules.

STEROID BANS. Virtually every amateur and professional athletic governing body has enacted a prohibition against the consumption of anabolic steroids. Enforcement of these prohibitions is difficult, and often entails an arms race of its own, as those who devise tests for the drugs struggle to stay ahead of others who devise techniques for masking them. Yet there is little question that most athletes, even those who currently take steroids, would be delighted to learn that a fail-safe method of detecting these drugs had been discovered.

ARBITRATION AGREEMENTS. In the business world, contracting parties often sign agreements that commit them to binding arbitration in the event of disputes. In the process, they waive the option of pursuing their interests as fully as they might later wish to. In return, however, they avoid battles in which each side wastes a fortune on largely offsetting legal maneuvers. The legal system itself sometimes takes steps to limit spending on litigation. For example, a federal judge in South Dakota recently announced—presumably to the approval of litigants—that he would read only the first 15 pages of any brief submitted before his court.

Many forms of collective action—both laws and informal social norms—have a direct impact on the specific consumption imbalances that are our focus here. For example, it has been a common practice in human societies over thousands of years to enact sumptuary laws and to levy special taxes on luxury goods (more on these practices in chapter 13). And many communities have social norms that discourage conspicuous consumption.

The power of these norms became vividly apparent to me several years ago when they led me to pass up what otherwise would have been an irresistible consumption opportunity. A relative in California had bought a new Porsche 911 cabriolet during a visit to France. Because the franc was then trading cheaply against the dollar, he paid only $26,000 for essentially the same car that would have cost him $70,000 had he purchased it in the United States.

Actually, there was one important difference between the car he bought in Europe and the one he would have bought here. When he returned to California he discovered that he could not register his car there because it had been produced for the European market. California dealers had successfully lobbied for a law that made such cars illegal even if retrofitted to satisfy all California pollution regulations. As a stopgap measure, he registered it in Oregon, but in time this led to difficulty with his insurance company. In the end, he decided to sell the car and, being a family member, I had a chance to buy it for just a small fraction of its original market value (by then it was three years old). And since my home state of New York does not prohibit retrofitting European car models, I could have owned and operated it in full compliance with the law.

I was sorely tempted. Yet my small upstate college town has a strong, if usually unstated, social norm against conspicuous consumption. People here are far more likely to drive Volvos than Jaguars, and although ours is a cold climate, we almost never see anyone wearing a fur coat. At that time, a red Porsche convertible really would have been seen as an in-your-face car in a community like ours. Although I have never thought of myself as someone unusually sensitive to social pressure, I realized that unless I could put a sign on the car that explained how I happened to acquire it, I would never really feel comfortable driving it.

I still wonder whether I made the right decision. In the years since this episode, a number of other Porsches have materialized here, and seeing them always kindles a twinge of regret. But what is not in question is that, at the time, there would have been a social price to pay had I bought it.

There are other social norms whose effect, if not their explicit purpose, is to discourage excessive effort. For example, Christianity, Judaism, and many other religions of the world embrace Sabbath norms, which enjoin practitioners to set aside a day each week for rest and worship. Such norms may be viewed as early precursors of blue laws, which mobilized the state's enforcement powers toward similar ends. In both cases the effect is to limit the extent to which people can trade leisure time for additional income.

The overtime provisions of the Fair Labor Standards Act in the United States serve a similar purpose. These provisions, which require employers to pay a 50 percent wage premium when workers exceed 8 hours on any given day or 40 hours in any given week, provide a strong incentive to limit the amount people work. Similar legislation exists in many other Western countries. To the extent that conspicuous consumption—and hence the longer hours required to finance it—is more attractive to individuals than to society as a whole, these provisions help narrow the incentive gap.

Social Security legislation attacks the savings deficiency that I have attributed to concerns about relative consumption. As noted earlier, the system is not really a savings plan, but rather an income transfer from workers to retirees. From each individual worker's perspective, however, it is the functional equivalent of a forced savings plan. The worker loses 15 percent of her weekly income to the payroll tax, which she then recoups in the form of benefit payments during retirement. Whatever its explicit intent, one effect of the program is to help insulate people from a tendency to consume too much. Their payroll tax payments are simply not available to bid for houses in better school districts.

Consider also the effects of safety regulations, which constrain workers' ability to accept riskier working conditions in return for higher pay. The problem is that although people want to avoid illness and injury, they also want their children to keep up with (or exceed) community standards with respect to education and other important advantages. Taking a riskier job will often enable parents to come up with a down payment for a house in a better school district, and even if luck turns against them, insurance will pay the bills. From a collective perspective, however, trading safety for higher wages is a false bargain, in the same way that working longer hours and saving less are. For when all parents accept riskier jobs to obtain higher wages, they succeed only in bidding up the prices of houses in the better school districts. Laws that limit the risks we can take are attractive not because we are too stupid to be concerned about our safety, but because the individual incentives we face are misleading.

Skeptics may complain that the legislative histories of these laws offer little explicit support for the interpretations I am giving them. For example, the legislative history of the Fair Labor Standards Act makes no mention of conflict between individual and group. Rather, it suggests an intent to spread existing employment opportunities more equitably across workers. Safety regulation, likewise, is typically defended not as a device for closing incentive gaps but as a way to protect workers from exploitation from employers with market power. And the legislative history of the Social Security Act makes no mention whatever of concerns about relative income.

But what laws do and what legislators say they want them to do are often two different things. In the case of the Fair Labor Standards Act, for example, recent studies have shown that contrary to statements in the legislative history, overtime provisions typically have done little to distribute jobs more equitably.[3] Likewise, if protection against exploitation were the real purpose of safety regulations, then these regulations should have least impact in the most competitive labor markets. It is in these markets, after all, that employers face the strongest incentives to cater to workers' concerns about safety, even in the absence of regulation. Yet the evidence is clear—whatever the ultimate purpose of safety regulation may be, its impact is greatest in precisely those labor markets that by traditional measures are most competitive.[4]

Given the energy with which society has tried to extinguish people's concerns about relative position, it is hardly any surprise that legislators have not offered these concerns as a rationale for the laws they propose. Of course, this does not mean that we can always infer a law's intent by looking at its consequences. Even so, laws with bad consequences are more likely than others to be overturned eventually, and although there are many ways in which the laws we have discussed might be improved, there seems little sentiment in favor of eliminating them.

That fact alone should be troubling to believers in the efficacy of Smith's invisible hand, which stresses the deep harmony between individual and collective interests. For example, in orthodox economic models, which assume that workers do not care about relative position, it is not clear why anyone would favor overtime laws. If workers disliked working long hours, competition should result in a satisfactory overtime premium, even without regulation. Alternatively, if workers really wanted to work long hours, they would presumably not support a law that discourages employers from having them do so. According to economic orthodoxy, an overtime law is thus either harmful or irrelevant. And similar conclusions follow with respect to safety regulations. If free trade in private markets produced the best possible allocation of resources, then these laws should make matters worse, not better, and we should expect workers to clamor for their repeal.

Yet these laws have stood the test of time, and continue to receive active support from the very same people whose behavior they most constrain. This pattern becomes coherent if we view these laws as attempts to resolve conflicts between individuals and groups.

Adam Smith was the greatest economist who ever lived. But although he is most widely remembered for his account of why the individual pursuit of self-interest often promotes social ends, he was under no illusions that this is *always* the case. Note for example, his circumspect description of the entrepreneur who is led by the invisible hand "to promote an end which was no part of his intention":

> Nor is it *always* the worse for society that it was no part of it. By pursuing his own interest he *frequently* promotes that of society more effectively than when he really intends to promote it.[5] (Emphasis added.)

Many of Smith's modern disciples are considerably less circumspect regarding the efficacy of the invisible hand. Yet despite their optimism, the plain fact remains that many behaviors serve individual interests at the expense of society as a whole. An important class of such behaviors are those whose payoffs are highly dependent on context. And in view of the pervasive importance of context, there can simply be no presumption that free-market exchange yields the socially optimal mix of houses, cars, savings, leisure, safety, or autonomy in the workplace.

The evidence we have seen suggests that concerns about relative position are a powerful element of human nature. Given the intensity of these concerns, we are confronted at almost every turn with opportunities to pursue actions that are smart for one, dumb for all. We have no reason to hope that the resulting distortions will be small, and much evidence for believing that they are large.

I hasten to add that the mere fact that the invisible hand may be flawed does not imply that alternatives to free-market exchange will necessarily be any better. Indeed, as the unhappy experience of the collectively managed economies vividly illustrated, at least some alternatives are vastly worse.

Yet we must also not lose sight of the fact that we have tinkered with the market system in the past to good effect, as when environmental legislation gave us cleaner air and water. And given the scale of the waste inherent in our current consumption patterns, we would be foolish not to explore the possibility that similar opportunities remain to be exploited.

CHAPTER 12

SELF-HELP?

Economists and a growing number of other social scientists and policy analysts use the well-informed, dispassionate, rational-actor model to explain and predict human behavior. Yet much human behavior is not well captured by this model. For example, the annual Darwin Award is granted posthumously to the individual whose death from ill-considered behavior best protects the human gene pool from degradation. One winner was crushed to death by a soft drink machine as he sought to shake a free Coke from it. Another was extinguished when his car, equipped with a jet assisted take-off unit, became airborne and crashed into a mountainside.

If our only problem were that we're not as clever as the economist's hypothetical rational actor, the errors we make would be unsystematic, and the rational-actor model would still predict reasonably well. We might buy too much of something on one occasion, but we'd buy too little on another, and thus end up with roughly the right amount on average.

Yet we face several other important difficulties in addition to our limited mental computing power. For one thing, we tend to have much more information about some opportunities than others. We also find it hard to predict how we will adapt over time to new experiences. And even if we had all the relevant information and could make all the relevant predictions correctly, we would still discover that the best choices often require patience and discipline to execute. The bad news is that

any one of these difficulties will bias our choices in favor of conspicuous consumption. In combination, they may create a substantial imbalance. The good news is that to the extent that such an imbalance
results from faulty choices by individuals, there may be opportunities
to improve matters through unilateral action.

BIASED INFORMATION

The classical rational-actor model assumes that the decision maker is
perfectly informed not only about the existence of all relevant alternatives but also about their respective costs and benefits. No one really
takes this assumption literally, of course, and even the most ardent
free-market economist would concede that people may decide imper-
fectly when they are unaware of potentially superior alternatives.

This turns out to be a more serious problem for some kinds of
products and activities than others. Most of what I have been calling
conspicuous consumption items are produced by private firms for sale
in the marketplace. Producers of these products have strong incentives
to employ commercial advertising and other forms of communication
to tout their offerings. Procter & Gamble alone spends more than $2
billion a year promoting its various toothpastes, soaps, and detergents.
Kellogg spends more than half a billion dollars a year plugging its
breakfast cereals and other products. And Anheuser Busch spends almost the same amount to promote its various brands of beer. Altogether, the top 100 U.S. advertisers spent more than $50 billion in
1995 alone.[1]

Social critics have long complained that the notoriously inflated
claims of these advertisers hardly provide a sound basis for choosing
among their products. It is mathematically impossible, after all, for
every headache remedy to offer the fastest relief, for each brand of de-
tergent to yield the whitest whites, and so on. But since advertising hy-
perbole is common knowledge even among children, most of us
discount advertising claims, and it thus seems unlikely that even fledg-
ling consumers are seriously misled.

What is more, advertising may actually be more informative than might appear. The mere fact that a product is advertised at all constitutes a credible signal about its ability to please buyers, because producers do best when they focus their advertising dollars on those products they predict that consumers will like most. A single, 30-second spot during the 1998 SuperBowl cost $1.3 million, and it is not uncommon for national television advertising campaigns to cost upwards of $10 million. These sums are poorly spent to promote products that consumers won't want to buy a second time. So quite apart from what advertisers may claim about their products, their decision to back them with expensive promotional efforts is informative. All things considered, the information we have about the various products for sale in the marketplace may not be all that bad.

The picture is strikingly different, however, with respect to the information we have about inconspicuous consumption items. We have seen that increases in time spent with family and friends, safety and autonomy in the workplace, urban parkland, freedom from traffic congestion, and a host of other items confer significant and lasting increases in human satisfaction—much larger and more enduring increases than we get from comparable investments in bigger houses and more expensive cars. Yet because inconspicuous consumption items typically are not offered for sale in the marketplace, we do not hear a steady stream of advertising messages touting their benefits.

There are exceptions, of course. For example, the most effective strategy for the marketers at Disney World may be to remind people of the joys of family vacations together. And private employers may sometimes sponsor ads proclaiming their satisfying work environments. For example, in the background the chorus sings "Dow helps you do good things" as we watch the young college graduate basking in praise for having developed a new strain of corn that will curb world hunger. On balance, however, there can be little doubt that advertising messages focus more heavily on conspicuous consumption than on inconspicuous consumption.

This focus does not *guarantee* a bias in our consumption choices. After all, if we really want to spend more time with family and friends, and less time climbing the career ladder, we always have that option.

Yet most of us are surprised to discover how strongly our choices and evaluations are influenced by information that we happen to have readily at hand. For example, students who are shown brief violent cartoons by experimenters are more likely than others to employ physical violence when involved in disputes with their classmates.[2] And subjects in jury experiments who are shown slasher films, such as *Nightmare on Elm Street* and *Texas Chain Saw Massacre,* are considerably less likely than control subjects to express sympathy for a rape victim.[3]

The information to which we are exposed can affect our responses even when we have every reason to believe that it is manifestly irrelevant. In one remarkable experiment, for example, the psychologists Daniel Kahneman and Amos Tversky showed that people's responses to an estimation problem were strongly influenced by a number they knew to be completely random. The specific problem they posed to subjects was to estimate the percentage of African countries in the United Nations.[4] But before even asking this question, Kahneman and Tversky had subjects spin a random number wheel with an indicator that was equally likely to stop on any whole number between 0 and 100. Each subject surely knew that this number had no possible bearing on the correct answer to the question. Yet subjects who got 10 when they spun the wheel gave an average response of 25 percent, whereas those who got 65 gave an average response of 45 percent!

The number produced by spinning the wheel had influence not because people thought it relevant but simply because it was *available.* Most Americans simply don't know the percentage of African countries in the United Nations. The number from the spinning wheel provided a handy reference point for making a guess.

I do not mean to suggest that we are not creatures of free will on some meaningful interpretation of the term. Clearly any of the subjects in the Kahneman and Tversky experiment could have responded differently had they felt motivated to do so. Yet that cannot obscure the fact that many decisions we make depend on the information to which we are exposed. And if that information is biased, there is every reason to expect that our decisions will also be.

The notion that advertising messages may distort our consumption decisions is hardly new. Four decades ago, this charge formed the central thesis of John Kenneth Galbraith's influential book, *The Affluent Society*. And as Galbraith forcefully emphasized, the producers of conspicuous consumption goods do not merely *inform* us of the merits of their products. They also attempt to *persuade* us to believe we need them, using all the tools in the modern social psychologist's arsenal. Information of the sort they provide us is likely to have considerably more impact than a digit from a random number wheel.

Yet even in the absence of advertising messages, we would still have more information about conspicuous consumption than about inconspicuous consumption. We see our neighbors' houses and cars, but not how much they save, or how much autonomy they have in their jobs, or whether those jobs leave them with time and energy to read books to their preschoolers at bedtime. (Hence, in part, my reason for describing the latter items as inconspicuous consumption.) Because the things we see most often are most readily available in memory, they tend to have disproportionate influence on our spending decisions. And this too implies a bias in favor of conspicuous consumption.

PREDICTING ADAPTATION

In many cases, we can make intelligent choices between a pair of alternatives if we can predict how each member of the pair will affect us at the moment of decision. For example, in choosing between rice and potatoes as a starch for the evening meal, we need only predict which one will satisfy more on that occasion. And most of us are pretty good at this.

In many other cases, however, intelligent choice requires that we predict not only which alternative will satisfy more in the moment of decision but also how the experience of each would evolve over time if chosen. Consider, for example, the choice between two otherwise identical houses, one with a commanding view of city lights and the other with no view to speak of. Given that most people like views, the house that has one will naturally carry a higher price tag. Is it worth it?

It is a relatively simple matter to gauge our subjective impressions of the immediate impact of the view just by inspecting the two houses. And if the view has little immediate impact, the best choice is probably the house without one, especially if the house with the view costs, say, $50,000 more. (Recall from chapter 2 that the premium for a view is several times that amount for many upmarket private residences.)

But suppose you are financially comfortable and find the view utterly breathtaking, so much so that you can think of nothing else you could buy for $50,000 that would have similar impact. If you also feel comfortable about your current level of charitable giving and feel secure about your retirement savings, the house with a view might then seem the most attractive—indeed, even the most prudent—choice.

But now suppose you read an article in which people who owned houses with stunning views were surveyed and reported that, after having lived with their views for several months, they scarcely even noticed them. Would that give you pause?

I hasten to add that I know of no such article. Despite considerable searching, I have never been able to find a study that has evaluated how people actually respond over time to views that seem stunning initially. In lieu of such a study, I always ask friends and acquaintances who have views how they have adapted to them over time. Remarkably, almost all report that even after the initial thrill dies down a bit, their views remain an ongoing source of pleasure and excitement.

One might be skeptical of these responses on the grounds that many people would find it too painful to admit that they had paid a lot for views that they quickly ceased to enjoy. Yet many of these same people make essentially similar admissions with respect to expensive paintings they own.

When I press them to explain the difference, many say something to the effect that, whereas paintings have a static quality, their views are dynamic, changing with the time of day, the seasons, the weather, even the quality of the air. In most places, picture-postcard weather—those crystal-clear days on which views are at their spectacular best—comes only sporadically, thus helping to maintain a sense of scarcity and appetite. A painting, by contrast, can be studied to one's heart's content at any time. Ironically, the owner of an expensive painting may discover that she enjoys it less when it hangs on the wall of her living room than if she were to encounter it only a few times a year in a local museum.

My point is not that the casual responses of friends settle the question of how people adapt over time to having houses with views. Rather, it is that if one were considering whether to buy such a house, it would be good to know something about this. Yet adaptation scarcely merits any attention at all when people confront purchase decisions.[5] Typically we seem to estimate the attractiveness of a good or activity by trying it and seeing how it affects us. When considering a house with a view, for instance, we sit in its living room and stare out for a while; when considering a new car, we take it for a test drive; and so on. And on the basis of these initial impressions, we then make our purchase decisions.

Does ignoring adaptation make some choices misleadingly attractive relative to others? The answer will clearly depend on whether we adapt differently over time to experiences in different categories. If we do not, then failure to account for adaptation will introduce no bias. For example, if the initial impression of every activity overstated its eventual attractiveness by a factor of, say, three, then all activities would be disappointing, but our choices among them would not be distorted.

Distortions surely will result, however, if we adapt more fully in some areas than in others. Thus, if we choose among potential experiences in accord with how strongly we react to them initially, the logical implication is that we will invest too heavily in experiences whose attractiveness declines steeply over time and too little in those whose attractiveness declines less steeply, or even grows, over time.

A central, if often implicit, theme in the psychological literature on the determinants of life satisfaction is that adaptation is highly variable across categories. The categories I have called conspicuous consumption are typically most attractive in their initial stages, falling off sharply thereafter. For example, although it is clear that most people experience a rush of satisfaction when they first acquire television sets with bigger screens, refrigerators with greater capacity, or loudspeakers with greater dynamic range, these feelings almost invariably tend to decay rapidly. Once we become accustomed to the bigger TV, the more spacious refrigerator, or the better loudspeakers, their favorable features fade into the background. We are no longer conscious of them. This helps to explain why, as we saw earlier, the average level of subjective well-being within a country remains remarkably stable even in the face of manyfold increases in material-goods consumption.

By contrast, the time profiles of our reactions to increases in many forms of inconspicuous consumption have essentially the opposite configuration. For example, our subjective experience of vigorous exercise or of learning to play a musical instrument may even be mildly aversive at first, but will gradually become pleasurable, and ever more so as additional time passes. To the extent that we ignore our tendencies to adapt differently in different spheres, we will spend too much on conspicuous consumption, and too little on inconspicuous consumption.

Consider, for example, a man trying to decide whether to trade in his Toyota Corolla for a new Porsche Boxster. He could meet the payments on the new car by working an additional Saturday each month, which would mean not spending that Saturday with friends. Orthodox economic theory suggests that he will work the extra Saturday if the satisfaction afforded by the Porsche outweighs the satisfaction provided by the company of his friends. But never having owned a Porsche, he cannot be sure how that experience will affect him. Nor can he know how things will evolve if he continues to spend the extra Saturday with friends. In both cases, he must make rough guesses about the future.

Introspection may provide reasonably good estimates of how these experiences will affect his satisfaction in the short run. But in the problem at hand, the relevant short- and long-run effects are likely to be different. Because the Porsche is much faster and handles much better than his Toyota, his test drive will provide an initial thrill. Over time, however, he will grow accustomed to the new car's capabilities and this capacity to stimulate will decay. The contribution to subjective well-being of additional time spent with friends will have a markedly different time profile. As relationships continue over time, the satisfaction they provide tends to increase, rather than diminish.

In the long run, then, extra time spent with friends might well prove the better choice. Yet the short-run increment in satisfaction might easily be higher with the new car. And because these short-run effects are the most vivid and readily available sources of information at the moment of decision, they will tend to bias choice in favor of the car.

Failure to take adaptation into account has similar implications for the decision about how much to save. Here the problem stems from how the amount we consume now affects our ability to derive pleasure from a given consumption level later on. By way of illustration, consider the following hypothetical choice between two different consumption profiles that could be financed from the same stream of lifetime earnings. In each case, suppose that you and all others in your age cohort earn a salary of $50,000 each and every year from age 21 until retirement at 65. In one instance, suppose that you and others spend exactly your salaries of $50,000 each year, as shown by the level consumption profile labeled A in the figure below. Alternatively, suppose you and others start out by saving $10,000 a year (or, to put it another way, suppose you start out by consuming only $40,000 a year), then gradually diminish your rate of saving until, by middle age, you begin drawing down your savings in ever larger amounts to finance additional consumption. If we ignore for simplicity the fact that your savings generate interest, this pattern yields the rising consumption profile labeled B in the diagram. Note that although profile B starts out $10,000 lower than profile A and ends up $10,000 higher, total lifetime consumption is the same on each profile. Which one would you choose (assuming that, in either case, you receive the same generous pension during retirement)?

When I put an essentially similar question to a sample of more than 100 Cornell seniors a few years ago, almost 80 percent chose B, the rising consumption profile. Evidence suggests that this profile would indeed be the more satisfying of the two.[6] Here again, the idea is that our evaluations of almost everything—including material living standards—depend on our frames of reference. One frame of reference for evaluating our material standard of living involves comparing what we currently have to what others have. But since everyone is assumed to follow the same consumption profile in this example, this comparison adds nothing of interest. A second frame of reference involves comparing what we currently have to what we ourselves had in the recent past, and it is this frame of reference that proves decisive

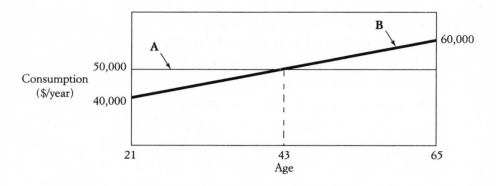

STATIC AND RISING CONSUMPTION PROFILES

for the problem at hand. For example, someone who consumes $50,000 this year is more likely to be satisfied with her standard of living if she consumed $45,000 last year than if she had consumed $55,000. People who consume too much too soon thus establish a more demanding frame of reference within which their later consumption must be evaluated.

The more we save during the early course of the life cycle, the steeper, and hence more satisfying, our consumption profiles will be. As obvious as this might seem, however, most of us never consciously consider the extent to which our current spending habits affect our evaluations of future living standards. To the extent that we ignore this relationship, we will tend to save too little. Here again, our failure to take adaptation into account leads to costly, and avoidable, errors. Individuals acting alone could mitigate this problem by simply saving more.

Perhaps the most vivid example of failure to account for future adaptation is the drug abuser's failure to anticipate increasing tolerance to his drug of choice. Thus a cocaine abuser typically gets launched on his downward spiral in the expectation that repeated ingestion of the drug will yield the same rush of euphoria he experienced on his first trial. He quickly discovers, however, that larger and larger doses are required to produce this effect. And before long, it becomes necessary to ingest prodigious quantities of the drug merely to avoid feelings of profound dysphoria. We may be sure that fewer people would take the first steps along this miserable trajectory if their patterns of future adaptation were clear to them at the outset. Our tendency to allocate too many resources to conspicuous consumption is in this sense no different in kind, though of course profoundly different in degree, from the addict's problem with cocaine.

THE EXECUTION PROBLEM

Suppose, for the sake of discussion, that we set aside the various decision errors to which we seem prone. And let us also assume away the various arms-race and related contextual problems that might lead us to spend too much on conspicuous consumption—as in the case of job seekers who feel forced to wear custom-tailored suits in the hope of making favorable first impressions. In other words, suppose we knew precisely how to allocate our resources to maximize life satisfaction, and could achieve that outcome by taking unilateral action. We would still confront one more formidable hurdle, which is that inferior consumption patterns are often painfully *tempting*. We could know exactly what is best for us and yet still have a hard time executing the right choices.

The case of addictive drugs again provides an instructive analogy. Thus people in recovery from abuse of alcohol, cocaine, heroin, and other drugs are typically highly vulnerable to relapses, even long after having overcome their acquired tolerance for these drugs. The problem confronting these people is surely not biased or incomplete information; nor is it any failure to anticipate the pattern of adaptation that awaits them. After all, they have already experienced the perils of these drugs firsthand. Rather, their peculiar difficulty is that whereas the rush of euphoria from taking the drug comes right away, the various costs come later. They *know* the drugs may cost them their jobs and their families. But not right away. They want to say no, but believe they can always say no tomorrow.

In this respect as well, our decisions regarding ordinary consumption goods are often no different in kind from recovering addicts' decisions regarding drugs. Thus the psychologist Martin Seligman has coined the term *salted-nut syndrome* to describe our tendency to continue eating salted nuts well past the point at which they spoil our appetites for the upcoming meal. We *know* we should put the nuts away sooner. But it is all too easy to eat a few more before taking that step.

The psychiatrist George Ainslie has argued that human and animal nervous systems are simply hardwired to prefer the poorer but earlier of two goals, when the earlier goal is close at hand. [7] This pattern was originally demonstrated by Ainslie's collaborator, the late psychologist Richard Herrnstein, who studied what pigeons do when given a chance to choose the smaller but earlier of two morsels of food. Herrnstein's pigeons could peck one button and get a small morsel of food after a given delay, or they could peck a second button and get a larger morsel after a somewhat longer delay. The larger morsel was the right choice in the sense that the extra nourishment it provided was far more than enough to compensate, in nutritional terms, for the slightly longer wait. Herrnstein found that if the delay before receiving the smaller morsel was sufficiently long, the birds were "rational," always passing up the smaller morsel in favor of the larger one. But as the waiting time for both morsels grew shorter, there inevitably came a point at which the birds switched. Once the smaller, earlier morsel became imminently available, it became irresistible.

Similar preference reversals are widespread in everyday human behavior. For example, the dieter vows before dinner to forgo dessert, but then changes his mind when the dessert trolley arrives. That his subsequent expression of regret at having done so is genuine is supported by the fact he deliberately avoids keeping tempting desserts on hand in his own kitchen. In the same vein, we may note that executives who order their lunches in the morning typically order smaller portions than those who wait until noon.

Similar evidence confirms the suspicion that drug abuse appears to be largely a consequence of the spurious attractiveness of poorer but earlier rewards. For example, experimenters have found that alcoholics are much less likely to drink when they are required to do a small amount of work, or receive a mild electric shock, *before* drinking.[8] These are the very same alcoholics who are not deterred by the knowledge that far more devastating costs will surely befall them *after* drinking.

That self-control problems are widespread is further evidenced by the sheer variety of tangible means by which individuals have attempted to solve them. Consider, for example, the person who wants to get out of bed on time for work, but has trouble summoning the will to do so when her alarm goes off. Morning after morning, she flips the alarm off, rolls over, and goes back to sleep. The economist Thomas Schelling observes that many people solve this problem by moving their alarm clocks out of easy reach, thus making it impossible to turn them off without getting out of bed.[9] By the same token, fearing they will gamble too much, many people limit the amount of cash they take to Atlantic City. Fearing they will stay up too late watching TV, they move the television out of the bedroom. In varying degrees, Ainslie argues, we are all addicts of a sort, battling food, cigarettes, alcohol, TV sportscasts, detective novels, and a host of other seductive activities.

As with our failure to forecast adaptation, self-control problems would cause no bias in our spending patterns if they arose with equal force for every activity. Yet here again, our failures differ across categories; some goods are simply harder to resist than others. When we see a *New Yorker* cartoon that portrays a wary grocery shopper entering an aisle marked with a sign warning "Caution, potato chips ahead," we know instantly what the artist had in mind. Signs warning "Caution, brown rice ahead," or "Caution, soy flour ahead," would have been simply unintelligible.

For present purposes, the important point is that the more conspicuous a consumption opportunity is, the more difficult the corresponding self-control problem is likely to be. It is not the ordinary good that proves so tempting, but the one that is in some way distinctive. Thus the person who knows he needs to save more for retirement will not be tempted to stock up on safflower oil, but may give in and buy a sleek new sailboat, or a set of titanium golf clubs. The attraction of the distinctive product is in this way similar to the attraction of the salted nuts: In people with a taste for them, both ignite powerful appetites. In each case it may be clear that a better outcome will result by abstaining, yet that knowledge alone may fail to summon the necessary restraint.

That saving in particular gets short shrift because of self-control problems is further evidenced by the enormous costs that many people incur because of their inability to postpone purchases even briefly. Someone carrying credit-card balances totaling $10,000, for example, will incur as much as $1,800 a year or more in interest payments. If instead she had postponed her purchases until she could pay for them out of savings, and then used that $1,800 to buy treasury bonds paying 5 percent interest each year, she would have had an extra $10,443 after 5 years, an extra $62,494 after 20 years.

The telltale footprints of self-control problems are also evident in the steps many of us take to prevent ourselves from spending too much. As the economists Richard Thaler and Herschel Shefrin have suggested, people who want to save for Christmas gifts, yet find they deplete their savings whenever a tempting purchase opportunity arises, sometimes respond by joining "Christmas clubs," special savings accounts that prevent them from making withdrawals before a specified date in late autumn.[10] We also buy whole-life insurance policies, which pay submarket rates of return and impose substantial penalties on withdrawals before retirement. And we find it attractive to work for employers who essentially force us to contribute to pension plans. If self-control problems did not make it difficult to achieve our well-considered savings goals, we would be less inclined to surrender our autonomy in these ways.

To recapitulate briefly, it appears that human decision making is flawed in specific ways that bias our choices in favor of conspicuous consumption. One source of bias is that we have more information about conspicuous consumption than about inconspicuous consumption, not only because conspicuous consumption is often literally more visible but also because producers focus their commercial messages on the attractions of conspicuous consumption. A second source of bias results from our failure to account for the different adaptation profiles that characterize different forms of consumption. And finally, our choices tend to be biased because conspicuous consumption is simply more tempting than inconspicuous consumption.

If the bias in our current consumption patterns were the exclusive result of arms-race problems of the sort discussed in the preceding chapters, it would be fruitless to seek remedies based on unilateral actions by individuals. Unilateral action seems altogether more promising, however, if the imbalance stems at least in part from our own human frailties. And herein lies the attraction of the voluntary simplicity movement, which urges a retreat from the rat race for career advancement and accumulation of material goods.

THE VOLUNTARY SIMPLICITY MOVEMENT

Since the dawn of the industrial age, movements have organized sporadically to promote simpler modes of living. Prominent examples include the Arts and Crafts movement, led by John Ruskin and William Morris in reaction against what seemed to them an overmechanization of life in late-nineteenth-century England; and the offshoot Craftsman movement championed by Gustav Stickley, Elbert Hubbard, and others in the early-twentieth-century United States. But owing perhaps to their limited capacities to communicate directly with the masses, these and other similar movements dropped from sight relatively quickly, never having achieved more than fringe status.

The current back-to-basics movement, which was launched with the publication of Duane Elgin's *Voluntary Simplicity* in 1981, may itself run a similar course in time. Yet so far it has managed to attract far more attention and interest than the earlier ones. In the last decade, literally scores of similar books have echoed Elgin's call—among them, *Your Money or Your Life,* a 1992 volume by Vicki Robin and the late Joe Dominguez that is regarded by many as the movement's most influential title; and Sarah Ban Breathnach's *Simple Abundance,* which has been entrenched on various *New York Times* bestseller lists since it appeared in hardcover in 1995. Many bookstores now have entire sections entitled "Simplicity," and there are at least four large newsletters on the subject with burgeoning subscription lists. The first national Voluntary Simplicity Conference was held in Washington, D.C. in May 1997.

As this beehive of activity suggests, the voluntary simplicity, or downshifting, movement has registered impressive growth. For example, in a 1995 survey sponsored by the Merck Family Fund, 28 percent of respondents reported that they had made changes in their lives in the last five years that resulted in their making less money—either by working shorter hours, by moving to a lower paying job, or by working at home.[11]

Although the movement is most active in the United States, it is also growing rapidly in England. Thus a survey by the Henley Center for Forecasting reported that 6 percent of Britons have voluntarily reduced their income in the past year and another 6 percent intend to.[12] Gerald Celente, editor of *The Trends Journal,* predicts that 15 percent of all persons worldwide will be practicing voluntary simplicity by 2005, up from 2 percent today.[13]

What, exactly, does the voluntary simplicity movement urge people to do? As the jacket flap copy of one recent book described it, the movement's main message is that "less—less work, less rushing, less debt—is more—more time with family and friends, more time with community, more time with nature."[14] Although some authors occasionally mention public-policy measures that might further their agenda, the simplicity movement is quintessentially a self-help movement. It lays out strategies that individuals, acting alone, can follow. For instance we are urged to cut back our hours, switch to part-time jobs, or run businesses out of our homes. And many movement books (such as *Cut Your Bills in Half: Thousands of Tips to Save Thousands of Dollars,* a 1989 title by the editors of Rodale Press) offer concrete strategies for remaining financially solvent in the process. We should save more and pay down our mortgages; or perhaps sell our houses and buy smaller ones in less expensive areas; and instead of eating in expensive restaurants so often, have potluck suppers with friends; and so on.

To a remarkable degree, the passionate, almost evangelical, urgings of voluntary simplicity movement authors coincide with the prescriptions of the dispassionate analyst whose goal is to prevent people from making decisions based on biased or incomplete information. And to the extent that our current emphasis on conspicuous consumption is the result of bad personal decisions, someone who followed the movement's advice could expect to be pleased with the results.

Another aspect of the simplicity movement is consistent with the idea that bad decisions result not just from biased information and faulty reasoning but also from lack of patience and discipline. Thus the movement promulgates its message not just in books, newsletters, and other print media, but also through *simplicity circles,* its term for groups of people who meet periodically to share thoughts and offer mutual support as they strive to adopt simpler modes of living. These groups are eerily similar to Alcoholics Anonymous and various other 12-step programs whose goals are to inform, indoctrinate, and provide emotional support. If the alcoholic's problem is that he finds it difficult not to drink, he can turn to fellow AA members for support. By the same token, if someone finds that she has difficulty resisting the temptations of the marketplace, she can find comfort and support in the company of fellow circle members.

In purely practical terms, then, the voluntary simplicity movement appears well designed for attacking the individual-level problems that lead to unbalanced spending patterns (though, to my knowledge, none of the movement's proponents has ever described it in anything like these terms). What is more, the movement's recommendations—if everyone were to follow them—are squarely consistent with the evidence we have seen about how changes in consumption patterns would affect life satisfaction, though here again, movement proponents typically do not argue their case in these terms.

THE DOWNSIDE OF DOWNSHIFTING

If individual decision errors were the only, or even the most important, source of our spending imbalance, people who followed the voluntary simplicity movement's program would experience uniformly favorable results. And as word of their successes filtered out, we would expect the movement to spread like a prairie fire. Yet although the downshifting movement has shown impressive growth, it remains small. And although it has transformed consumption habits dramatically in many individual cases, it has not, in fact, had much impact on our overall spending patterns. On the contrary, as a nation we are logging more hours at the office and spending at a higher rate than ever before.

There is a good reason that simplicity movements through the ages have had trouble catching fire. As we saw in the preceding chapters, there are many instances in which spending differently would improve matters if everyone did so, yet would make matters worse for any individual who acted alone. You want an interesting job, one that is challenging and gives you opportunities to learn and grow as you work? Well, so do a lot of other people, and only rarely do these jobs go to people willing to work only part time. Many downshifters discover that the extra time they've captured by switching to a part-time job fails to compensate for the lower levels of engagement they experience while working.

Lack of good part-time jobs also forces many downshifters to become jacks-of-all-trades. Thus Nanny Nehring Bliss, a 27-year-old practitioner of voluntary simplicity who lives with her husband in Bloomington, Illinois, "spends her days creating inexpensive staples in the kitchen, tending to the couple's worm compost in the basement, researching land opportunities on the Internet, and occasionally taking on a small writing or cooking project for pay."[15] Job specialization has its obvious downside, especially when carried to excess. Yet failure to specialize also entails costs, the most conspicuous of which is lower productivity. Because unspecialized work is typically so unproductive, it actually ends up being extremely costly in time, the very thing that downshifters are so eager to have more of.

Although Nehring Bliss (her real name), who does all her own baking, says that "five hours to make a loaf of bread does not seem like a long time," it is in fact a *very* long time. Even a minimum-wage worker can buy a terrific loaf of fresh bread at the bakery near my house for less than she earns in 15 minutes. Professional bakers are simply much more efficient than the rest of us at making bread, and relying on them to perform that task frees us up to spend more time on things we are comparatively good at doing. My point is not that professional bakers should be the only ones ever to bake bread, but rather that baking your own bread makes sense only if you find the experience itself enjoyable relative to other uses of your time. Similarly, it is by no means a mistake that many of us spend a lot of time playing tennis, or playing musical instruments, even though we never expect to compete with professionals in those areas.

But when all is said and done, we also need to be able to pay our bills. And we can all expect to meet those obligations in the shortest time—thereby freeing up more time to do whatever else we wish—if we concentrate at least a significant proportion of our efforts on those tasks we are best at. Specialization need not entail rigidly segmented, mind-numbingly repetitive work. Yet typically it does preclude spending most of our working time alternating between a variety of tasks we are not especially good at.

Someone who follows the latter route must thus expect to pay a price of one sort or another. Nehring Bliss has obviously found time to bake bread and tend to her worms. But she and her husband also have no health insurance and no retirement plan. And because they do not plan to have children, they needn't concern themselves with carrying a mortgage on a house in a good school district.

Back-to-basics movements almost invariably fail to appreciate that high productivity is a good thing because it offers the potential to free up more time for the things we most want to do. To the extent that the existing menu of part-time jobs makes it difficult to find opportunities to utilize one's skills and abilities to the fullest, a double penalty from switching to part-time work thus remains—lower pay not only because of working fewer hours but also because of being less productive during each hour worked. The first penalty can be offset by the benefits of the additional free time. But the second penalty is a pure loss. In the end, lower productivity inevitably means less freedom to pursue your own vision of the good life.

Some people, of course, do manage to cut back their hours without having to take a significant cut in their hourly wages. But even these people often confront unexpected difficulties. Having more free time, for example, invites opportunities for travel and other leisure activities, many of which are not cheap. Thus, as one freelance writer who works at home put it, "The more of life's pleasures you have time to participate in, the more they cost."[16]

Even many of the voluntary simplicity movement's money-saving tips tend to break down once more than just a few people begin to pursue them. For example, one author suggests that when shopping for groceries we should look for "big discounts on seconds: bruised fruit, day-old bread, dented tins and torn labels."[17] Yet only a small proportion of fruit, bread, canned goods, and other merchandise is in distressed condition, and once demand outstrips available supplies, the discounts for these products rapidly shrink.

Another problem is that many people already live so close to the margin that cutting back may entail painful compromises in the standard of care provided for children and ailing parents. Thus, notes author Mary McCarty, "I wish with all my heart I could slow down, volunteer for simplicity, and make my family less frantic. I just can't figure out how to do it without losing my job, neglecting the kids, or getting the house condemned by the board of health. . . . I [already] drive a 10-year-old car, live in a reasonably priced house and pack my lunch."[18]

For most of us, of course, it is *always* an option to move to a smaller house in a less expensive neighborhood. The problem is that such a move may entail costs far more troubling than having to get used to more modest living quarters. The cheaper neighborhood may be less safe, for example, or more polluted; and its schools may not be nearly as good as the ones in our current neighborhood. What is more, the cheapest housing is typically also more isolated geographically, and this often entails a significant increase in commuting time.

Individual moves to part-time or stay-at-home work also may prompt others to make additional demands on our time. "Because you work at home, others don't consider it real work," notes Marilyn Goldstein, who quit her corporate job to pursue her writing interests at home. "Therefore, they feel free to call and ask for a piece of all your spare time: to collect for Cancer Care because they're too busy in the office, drive them home from the service station after they drop off their cars for a tune-up, run them over to the airport, pick up the newspapers on the porch because they forget to cancel for their vacations, return last night's videos to Blockbuster, baby-sit for their cats. The simplified life suddenly demands a to-do list longer than the ones in the bad old moneymaking, money-spending, doing going running days."[19]

ONCE AGAIN: SMART FOR ONE, DUMB FOR ALL

I must not overstate the difficulties associated with voluntary simplicity. Our imbalanced consumption patterns no doubt stem in part from the fact that we are poorly informed, that we fail to anticipate how we will adapt to different experiences, and that we lack the patience and willpower to execute even our well-considered consumption plans. Voluntary simplicity can help mitigate all these problems.

Yet our consumption imbalance would persist even if we were perfectly informed, rational decision makers with limitless patience and willpower. The problem is that many important rewards in life depend on how much we spend relative to others. If we all cut back, we do better; but someone who cuts back unilaterally often does much worse. To the extent that choices that are smart for one are dumb for all, individual action, by itself, simply won't be enough.

CHAPTER 13

OTHER FAILED REMEDIES

Conspicuous consumption is misleadingly attractive to individuals and families in the same way that investment in military arms is misleadingly attractive to individual nations. Assuming we are lucky enough to avoid a nuclear holocaust, however, the waste that stems from spending too much on conspicuous consumption is vastly greater. An across-the-board reduction in the rate of growth in conspicuous consumption would, in time, free up literally trillions of dollars worth of resources annually. As we have seen, these resources could be used to support more time with family and friends, more freedom from congestion and pollution, greater autonomy and flexibility in the workplace, and increases in a variety of other forms of inconspicuous consumption that would enhance the quality of our lives.

The idea that as a society we can do better by spending less on conspicuous consumption is hardly novel. Indeed, for as long as we have organized ourselves into social groups—which is to say, for as long as we have existed as a species—we have employed one scheme after another to curb conspicuous consumption. Some of these schemes, such as sumptuary laws and social norms, accomplished the desired reductions only by creating other, more serious problems. Still others—such as luxury excise taxes—led to small improvements, but were themselves so costly to administer that the resulting gains largely dissipated. Our history of attempts to curb conspicuous consumption has been, in short, a largely failed one.

Yet there are grounds for hope. We may note, for example, that although many of our early attempts to reduce environmental pollution were also dismal failures, often imposing costs far greater than the minimal gains they achieved, we have in recent years begun to adopt a series of highly cost-effective environmental solutions. The key to this progress has been a better understanding of the incentives that led to excessive pollution in the first place. By the same token, our early attempts to curb conspicuous consumption failed largely because we failed to understand the incentive structure responsible for the problem. This incentive structure, it turns out, is closely analogous to the one that gives rise to the problem of environmental pollution. And this insight, as we shall see, suggests a disarmingly simple way to achieve a more balanced consumption mix.

THE LIBERTARIAN OBJECTION

Before considering the various collective steps by which societies have tried to limit conspicuous consumption, we must confront the objection that such steps can never be legitimately taken in a political democracy. This position is most prominently associated with the philosopher Robert Nozick and other contemporary libertarian thinkers, but its supporting arguments have been influential across a much broader spectrum. Because these arguments constitute one of the two major remaining obstacles to achieving a more sensible allocation of resources, they merit careful consideration. (The second obstacle, which we will take up in chapter 15, is the false belief that greater inequality promotes economic growth.)

In a nutshell, the libertarian position is this: Without disputing that satisfaction with material living standards may be heavily dependent on context, the libertarian objects that Tom's unhappiness about Bill's increased consumption simply does not constitute legitimate grounds for curbing Bill's consumption. Tom may be unhappy, but it is nonetheless Tom's responsibility to simply mind his own business. The libertarian argues that to restrict Bill's consumption because it makes Tom unhappy is essentially no different from telling Bill he can't wear a purple shirt because Tom doesn't like the color purple. Tough luck, Tom! Bill has a *right* to wear a purple shirt, and those who don't like it had just better get used to it.

This objection has considerable rhetorical force. After all, as parents most of us try to teach our children not to worry about what others consume. There will *always* be others with more, we tell them, and if you can't accept that gracefully, you're in for a lot of trouble. By analogy, it seems plausible that this might be the best posture for the state to assume as well.

Yet this ignores the fact that, unlike the wearing of a purple shirt, many forms of consumption cause not only injured feelings in others but also more tangible losses. Consider again the job seeker who gains a leg up on his rivals by showing up for his interview in a custom-tailored suit. Acting as individuals, the best response for his rivals may be to show up in custom-tailored suits as well. Even though all job seekers might strongly prefer the alternative of all spending less on their professional wardrobes, they are stuck with the extra expense.

Suppose it were somehow practical for all job seekers to meet and discuss the issue. And suppose they voted unanimously to prohibit interviewees from showing up in a suit costing more than, say, $300. On what grounds might we then conclude that this restriction is illegitimate? Because it violates the individual job seeker's freedom? That would be a strange objection indeed if each job seeker had just voted in favor of the restriction. If each had *wanted* to restrict his own freedom in precisely this way, disallowing their agreement would simply make them worse off.

Perhaps some would object that such an agreement could never command unanimous support in the first place. Thus there would always be *someone*—a fashion buff, say—whose purpose in wearing the custom-tailored suit had nothing to do with gaining advantage over his fellow job seekers. And because the restriction would make such persons worse off, they could hardly be expected to support it. As a practical matter, then, a proposal to limit wardrobe expenses might get a majority vote, but never a unanimous one.

Yet we do not recognize failure to achieve unanimity as a barrier to legitimate collective action in other spheres. Because most of us value cleaner air, for example, we require motorists to maintain emission-control equipment on their cars, even though some motorists don't care about air quality and would be delighted not to have to incur this extra cost. In these and countless other cases in which important common goals are at stake, we are prepared to restrict individual freedom in the name of the greater good.

Others might object that curbing people's freedom to do as they please is sometimes justified, but only in extreme cases such as environmental pollution, which, after all, is often a matter of life or death. Yet, as we have seen, the actions people take to meet community consumption standards often have grave consequences as well. For example, many parents reluctantly accept long hours at stressful jobs because that is the only way they can afford to buy houses in safe neighborhoods with good schools. We have no evidence that the stresses of these jobs, or the lack of time to maintain close personal relationships, or the inability to get enough sleep, shortens fewer lives than the damage inflicted by dirty air and water. Many lives would be extended and enriched if all parents felt freer to work shorter hours in less stressful jobs—an outcome that is attainable, at least in principle, through collective action. It simply makes no sense to say that such action is illegitimate because the stakes are too low.

Alternatively, one might object that an agreement limiting what job seekers spend on suits is bound to be unenforceable. After all, if wearing a better suit than others really does help you win the job, there will be powerful incentives to evade the spending limit. You could buy a suit off the rack, for example, and then make under-the-table payments to a tailor to recut it completely.

This objection might indeed prove decisive. But it concerns the *practicality* of the proposal, not its political legitimacy. Because certain kinds of action are impractical a high proportion of the time, it may prove tempting simply to dismiss them as illegitimate, thereby to avoid having to consider them repeatedly. Yielding to this temptation is costly, however, if it later forecloses consideration of similar actions that could meet the test of practicality. This is a point of more than passing theoretical interest for, as we shall see, collective restrictions of conspicuous consumption have often failed in the past for essentially practical reasons. When such restrictions prove impractical, we *should* reject them. But we should do so in the name of impracticality, not illegitimacy.

Finally, we must consider the "slippery-slope" argument against attempts to restrict human behavior. This argument holds that even though the benefits of regulating behavior might appear to outweigh the costs in a specific instance, regulation is still a bad idea because of the unfavorable precedent it will set. Once we restrict people's behavior in some minor way and they grow accustomed to that, the stage is set for further encroachment on personal freedom. And little by little, Orwell's *1984* nightmare becomes a reality.

Regulation may indeed be a slippery slope, yet it is one we are repeatedly forced to go part way down. And in case after case, going part way down this slope does not seem to have resulted in a slide all the way to the bottom. For example, although most of us concede the need for a law against yelling *fire* in a crowded theater when there is no fire, we continue vigorously to resist further attempts to curb our freedom of speech. Perhaps the slippery-slope problem receives too little attention when lawmakers debate legislation. But even if so, this would not imply that small collective steps to curb conspicuous consumption are politically illegitimate.

To acknowledge that important economic, psychological, and even physical rewards are significantly affected by the spending of others is simply to note an obvious fact of the human condition. Because each individual's consumption affects the frame of reference within which others must make important choices, this frame of reference is no less a legitimate object of public concern than the quality of our air and water. In the absence of collective action to change individual incentives, our likelihood of achieving the most sensible allocation of our time and money is no higher than our likelihood of enjoying acceptably clean air and water in the absence of environmental regulation.

We will think more productively about collective action to curb conspicuous consumption if we eschew the rhetoric of political illegitimacy and focus instead on the practical consequences of specific proposals. Many proponents of radical social change will find this a difficult, even distasteful, posture. Most radical social change, after all, has come at the initiative of political extremists, for whom ideology is a far more natural lens through which to view the world. The change in social policy that is needed to transform our current consumption mix is a genuinely radical social change, if not in form, then at least in its ultimate consequences. Yet it is a change rooted not in ideology, but in what we may call *radical pragmatism*. We want change that *works*. And to see what works, we must first understand what has failed and why.

SUMPTUARY LAWS

More than four centuries before Christ, Roman laws attempted to restrain a broad array of expenditures, including even the amount that could be spent on funerals. In addition to restraining the sizes of mausoleums and the amounts spent on funeral meals, these laws went on to require that funeral pyres "shall be constructed from unfinished wood, not from polished wood."[1] Chinese law during the T'ang Dynasty prohibited commoners from taming peregrine falcons, a privilege that was reserved for the elite.[2] Chinese commoners were further restricted by a seventeenth-century law prohibiting them from wearing fine silks and from using gold or silver leaf on household articles and saddles.[3] In the Ottoman Empire, merchants were not permitted to wear furs, a restriction that did not apply to government officials.[4] And in medieval Europe it was illegal in many places for any but royalty to wear linen and lace.

These and other sumptuary laws were among the earliest and most ill-advised forms of collective action to curb conspicuous consumption. Perhaps the most obvious problem with them is that whenever they prevented escalation in one form of spending, they almost always stimulated evasive actions that were at least as costly.

Thus the prohibition against wearing linen and lace led to attempts to signal status by wearing costly buttons, which by the fourteenth century "were worn as ornaments and fastenings from the elbow to the wrist and from the neckline to the waist."[5] The appearance of gold, silver, and ivory buttons quickly became an indication of wealth and rank, leading some jurisdictions to pass further sumptuary laws restricting the use of buttons.[6]

Under the terms of another sumptuary law, people in parts of northern Europe in the late 1500s were permitted to dress in clothing of only a single color. To get around this law, people wore clothing with an outer layer dyed in one color and an inner lining dyed in another. They would then cut the outer layer in places to expose the inner layer—all perfectly legal under the terms of the law. Thereupon they would pull the linings through the slashings and puff them out for emphasis.[7]

During the Tokugawa period of Japan (1603–1867), members of the increasingly prosperous merchant class "were barred by sumptuary laws from wearing jewelry as well as certain kinds of clothes and from owning certain kinds of traditional fine art works, all of which were reserved for those who held the rank of samurai and above."[8] In response, the merchant class simply developed its own art forms, among them the exquisitely detailed miniature sculptures called netsuke. And there was essentially no limit on what one could spend on ever more elaborately carved netsuke.

Medieval Florence had a sumptuary law that limited the number of courses served during the evening meal. This law quickly inspired the pastry-wrapped meat-and-pasta torte and many other elaborate one-dish meals, which were no less time-consuming and expensive to prepare than the multicourse meals they replaced.[9] When the Venetian Senate prohibited women from wearing dresses made from silver or gold cloth in 1443, many responded by wearing detachable sleeves made from the forbidden fabrics.[10]

Aside from the fact that close substitutes for banned activities often robbed sumptuary laws of their intended effect, these laws were problematic in other, more troubling, ways. For example, the laws made no allowance for the fact that the costs of not engaging in a prohibited activity might be extremely high for some people. Thus, whereas many people may buy expensive sculpture simply because it provides a convenient means of putting their wealth on display, there are others of modest means for whom sculpture is a heartfelt passion. These people are willing to forgo many of life's ordinary pleasures to acquire fine sculpture, and a law that prohibits them from doing so inflicts gratuitous injury.

Another difficulty is that sumptuary laws were typically profoundly undemocratic, enacted to insulate those in positions of power and privilege from emulation by their social inferiors. It is this aspect of these laws that seems to have inspired Adam Smith's contempt for them. Thus, as he put it in *The Wealth of Nations,*

> It is the highest impertinence of kings and ministers to pretend to watch over the economy of private people and to restrain their expense, either by sumptuary laws or by prohibiting the importation of foreign luxuries. They are themselves always and without exception, the greatest spendthrifts in the society. Let them look well after their own expense, and they may safely trust private people with theirs. If their own extravagance does not ruin the state, that of their subjects never will.[11]

In the end, the various difficulties with sumptuary laws led most jurisdictions to strike them from their books. Thus, as the sociologist Alan Hunt wrote, "Between the early seventeenth century and the end of the eighteenth the 'typical' sumptuary law. . . disappeared from all countries, both East and West."[12] But the legacy of sumptuary laws lives on in memory—so strongly that all subsequent attempts to curb conspicuous consumption have carried a heavy burden of guilt by association.

SOCIAL NORMS

By processes that remain poorly understood, human societies throughout history have managed to implement social norms that alter individual incentives to engage in various activities.[13] A specific target of many of these norms has been our tendency to overemphasize conspicuous consumption. Many religious doctrines, for example, exhort us not to envy or covet our neighbor's possessions. Specific groups, such as Puritans, the Amish, and the Quakers, went considerably further. For example, John Woolman, a prominent Quaker leader in the eighteenth century, "decried excessively lengthy workdays, and cautioned employers not to work others too hard."[14]

Although social norms are often articulated most clearly by religious institutions, they also spring from secular sources. And such is the variety of concerns they address that a single behavior is sometimes the target of two or more very different social norms. For example, wealthy people in some communities refrain from wearing fur coats in public not only in deference to social norms urging concern for animal rights but also because of social norms that brand these coats as ostentatious.

Many observers favor informal collective action of this sort on grounds that it is much less coercive than the alternative of formal sumptuary laws and other regulations that employ state power to limit conspicuous consumption. In one sense, however, this might be seen as a disadvantage, since a central problem with sumptuary laws was that they were so easy to evade. Yet social norms, in some settings, are actually far less easy to evade than sumptuary laws. By virtue of being less formally and explicitly codified, norms do not invite the same legalistic maneuvering that laws do. For example, if the target of a social norm is ostentatious consumption (defined by the familiar "we-know-it-when-we-see-it" criterion), one cannot escape ostracism by merely shifting from lace to gold buttons.

The other side of this coin, of course, is that social norms are often highly coercive in the same gratuitous way that sumptuary laws were. Thus a sports-car enthusiast who consumes at a generally modest level may be discouraged by social pressure from buying the one luxury that would most genuinely enrich his experience.

If social norms sometimes work too well, at other times they do not work at all, especially in the large and relatively fluid social environments in which most of us currently live. As the political scientist Robert Putnam has emphasized, the depth and breadth of our social ties have weakened in recent decades, making us ever less dependent on other people's good opinions of us.[15] Even in small towns, long-standing norms against conspicuous consumption have begun to break down under the weight of greater mobility and increasing dispersion in the distributions of income and wealth. For example, the norm that prevented me from buying a bargain Porsche in the late 1980s did not prevent me from buying a BMW in the mid-1990s.

To be sure, I would be more comfortable if others knew that I bought the car not to flaunt my economic good fortune but for other, more practical reasons. As I was about to buy a new Volkswagen Jetta to replace the seven-year-old one I had just given to one of my sons when he graduated from college, I met a man who was trying to sell his year-old BMW sedan. His asking price was about the same as the sticker price of the Jetta, and the three years remaining on the car's bumper-to-bumper warranty were as much coverage as I'd have gotten on the brand new Jetta. On top of that, the BMW accelerates more briskly, handles more surely, brakes more swiftly, and gets much better ratings in crash tests. After comparison test drives, I instantly realized that the only reason for not buying the BMW was my apprehension about what others might think.

In the late 1980s, that might have been enough. But there are many more upmarket cars on the streets of Ithaca these days, and whatever resentments these cars still kindle are now spread awfully thin. They have not completely disappeared. A chemistry professor friend who drives a red Porsche convertible here tells me, for example, that people still occasionally make obscene gestures at him when he pulls up in traffic. Yet what seems clear, at any rate, is that if social norms against conspicuous consumption have begun to unravel even in small college towns, they hold little promise of restraining the emerging consumption patterns in modern industrialized nations.

LUXURY TAXES

Another obvious way to discourage conspicuous consumption is to tax it, and this strategy has also been widely employed in societies past and present. The Roman Empire under Augustus, for example, had a 4 percent tax on the purchase of slaves.[16] One of the earliest luxury taxes in Colonial America was a levy on private carriages, which were owned almost exclusively by the wealthiest households. These carriages were taxed according to the number of wheels they had, a rough proxy for how much their owners had spent on them.[17] At the end of World War I, France imposed a 10 percent luxury tax on 25 consumer items irrespective of their price, and on another 77 items if their respective prices exceeded given thresholds.

These early luxury taxes were considerably smaller than the largest ones levied by many contemporary societies. In the recent past, for example, Algeria has imposed a 66.7 percent tax on perfumes and small cars, and a 150 percent tax on large cars, caviar, and "precious objects." Australia imposes a tax of 40 percent on perfumery, jewelry, cars, and motorcycles and 50 percent on audio and photographic equipment.[18]

The U.S. government's most recent foray into luxury taxation was launched in 1991 by the levy of a 10 percent tax on all expenditures for autos, boats, aircraft, furs, and jewelry above the following thresholds: autos, $30,000; boats, $100,000; aircraft, $250,000; and furs and jewelry, $10,000. Under this scheme, for example, the luxury tax on a $50,000 car would be $2,000—10 percent of the $20,000 by which the car's purchase price exceeded the threshold defining luxury autos.

As a means of discouraging conspicuous consumption, luxury taxes offer one important advantage over sumptuary laws and social norms—namely that they are far less coercive. Our problem is not that the auto enthusiast spends too much on his car but rather that, as a nation, we could spend considerably less on cars without experiencing any measurable decline in satisfaction. A luxury tax on cars gives each of us—enthusiasts and others alike—an incentive to spend less. But unlike an outright legal prohibition or the stern social norm, the tax preserves the enthusiast's option to indulge his heartfelt passion.

Adam Smith liked luxury taxes, not because he imagined they might change people's behavior significantly, but because he realized that governments have to tax *something* and felt that luxuries were particularly easy targets. Smith thus favored taxes on housing because the opulent mansions of the wealthy are a prime instance of the "luxuries and vanities of life."[19] He also favored higher taxes on private carriages than on commercial traffic, citing the former as examples of the "indolence and vanity of the rich."[20]

Yet, despite their widespread use, luxury taxes on specific products also entail at least two important practical disadvantages. One is the need to employ the political process to decide which products are to be taxed at which rates. Once this question is opened up for public debate, the ugly battle for preferential treatment inevitably begins. In the United States and most other democracies, corporations must hire high-priced lobbyists and consultants to make sure the arguments for their respective positions receive the fullest possible attention of elected representatives. And, no surprise, *every* producer manages to come up with a long list of reasons for classifying its particular product as a necessity. The typical result is both enormously expensive and demonstrably at odds with the requirements of intelligent public policy.

Consider, for example, the U.S. government's position on owner-occupied housing. Such housing has always received generous tax concessions on the grounds that home ownership strengthens ties to the community. But why should the same concessions be granted to mansions costing several millions of dollars? Or to vacation homes at the seashore? And why, similarly, should people who live on modest houseboats be subject to the same luxury tax as those who purchase pleasure craft with eight-figure price tags?

Consider also that the U.S. luxury tax exempts aircraft used at least 80 percent of the time for business purposes. This means that the owner of a $37 million Gulfstream Jet who flies from New York to Hong Kong on business each week can fly his family from New York to Florida each weekend tax free. By contrast, the person who makes only the same New York to Florida trip each week in his $500,000 Cessna must pay the full luxury tax.[21]

Another problem with taxing luxuries on a case-by-case basis is that it invites the same kind of evasive responses we saw with sumptuary laws. The American luxury tax on autos, for example, does not apply to sport-utility vehicles, which are officially classified as trucks. Is it any wonder, then, that the explosive growth in sales of these vehicles coincided almost exactly with the imposition of this tax?

Loopholes and inconsistencies are by no means the exclusive province of the American tax system. In England, for example, men's shaving products are exempt from consumption taxes but women's tampons are not. England also exempts foodstuffs from excise taxes, with the exception of "ice cream, confectionery including chocolate products, crisps and prepared nuts," the idea being that items in the latter category are luxuries. This led the manufacturer of a "chewy bar" to petition for an exemption on the grounds that its product contained essentially the same ingredients as many tax-exempt breakfast cereals and that, in any event, its sugar content was too low to qualify as confectionery under the law. A court found in favor of this manufacturer, but the tax law was subsequently amended to make the product taxable once again.[22] All this quibbling over what should be taxed is enormously wasteful—so much so that it may well dissipate any savings from the resulting reductions in conspicuous consumption.

A second, and related, problem with case-by-case taxation of luxury items is that it injects an inescapable element of arbitrariness and capriciousness into our public debate. Is a $300 ticket to an evening performance of the Metropolitan Opera a frivolous luxury? Perhaps for some people, but what about for the Des Moines school teacher who has saved 20 years for the thrill of a lifetime? No two of us are alike, and what is one person's luxury is another's necessity. It is a fool's errand to suppose that a defensible definition of a luxury can be crafted for practical implementation. Saddling legislators with this task guarantees further erosion of the public's confidence in the integrity of government. Fortunately, however, a far simpler and better solution is at hand.

CHAPTER 14

LUXURY WITHOUT APOLOGY

The problem of excessive environmental pollution is caused by an incentive gap virtually identical to the one that gives rise to excessive conspicuous consumption. And once we understand the link between these two problems, we can use the lessons of our experience in the environmental domain to help craft better solutions to the conspicuous consumption problem.

By way of illustration, consider an individual weighing the decision of whether to drive to work or take the bus. This person has no reason to believe that his decision will have any measurable impact on air quality in his city. Thus, if he drives to work, the smog index will be essentially the same as if he takes the bus. If driving to work is considerably cheaper, or more convenient, he will drive. This is problematic because when millions of motorists simultaneously reach the same conclusion on this basis, the impact on air quality is far from negligible. If the same issue were decided not individually but by referendum, each individual might strongly prefer the option of each taking the bus to the alternative of each driving.

In the environmental domain, the fundamental incentive gap is that driving appears more attractive to individuals than to society as a whole. The problem is not that individual consumers care only about convenience and not about air quality. Even though they may care very much about air quality, their unilateral actions do not have any measurable impact on smog.

Note the virtually identical incentive gap in the job seeker's decision about whether to buy a custom-tailored suit. His natural focus is on whether the suit will increase his odds of landing the job he wants by enough to compensate for its extra cost. If the contest for the job is likely to be close, or if it is one he cares deeply about, it will be worth it for him to spring for the better suit. This is problematic because when other job seekers simultaneously reach the same conclusion, no one gains an edge, and the extra expenditures go for naught. In the consumption domain, as in the environmental domain, the incentive problem is that many activities are more attractive to individuals than to society as a whole. In the environmental domain, individual actions contribute only negligibly to overall air quality. In the consumption domain, individual spending decisions have only negligible effects on community consumption standards. But in each case, the aggregate effects of individual actions are far from negligible.

Our first attempts to solve the problem of excessive pollution were much like our first attempts to solve the problem of excessive conspicuous consumption. The Clean Water Act of 1971, for example, established a deadline by which each producer had to remove 90 percent of its base-year emissions of toxic wastes flowing into the nation's rivers. By issuing an across-the-board prohibition on specific acts of pollution, this law was essentially like the early sumptuary laws, which issued across-the-board prohibitions on specific forms of consumption. And, as we might have expected, the problems with both approaches are strikingly similar.

For example, one wasteful aspect of the sumptuary laws was the indiscriminate way they required cutbacks in consumption, even from those with a passionate attachment to the forbidden product or service. The original Clean Water Act was wasteful in an exactly parallel way. Whereas the goal of an intelligent environmental policy is to achieve a given reduction in pollution at the lowest possible cost, the Clean Water Act required the same 90 percent cutback from producers for whom curtailment was costly as from others for whom curtailment was cheap.

Other early environmental legislation empowered regulatory agencies to issue specific requirements regarding the kinds of equipment companies could use and the kinds of fuels they could burn. For instance, some regulatory commissions required the use of costly scrubbers that remove much of the soot and other pollutants from the chimneys of coal-fired electric generators. Others required utilities to burn only low-sulfur coal.

Although the intent of these actions was clearly benign, here too the result was often extremely wasteful. Government regulators are in no better position to advise companies about the use of sophisticated technologies for curbing pollution than they are to come up with sensible definitions of what constitutes a luxury good. Low-sulfur coal may be the cheapest way to reduce acid rain in one case, but in another case it is to install more-thorough scrubbers on the smokestacks. The people in charge of the day-to-day operations of these businesses are likely to know far more about alternative technologies than government regulators do. Here again, the lesson is the same as with attempts to require equal proportional pollution cutbacks. Trying to micromanage individual companies' pollution-abatement efforts generally results in wasteful outcomes.

This lesson has at last been absorbed by environmental policy analysts and the legislators they advise. Instead of requiring equal proportional cutbacks on the part of each firm, and instead of trying to micromanage each firm's abatement strategy, they now focus on policies that try to reduce each firm's incentive to pollute. Firms pollute not because they derive pleasure from fouling the environment, but because clean production processes are almost always more costly than dirty ones. Instead of prohibiting firms from polluting, or requiring specific pollution-control technologies, the growing trend is simply to tax firms on the basis of how much they pollute (or, equivalently, to require them to purchase effluent permits).

The result is to provide each firm with an incentive to cut back its pollution in the most cost-effective way it can, because its annual tax bill falls by each ton of pollution it manages to filter out. Firms that can reduce pollution cheaply will thus tend to specialize in pollution abatement. Those for which pollution abatement is most costly, however, soon discover that the amount they save in pollution taxes is often less than the cost of lowering pollution, and so these firms continue to pollute. In terms of our environmental concerns, this is perfectly acceptable because what counts is the total amount of pollution, not who put it there.

The tax approach to pollution control also addresses our concerns about fairness. For example, the firms that invest heavily in pollution abatement are rewarded in the form of lower tax payments. And other firms that find curtailing pollution too costly don't get off the hook because they end up paying the lion's share of pollution taxes.

Another advantage of the tax approach is that it provides strong incentives to develop new abatement technologies. For instance, whereas a firm required to install smokestack scrubbers or burn low-sulfur coal can relax once it meets those requirements, a firm that is taxed on each ton it emits is under continuing pressure to find cheaper ways of curbing its pollution.

With increasing frequency, environmental regulators have been abandoning the inefficient command-and-control approach in favor of effluent taxes and other incentive-based policies. The results have been exactly as predicted: The costs of a given level of pollution abatement are lower—often dramatically so—under the new incentive-based systems.[1]

In a hypothetical world with only a single conspicuous-consumption good—say, cars—the analogy between luxury taxes and pollution taxes would be virtually exact. The problem in each case is that we have too much of something in the absence of collective action—too much of the conspicuous consumption good in one case, too much pollution in the other. Each problem exists because of an incentive gap. Both conspicuous consumption and activities that pollute are more attractive to each individual than they are to society as a whole.

With a tax on the luxury good, people would have an incentive to spend less of their incomes on it and more of their incomes on inconspicuous consumption—just as, with a tax on pollution, firms have an incentive to emit less pollution. Note that in both cases, the tax tends to distribute the burden of adjustment in a fair and efficient manner. Just as a pollution tax concentrates pollution abatement in the hands of those who can accomplish it most cheaply, so a luxury tax concentrates the reduction in conspicuous consumption in the hands of those consumers best equipped to adjust. The consumers who don't care that much about cars will find that their best bet is to scale back their automobile expenditures significantly, thereby to escape the burden of the tax. And those for whom such cutbacks would be most painful will elect to pay the tax to continue to pursue their passion.

Unfortunately, however, there is not just one conspicuous good but many. If we taxed bright silks, people would simply move to gold buttons, just as the medieval Europeans did. To complicate matters further, what is a conspicuous-consumption good for one group of consumers may not be for another. The cold fact is that we have no reliable formula for defining what constitutes a conspicuous consumption good for purposes of taxation. And as we have seen, attempts to use the political process to classify specific goods as luxuries or necessities for tax purposes is to invite a free-for-all that would dissipate most, if not all, of what we hoped to gain. Fortunately, however, we can attack the problem without having to settle such questions on a case-by-case basis.

THE PROGRESSIVE CONSUMPTION TAX

Because we ignore the fact that our own spending influences the frame of reference that defines an acceptable living standard, certain forms of private consumption currently seem more attractive to us as individuals than to society as a whole. The simplest solution is to make those forms less attractive by taxing them, not on a case-by-case basis as we have in the past, but by a single levy on the total amount that families spend each year. Many European nations already have a value-added tax, which is essentially a national sales, or consumption, tax.

The problem with the value-added tax is that, like all sales taxes, it is highly regressive because the rich tend to save a significantly higher proportion of their incomes than the poor.[2] And because the value-added tax imposes a disproportionate burden on low-income families, the highest feasible tax rates under this approach are far too small to have much impact on the spending habits of the well-to-do. The value-added tax rate in most European countries, for example, is 17.5 percent, which although considerably higher than state sales tax rates in the United States, does not put much of a dent in sales of Patek Philippe wristwatches. Another problem is that with an ever larger proportion of total earned income now flowing into the hands of those atop the economic totem pole, exclusive reliance on sales taxes could never generate enough revenues to cover even the most fat-free government budget.

It is possible in principle, of course, to make sales taxes less regressive by exempting specific necessities and putting surcharges on specific luxuries. Indeed, most European nations have exemptions for food, children's clothing, and certain other items, and England levies luxury surcharges on a schedule of high-end goods. As we have seen, however, these steps invariably generate costly political battles that dissipate many of the resources we are trying to redeploy.

A natural alternative to a flat sales tax collected at the cash register (or from producers, as in the case of the value-added tax) is a single progressive tax levied on the total amount each family consumes each year. Proposals for precisely this tax have surfaced at many points during the last 300 years, and have almost invariably drawn praise from the leading economic and political thinkers of the day. Writing in *Leviathan,* for example, Thomas Hobbes made clear his view that consumption taxes were desirable for reasons similar to those I suggest here:

> For what reason is there, that he which laboureth much, and sparing the fruits of his labour, consumeth little, should be more charged, than he that living idly getteth little and spendeth all he gets: seeing the one hath no more protection from the Commonwealth than the other? But when the Impositions are layd upon those things which men consume, every man payeth Equally for what he useth: Nor is the Commonwealth defrauded by the luxurious waste of private men.[3]

Invariably, however, these early enthusiasms for consumption taxes were quickly dampened by what appeared to be almost insurmountable practical difficulties. Principal among these was the daunting belief that the only way a person could document how much he consumed would be to save an auditable receipt for each and every purchase he made during each tax year. If one's tax were based on the total thus documented, however, what incentive would a tax evader have for saving more than some minimal proportion of his receipts? Again and again, economists reluctantly concluded that a progressive tax on total consumption could never be implemented. Thus John Maynard Keynes wrote that although the idea of a tax on total expenditure is "theoretically sound, it is practically impossible." John Stuart Mill, Alfred Marshall, and Alfred Pigou had voiced similar concerns in the nineteenth century.[4]

But these skeptics were wrong. As the economist Irving Fisher saw clearly during the early 1940s, a system of progressive consumption taxation could be achieved by a simple one-line amendment to the federal tax code—making savings exempt from tax. This is so, Fisher realized, because of a basic accounting relationship. Roughly speaking, there are only two things a family can do with its income: spend it or save it. The amount a family consumes each year is thus the difference between the amount it earns and the amount it saves.

Truth be told, it is more complicated than that but only slightly. Thus, as Irving Fisher and his brother Herbert put it in their 1942 book:

> How do we figure the amount we spend in a day? We need only two data:
>
> 1. The amount we had to spend; that is, what we had or received during the day.
> 2. The amount we did not spend; that is, the amount left over as determined by counting at the end of the day. . . .
>
> We propose, then, to reckon taxable spendings, not by adding together the separate items spent for food, clothing, rent, amusements, etc., but by adding together the gross receipts from all sources and then deducting all items of outgo other than "spendings." The chief deductions under this proposal are: investments, taxes paid during the taxable year, and proper exemptions for the taxpayer and his dependents.[5]

By *investments,* the Fishers meant net deposits into savings accounts. These would be much like today's IRAs or 401(k) retirement accounts, with the important exception that they could be drawn down, if desired, before retirement. Administratively, a progressive consumption tax is therefore essentially the same as the progressive income tax currently in place in most countries. (In either case, the current tax structures of most countries could, and should, be simplified further, but that is a separate issue.)

As the Fishers recognized, the progressive consumption tax thus defined is essentially a luxury tax, but without the devastating cost of having to define and tax specific luxury goods on a case-by-case basis: "Such a luxury-spending tax is more truly a luxury tax than any excise tax on specific luxuries, such as costly automobiles, opera tickets, or Oriental rugs. To define satisfactorily specific objects as 'luxuries' is impossible; but to measure satisfactorily what constitutes luxurious *spending*, and with definite gradations, is easy."[6] Approaching the tax problem in this way completely eliminates the costly battle over which goods are to be exempt and which are to be taxed at premium rates. The simple and elegant idea is that the first dollars a family spends go for the things it needs most, and that additional spending buys things that, *in the family's eyes,* are simply less important.

The following example illustrates how a progressive consumption tax would work for a family of four if the standard deduction were $7,500 per person. With a total standard deduction of $30,000 per year, the family's taxable consumption would be calculated as its income minus $30,000 minus its savings minus its tax. A family whose income was no more than $30,000 plus the amount it saved (where annual savings would be defined as net deposits into the family's 401(k)-like account) would thus owe no tax at all under this plan. It could purchase basic necessities—defined not by legislators but by its own members—essentially tax free. Once its total consumption passed the taxable threshold, it would then begin to pay tax on each additional dollar of consumption, at a rate that escalated gradually as the amount of total consumption increased. For instance, the tax rate on families with positive taxable consumption might begin at 20 percent and then gradually escalate in the manner shown in the table below.

TAX RATES ON TAXABLE CONSUMPTION

Taxable Consumption	Marginal Tax Rate
0–$ 39,999	20 percent
$ 40,000– 49,999	22
50,000– 59,999	24
60,000– 69,999	26
70,000– 79,999	28
80,000– 89,999	30
90,000– 99,999	32
100,000–129,999	34
130,000–159,999	38
160,000–189,999	42
190,000–219,999	46
220,000–249,999	50
250,000–499,000	60
500,000–999,999	70

Given this rate schedule, the table below shows how much tax families with different income and savings levels would pay.

ILLUSTRATIVE INCOME, SAVINGS, AND TAX VALUES UNDER A PROGRESSIVE CONSUMPTION TAX

Income	Savings	Taxable Consumption	Tax
$ 30,000	$ 1,500	0	0
50,000	3,000	$ 14,167	$ 2,833
100,000	10,000	49,836	10,164
150,000	20,000	81,538	18,462
200,000	40,000	104,328	25,672
500,000	120,000	258,000	92,000
1,000,000	300,000	458,000	212,000
1,500,000	470,000	654,588	345,412

In line 2 of this tax table, for example, note that the family's taxable consumption ($14,167) is equal to its income ($50,000) minus its savings ($3,000) minus its standard deduction ($30,000) minus its tax ($2,833). Because the family's taxable consumption was less than $40,000, the IRS computed the family's tax as 20 percent of its $14,167 taxable consumption, or $2,833. Similarly, the tax liability of the family shown in line 3 of the table is computed as 20 percent of its first $40,000 of taxable consumption ($8,000) plus 22 percent of the remaining $9,836 ($2,164), for a total of $10,164.

At first glance this might seem confusing, because it would appear that a family would have to know its tax to compute its taxable consumption, yet could not compute its tax without first knowing its taxable consumption! Fortunately, however, taxpayers need not actually jump through the mathematical hoop of computing taxable consumption. Just as they do now, IRS accountants would solve the necessary equations and publish a table telling each family how much it owes on the basis of the simple difference between its income and its savings. Thus the family in line 2 that reported $50,000 of income and $3,000 of savings would go directly to a table that says it owes $2,833 on the $47,000 difference.

Unlike the value-added tax or the national sales tax, the consumption tax shown here is a progressive tax. Its escalating marginal tax rates on consumption, coupled with its large standard deduction, assure that total tax as a proportion of income rises steadily with income, even when the savings rate is sharply higher for high-income families. Further progressivity would be achieved to the extent that wealthy families drew down their savings to support high consumption levels during retirement.

If a progressive consumption tax is to curb the waste that springs from excessive spending on conspicuous consumption, its rates at the highest levels must be sufficiently steep to provide meaningful incentives for the people atop the consumption pyramid. For unless their spending changes, the spending of those just below them is unlikely to change either, and so on all the way down.

Most noneconomists have no difficulty accepting the validity of the economist's law of demand—which says that when the price of a good rises, we buy less of it—as a description of the behavior of ordinary people. Many are skeptical, however, that price could have much of an impact for people worth tens or hundreds of millions of dollars. It is true that many of these people would have difficulty spending their incomes even if they shopped continuously. Yet even the wealthiest people respond to price signals.

For example, in Manhattan, where real estate prices are several times higher per square foot than in most other American cities, the wealthy buy much smaller houses than their counterparts elsewhere. Whereas even a 5,000-square-foot brownstone is expansive by the standards of the wealthy residents of the Upper East Side, people with similar incomes in Los Angeles often buy 10,000- or even 15,000-square-foot houses. And even these houses pale in comparison with the largest dwellings in cities with relatively low land prices. As noted earlier, Microsoft Chairman Bill Gates has just built a 45,000-square-foot residence on the shores of Lake Washington, just east of Seattle.

Gates has a current net worth of more than $40 billion. If he were to move to Manhattan he could certainly *afford* to build just as large a house there, even if New York prices were five times as high as Seattle's. Yet he would almost surely not build such a house in Manhattan. Given the relatively small dwelling sizes of Manhattan's wealthy (which, again, are a direct consequence of the high real estate prices there), a 45,000-square-foot house would just be *unseemly,* even for a multibillionaire.

The resources that would be saved if a progressive consumption tax were to induce wealthy and upper-middle-class families to build smaller houses are real resources. And as we have seen, they can be put to good uses—indeed, much better uses than the ones to which they are currently being put.

An American CEO needs a 15,000-square-foot mansion only because others of his station in life have houses that large. To have a lesser dwelling would risk social embarrassment, or raise questions about the health of his business. Yet if *all* CEOs were to build smaller houses, no one would be embarrassed in the least. Indeed, many CEOs might even *prefer* to have smaller houses. It is a nuisance, after all, to have to recruit and supervise the staff needed to maintain a large mansion.

A similar logic applies to the wealthy person's decision about which car to buy. If he is *really* wealthy and of sporting temperament, he will want one that handles well, accelerates rapidly, and—perhaps most important—stands out in a crowd. Under our current tax structure, he might consider the Ferrari 456 GT. With its 437 horsepower, 5.5 liter,

48-valve, V12 engine, it accelerates from zero to 60 in about 5 seconds, and its $207,000 sticker price assures that the valets at Spago will try to elbow one another aside for a chance to park it.

Just as high real estate prices lead the wealthy to buy smaller houses, a steeply progressive consumption tax would lead them to spend less on automobiles. The erstwhile Ferrari driver, for example, might turn instead to the Porsche 911 Turbo, the base model of which currently sells for "only" $105,000. The 911 is even faster than the Ferrari, and it is also more surefooted. Its only real drawback, from the perspective of the ultrarich, is that its bargain-basement price has made it an almost common sight in the circular driveways of many neighborhoods. Under a progressive consumption tax, the Porsche would acquire precisely the rarefied status of today's exotic cars, which was all that kept it from being attractive to Ferrari buyers in the first place.

A numerical example is instructive. Suppose we taxed additional consumption at the highest levels at a rate of 70 percent—that is, for total consumption beyond some level, an extra dollar of consumption would mean an extra 70 cents of tax. And suppose that, because a consumption tax exempts savings, the person who would have spent $207,000 on a Ferrari now decides to invest a little more in the stock market and spend a little less on his car. If he buys the Porsche, his outlay, including the consumption tax, will be $178,500. In return, he gets a car that performs just as well as the Ferrari and, assuming others have responded similarly, is now also just as rare. As concerns both his motoring pleasure and his ability to signal his wealth, he is therefore just as well off as before.

In other ways, however, both he and the rest of us are better off. For one thing, he now has an additional $28,500 (the difference between $207,000 and $178,500) invested in his mutual fund, which will accumulate dividends and capital gains not taxed until he spends them. What is more, the government acquires additional tax revenue to pay down the federal debt, reduce the tax burden on low- and middle-income families, and/or restore neglected public services.

A major advantage of using the progressive consumption tax to help curb the growth of conspicuous consumption is that, unlike sumptuary laws and social norms, it preserves the aficionado's ability to indulge a particular passion in the material domain. Under current arrangements, the person who might skimp in other areas to buy the sports car or sailboat of his dreams is often dissuaded from doing so by the knowledge that this purchase may kindle resentment in others. With a progressive consumption tax in place, by contrast, he could enjoy his luxury without apology. The extra tax he pays is full penance for any injury, real or imagined, that his purchase may cause.

Painful Dislocations?

It might seem natural to worry that a tax that curbs consumption might lead to recession and unemployment. This is not a serious concern, however, because any money that is not spent on consumption will instead be saved and invested. The result is that some of the people who are now employed to produce consumption goods will instead be employed to produce capital goods—which, as we saw in chapter 7, will increase the economy's productive capacity in the long run.

The progressive consumption tax will also change the *kinds* of consumption goods we produce. If the tax is sufficiently progressive, it will collect more revenue than our current system does from those at the top of the economic pyramid and less from those at the bottom. This means that carpenters will spend less of their time building mansions for the superrich and more of their time building housing for others; and that fewer of our health-care dollars will be spent on liposuction and tummy tucks, and more on the treatment of people who actually have illnesses.

The government knows how to stimulate the economy when recession threatens. Indeed, a central problem of the postwar era has been containing the inflationary pressures that result when demand grows more rapidly than the economy's capacity to produce goods and services. By stimulating savings and investment, the progressive consumption tax will increase the rate at which the economy's productive capacity grows, and thus reduce the threat of inflation.

Virtually all important transition issues would be ameliorated by introducing the progressive consumption tax gradually—with phased increases in the amount of savings a family could exempt and phased increases in the highest marginal tax rates. Following this approach would eliminate the possibility of triggering a recession and prevent existing producers of luxury goods from being forced to endure painful cutbacks. Such a gradual phase-in would result not in an absolute decline in the amount of resources devoted to the production of conspicuous consumption, but in a reduction in *the rate of growth* of resources devoted to it. This approach would help overcome the status-quo bias inherent in our natural tendency to resist cutbacks in our customary spending patterns.

If a progressive consumption tax affected only the consumption decisions of the superrich, its benefits would be minimal. But such a tax would have much broader impact. Indeed, it would produce a cascade of similar savings all the way down the consumption pyramid. If we continue for several more decades on our current trajectory, the replacement for today's Ferrari 456 GT will sell not for $207,000 but for more than $400,000. Those who are content to drive the $105,000 Porsche 911 Turbo today will move up to a car something like the Ferrari 456 GT. Likewise, those who drive the $72,000 Porsche Carrera today will move up to a car like the 911 Turbo. The current drivers of the $45,000 Porsche Boxster will trade up to a car like the Carrera. Today's drivers of the BMW Z3 (about $30,000) will move up to something like the Boxster. And today's entry-level sports-car drivers will move up from the Mazda Miata (about $23,000) to a car more like the Z3.

Given the decisive role of context in the evaluation of product adequacy, we can safely predict that these moves will not yield any lasting increment in driver satisfaction. And yet they will substantially increase the total amount that drivers spend. If, for the sake of illustration, we assume that the current distribution of drivers across cars is as shown in the right column of the table below, a one-step across-the-board upgrade of the current sports-car hierarchy would result in an expenditure increase of more than 50 percent. That is, the sports car mix shown in the left column would cost over 50 percent more than the mix in the right column, even though the less expensive cars in the right column perform precisely the same services, in their context, as the more expensive ones would in theirs. From the collective vantage point, moving from the right column to the left column is a wasteful step, pure and simple.

The Unconstrained Sports-Car Hierarchy in 2010 (price, market share)	The Current Sports-Car Hierarchy (price, market share)
1. Tomorrow's Supercar, $414,000, 1% 2. Ferrari 456 GT, $207,000, 4% 3. Porsche 911 Turbo, $105,000, 15% 4. Porsche 911 Carrera, $72,000, 20% 5. Porsche Boxster, $45,000, 25% 6. BMW Z3, $30,000, 35% **Average price = $64,320**	1. Ferrari 456 GT, $207,000, 1% 2. Porsche 911 Turbo, $105,000, 4% 3. Porsche 911 Carrera, $72,000, 15% 4. Porsche Boxster, $45,000, 20% 5. BMW Z3, $30,000, 25% 6. Mazda Miata, $23,000, 35% **Average price = $41,620**

If we take no action, these upgrades will inexorably occur—as will others like them in other domains. A future version of the Patek Philippe Calibre '89 wristwatch, for example, will command twice its current price of $2.7 million. And tomorrow's Hermés Kelly alligator handbag will cost not $14,000 but $28,000. By contrast, with a phased introduction of the progressive consumption tax, the amount of resources devoted to producing these goods can be held near their current levels.

The point is not to put companies like Ferrari and Patek Philippe out of business, but simply to slow the rate at which additional resources are devoted to making *all* products—not just theirs—more opulent. As new ideas and technologies emerge, these products would continue to improve, even in the absence of continued spending escalation. But at a time when many truly pressing needs remain unmet, we must question the wisdom of spending billions of dollars to reduce zero-to-sixty acceleration times by another few tenths of a second, or to refine mechanical devices that will further attenuate the already negligible effect of gravity on timepieces.

A 50 percent expenditure savings is real money. If similar sums could be saved in every arena, simply by slowing temporarily the rate at which we increase spending on refinements, we could free up more than $2 trillion a year in an economy with annual consumption of more than $5 trillion. And because moving to a progressive consumption tax would also increase the rate at which we save for the future (more on this point in the next chapter), these gains would be just the beginning.

Incentives to Engage in Nonmarket Activity

A progressive consumption tax would also increase the incentive to engage in various forms of nonmarket activity. All incentives are relative, and because the progressive consumption tax makes it more costly, in relative terms, to engage in conspicuous consumption, it also makes it less costly to engage in inconspicuous consumption. For example, because the tax would mean that an additional dollar of cash wages would buy less if spent on conspicuous consumption goods, employers have an incentive to rearrange their compensation packages to emphasize untaxed quality-of-life benefits. Thus, by paying a little less in cash, which would have been taxed if spent, they can offer an extra week of vacation, which will not be taxed; or an extra measure of autonomy or safety; or a more private space in which to work; or perhaps even just a few extra parking spaces. Because the amount of additional conspicuous consumption goods people can buy by working longer hours would decline under a progressive consumption tax, they would have an incentive to work fewer hours and spend more time with family and friends or more time exercising or more time reading a good book.

Major Events Often Have Small Causes

Chaos theorists speak fancifully about how a butterfly's wings flapping in China might set off a chain of events that culminates in a hurricane in the Caribbean. Their point is that when numerous systems are interconnected in complex ways, even small changes can dramatically transform the landscape. Changes in spending are by no means exempt from this logic. Contrary to the assumptions of economic orthodoxy, the spending decisions of individual households are not made independently. Rather, as we have seen, they are strongly interconnected. When one family spends a little more, others follow suit, and their behavior influences still others, and so on. And when one family spends a little less, a similar pattern unfolds in reverse.

In any individual case, the response to the new incentives inherent in the progressive consumption tax might be small. But when one family reduces the rate of increase in the amount it spends on housing and cars, the same step immediately becomes more attractive to other families. And as they too begin to spend differently, they influence still others, in an ever-expanding network that, in time, feeds back onto itself. By virtue of these ripple effects, a tax that has only a small initial effect on any single family sets in motion a dynamic process that can radically transform our spending patterns.

Progressive Consumption Taxation Is Not a Fringe Idea

Since our future consumption mix under a steeply progressive consumption tax would be radically different from what it would be if we continued under current arrangements, this tax qualifies as an instrument of radical social change. Yet, in another sense, it is hard to imagine a less radical proposal. We have to tax *something,* after all, and even if we were to ignore the effects of the tax on the mix of goods and services we buy, there would still be powerful reasons for taxing consumption instead of income. The proponents of consumption taxation form an impressive list: David Hume, Adam Smith, John Stuart Mill, Alfred Pigou, and Alfred Marshall were among the early luminaries who extolled the virtues of progressive consumption taxation.[7] Contemporary economists of every political stripe have also voiced similar views. Thus conservatives like Nobel laureate Milton Friedman and Martin Feldstein, chairman of the Council of Economic Advisors under Ronald Reagan, are vocal advocates of consumption taxation;[8] so are liberals Kenneth Arrow, also a Nobel laureate; Laurence Summers, a Treasury Department official in the Clinton administration and winner of the economics profession's prestigious Clark Medal; and Lester Thurow, the best-selling author and former dean of MIT's Sloan School of Management. Liberals and conservatives disagree on many details concerning the consumption tax, including the extent to which it should be progressive (although virtually all forms of the tax that have been proposed are at least mildly progressive). But there is little disagreement on the principle that it is better to tax consumption than income.

Further indication that the progressive consumption tax is a mainstream idea is the fact that just such a tax was proposed in the U.S. Senate in 1995 under bipartisan sponsorship. Senators Pete Domenici (R, New Mexico), Sam Nunn (D, Georgia) and Bob Kerrey (D, Nebraska) called their proposal the USA tax, short for unlimited-savings-allowance tax. The USA tax is much like our current progressive income tax except that it exempts all personal savings from tax.

As with any new tax proposal, many details of the USA tax remain to be worked out. No matter how carefully crafted, it will affect different taxpayers differently, and protracted wrangling over specific provisions is therefore inevitable. Important transition issues, such as how to treat borrowings and how to treat existing savings and other assets, must be resolved. There is considerable room for disagreement on these issues. But as the economist Laurence Seidman has persuasively argued in his excellent book on the USA tax, practical solutions to these problems are at hand.[9]

Contemporary proponents of the switch to consumption taxation have focused their arguments on the fact that the tax would boost savings and therefore stimulate economic growth. This is true and would be reason enough for making the switch. Yet proponents of the USA tax have essentially ignored an even more powerful reason for switching: This tax, properly implemented, can stimulate radical changes in the ways we lead our lives. We currently waste literally trillions of dollars each year as a result of wasteful consumption patterns. Much of this waste can be curbed by the adoption of a steeply progressive consumption tax. Taking this step would greatly enhance every citizen's opportunity to pursue independent visions of the good life.

The catch? There is none. The extraordinary beauty of the progressive consumption tax is its ability to generate extra resources almost literally out of thin air. It is a win-win move, even for the people on whom the tax falls most heavily.

SO WHY DON'T WE ALREADY HAVE A PROGRESSIVE CONSUMPTION TAX?

One of the economics profession's Nobel laureates and most distinguished members—a man given to confident pronouncements—is the author of several bestselling books that have earned him a considerable sum over the years. Folklore has it that when one of his claims is greeted by the standard skeptic's rejoinder, "If you're so smart, why aren't you rich?" he delights in responding, "I *am* rich!" Though the skeptic's question backfires on such occasions, it is nonetheless a good one to keep in mind. We are prudent to be wary, for example, of investment advice urged on us by someone who appears to be in obvious financial difficulty.

My claims on behalf of the progressive consumption tax should inspire a similar skeptical question: If this tax is such a great idea, why don't we already have one? It would be an evasion to respond that many countries have roughly similar taxes, such as relatively steep sales taxes with exemptions for specific necessities and surcharges for specific luxuries. My claim, after all, is that these taxes are simply no match for a steeply progressive tax levied on total consumption expenditures.

I have already mentioned the importance of the misguided belief that it is illegitimate to tax one person's consumption because of its negative effects on others. By itself, this belief would not stand in the way of adopting a progressive consumption tax, for such taxes can be defended on other grounds. For example, Senators Domenici, Nunn, and Kerrey introduced their USA tax bill by touting its likely effects on savings. They made no mention of curbing conspicuous consumption.

For the USA tax to stimulate significant alterations in our consumption patterns, however, its rate structure would have to be much more steeply progressive than in the proposal introduced in the Senate. Such rates would be difficult to defend were it not for their promise to deliver significantly less wasteful consumption patterns. And so, in this sense, the belief that it is not legitimate to tax one person's consumption because of its negative effect on others has in fact stood in the way of a steeply progressive consumption tax.

But such a tax faces another far more important hurdle—namely, the belief that imposing sharply higher tax rates on the nation's most wealthy and productive citizens is a surefire way to cripple the economy. Although this belief is most deeply entrenched among conservatives, it has also won widespread acceptance among liberals. Indeed, it is no exaggeration to call this the single most influential belief driving economic policy in the late twentieth century. It was responsible, for example, for the dramatic reductions in the tax rates on top earners in both the United Kingdom and the United States during the Thatcher and Reagan administrations.

It is natural that voters find tax increases distasteful, and the belief that they will harm the economy has provided politicians with an irresistible opportunity to claim the moral high ground by denouncing them. Indeed, the risk inherent in proposing even a modest tax increase cannot have escaped the attention of any politician with a pulse, none of whom will have forgotten that when Democratic presidential candidate Walter Mondale proposed higher taxes on the rich, he went on to lose the 1984 election in a landslide. And many analysts insist that George Bush would have been a two-term president had it not been for his minor retreat from his "read my lips, no new taxes" pledge.

The belief that sharply higher taxes on the rich will cripple the economy is the fundamental premise of trickle-down economics. The fact that this premise is so widely accepted is a second important explanation for why we do not already have a steeply progressive consumption tax. Indeed, if this premise were in fact correct, it would also explain why we *should* not have such a tax. On the best available evidence, however, a steeply progressive consumption tax would not only not cripple the economy but actually invigorate it.

Yet it is what people *believe* about reality, rather than reality itself, that governs public policy decisions. And as long as the fundamental premise of trickle-down economics remains an entrenched part of the received wisdom, the adoption of a steeply progressive consumption tax will remain a political long shot.

CHAPTER 15

EQUITY VERSUS EFFICIENCY: THE GREAT TRADE-OFF?

No one is surprised to hear someone like Federal Reserve Chairman Alan Greenspan, a lifelong Republican, remark that "All taxes are a drag on economic growth. It's only a question of degree."[1] But this view is no longer confined to well-heeled conservatives. For example, even many staff writers for the *New York Times*—long known for its uncompromising soak-the-rich positions on tax policy—voiced essentially Greenspan's position during the 1996 presidential election campaign.

Indeed, the fundamental premise of trickle-down economics has become a bona fide staple of the conventional economic and political wisdom of the late twentieth century. Most liberals, and even many conservatives, have always believed that a more progressive tax structure would be desirable on equity grounds. Yet most liberals and virtually all conservatives now also believe that greater progressivity would entail significant penalties to economic growth.

In both the United States and the United Kingdom, concerns about efficiency appear to have trumped concerns about equity. Strongly influenced by trickle-down rhetoric, legislators in both countries voted to cut top marginal tax rates sharply in the 1980s, and despite slight upward revisions in the United States in 1991 and 1993, these rates remain the lowest among industrialized nations. We may therefore expect that proposals for a steeply progressive consumption tax will be greeted by prophesies of economic doom and gloom. Be-

cause many of the authors of these prophesies occupy respected positions in business, government, and the academy, we must consider
their arguments with care.

THE MYSTERIOUS RELATIONSHIP BETWEEN
EFFORT AND REWARD

The conventional view that tax equity comes at the expense of efficiency is predicated on the time-honored belief that people respond to
incentives. Thus, say the trickle-down theorists, when the rewards for
effort and risk taking are reduced by the imposition of higher taxes,
people will expend less effort and take fewer risks. In the standard
rhetorical flourish of trickle-down theory, the problem with steeply
progressive taxes is that they kill the geese that lay the golden eggs. Or,
as the economist Benjamin Higgins put it somewhat less colorfully,
"the rate of development is reduced, possibly to the point where even
the very level of welfare of the underdog, which the equity measures
are designed to help, is lowered instead."[2]

The trickle-down theorists are surely right that incentives matter.
When the price of gasoline doubled in the late 1970s, for example, the
proportion of cars sold with fuel-efficient four-cylinder engines rose
sharply. By the same token, when the price trajectory of gasoline re-
versed itself in the ensuing years, falling sharply relative to the price
trajectories for other goods, the market for cars with six- and eight-
cylinder engines began a robust comeback. We may not be the perfect
rational maximizers assumed by the abstract models of economic theory, but neither are we stupid. Just as most of us know enough to come
in out of the rain, most of us know enough to rearrange our spending
patterns when relative prices move significantly.

Yet the fact that we respond to incentives in a self-interested way
does not, by itself, imply that higher tax rates at the top will cause a
slowdown in economic growth. It is true that an increase in the tax
rates facing top earners means a reduction in the economic rewards for
taking risks and expending effort, just as the proponents of trickle-
down theory insist. As every basic economics textbook makes clear,

however, a fall in the after-tax wage rate simply does not lead to an unambiguous prediction about the quantity of effort supplied. Thus, whereas a lower real wage constitutes a reduction in the reward for effort and hence an incentive to work less, it also exerts an opposing effect: By making the individual poorer than before, it provides an incentive to work more to recoup his loss. Economic theory is completely silent on the question of which of these two opposing effects will dominate. The case for the conventional position must therefore be made on empirical grounds.

A number of episodes appear—at least superficially—to support the trickle-down theory's central premise. Perhaps the most vivid of these consist of responses to changes in state and local income tax rates. For example, conservatives in New York have warned since the 1950s that rising personal and corporate tax rates would prove costly to the state's economic vitality, and by most criteria these warnings have been remarkably on target. As one corporation after another has moved its headquarters from New York to some other jurisdiction with lower tax rates, the state's per capita income has continued a pattern of long decline in relative terms. All the while, Southern states with low tax rates have enjoyed a sustained economic boom. At the local and even state levels, at any rate, the fundamental premise of trickle-down economics appears largely confirmed. Higher tax rates seem to translate into lower rates of economic growth. And this, we may suspect, is an important reason for the widespread support that the fundamental premise of trickle-down theory currently enjoys.

Yet the observed responses to state and local tax changes tell us only that people are willing to substitute one location for another in response to tax incentives. They tell us nothing about their willingness to substitute leisure for effort, or about their reluctance to take risks for economic gain. If the top tax rates were increased significantly in *every* jurisdiction, would people work less, or would they be less willing to risk their capital? Or more important, in view of the reduction in barriers to labor mobility across national borders, would top earners in a given country be more likely to emigrate in response to an increase in their nation's highest tax rates?

For sufficiently high tax rates, the answer to even this question appears to be yes, at least if the early experience of countries like England and Sweden is any guide. With marginal tax rates well above 90 percent in the 1960s, both countries experienced costly outmigrations of talent.

Yet international labor flight is probably not an important constraint at the moment in the United States and the United Kingdom, both of which now have top marginal tax rates of roughly 40 percent— far lower than those in other industrial nations. For these countries, the important question for policy makers considering higher marginal tax rates is not whether top earners will flee, but whether their domestic economic decisions will be significantly distorted.

The case for such distortions is difficult to make on empirical grounds. If the net effect of a real wage reduction were to induce most people to supply significantly less labor, then the opposite should be true for a real wage increase. The cumulative effect of the last century's dramatic rise in real wages should thus have been a significant increase in hours worked. In fact, however, the length of the workweek is significantly lower now than in 1900.[3]

As noted earlier, the downward trend in hours worked leveled out shortly after World War II in the United States and has actually turned slightly upwards over the last two decades. This observation also casts doubt on the fundamental premise of trickle-down economics. After all, the wage of the median earner has declined slightly during the last 20 years—which, according to trickle-down theory, ought to have caused a reduction in work hours instead of an increase. By many accounts, the recent increase in hours worked is an attempt to recoup the loss of purchasing power that stems from lower wage rates.

Although comparisons across countries are inherently difficult to interpret, on balance we would also expect to see more effort supplied in countries with higher real after-tax wage rates if the fundamental premise of trickle-down economics were correct. Yet here, too, the numbers tell a different story. For example, even though Japanese CEOs earn less than one-fifth as much as their U.S. counterparts and face substantially higher marginal tax rates, there is no evidence that Japanese executives log shorter workweeks.

I stress again that none of these observations is inconsistent with the economist's claim that people respond to incentives. They do not rule out the possibility that people may work less if the top tax rate rises beyond some point. But taken as a whole, the empirical evidence is consistent with the claim that increases in the top U.S. and U.K. marginal tax rates would not cause wholesale reductions in effort.

TAX AVOIDANCE AND TAX EVASION

Another claim by trickle-down theorists is that high marginal tax rates compromise economic efficiency by channeling talent and effort into tax avoidance and tax evasion rather than productive work. Several writers saw evidence for this claim when the reduction in top U.S. tax rates enacted in 1986 was followed by a large increase in the amount of income declared by top earners.[4]

No one can deny that the payoff from a dollar invested in tax avoidance is higher when tax rates are high than when they are low. But although the Tax Reform Act of 1986 cut top tax rates, it also broadened the tax base significantly by eliminating a large number of deductions and exemptions. If a rational tax avoider knows about a legal deduction or exemption, she will almost surely claim it whether her tax rate is 40 percent or 60 percent. She may spend a little more effort searching out exemptions when the tax rate is higher, but her tax consultant is unlikely to advise her differently in the two cases. The post-1986 increase in reported income thus appears more plausibly explained by the fact that the act eliminated many existing loopholes.

Another potential efficiency loss is that higher tax rates also provide greater incentives for corporations to compensate executives with expensive perks. For instance, when top British marginal tax rates were higher than 90 percent, it was apparently not uncommon for companies to provide top executives with chauffeur-driven Rolls-Royces. For each executive, this perk might cost the company $50,000 per year, an amount most executives would hardly see fit to spend out of their own pockets. But since the after-tax value of an extra $50,000 in pay would have been less than $5,000 for these executives, a company-provided Rolls might nonetheless have seemed an attractive option.

Tax evasion is a serious problem. Yet in-kind compensation and similar behaviors must be monitored and controlled even with tax rates at their current, relatively low levels. More important, tax evasion of every sort will be sharply reduced if we tax consumption rather than income. Rather than spend $50,000 to provide an executive with a chauffeur-driven Rolls, the company can give her an extra $50,000 in cash, 100 percent of which she can then shelter by simply putting it into a mutual fund. By allowing people to shelter their savings completely from taxation, we thus eliminate much of the incentive to engage in tax evasion. Indeed, we have every reason to expect that tax evasion would be a less serious problem under a steeply progressive consumption tax than under today's only moderately progressive income tax.

On balance, it thus appears that the trickle-down theorist's case for the agonizing trade-off between equity and economic growth is far from compelling. There was never any solid theoretical support for the existence of this trade-off, and the empirical evidence, such as it is, would never change a skeptic's mind.

But the fundamental premise of trickle-down economics is not merely wrong. Rather, it has matters precisely backwards. For three independent reasons, the shift to a progressive tax on consumption would be more likely to *increase* economic growth rather than to inhibit it. The first reason is that taxing consumption will stimulate savings, and the resulting increase in investment will raise productivity.

How a Consumption Tax Stimulates New Savings

Proponents of consumption taxation have long stressed that it will increase savings, and they are right. Many of these same proponents, however, go on to predict that the increase will be small, and that the resulting increase in growth and well-being, though steady, will be small as well.[5] The latter predictions, however, are significantly off the mark.

Although switching to a consumption tax from an income tax would affect savings through several channels, most advocates of consumption taxation have focused on only two. The first, called the incentive effect, stems from the resulting increase in the monetary reward for saving. This effect is analogous to the effect on savings of an increase in the interest rate banks pay on savings. The second channel, called the postponement effect, stems from the fact that, by comparison to the current income tax, a consumption tax collects a larger share of a taxpayer's lifetime tax bill during the retirement years, when consumption is typically high relative to income. The consumption tax would thus not only *enable* the taxpayer to save more during his working years but also make it incumbent on him to do so. And if each individual has a larger savings balance on the date of retirement, total savings for society will be larger.

As past advocates of consumption taxes have conceded, however, both these effects are relatively small.[6] But even so, there are far more important channels through which a consumption tax would stimulate additional savings. One is the so-called horizontal-redistribution effect, whereby a consumption tax would stimulate savings by putting more resources in the hands of those whose savings rates were highest to begin with. Thus the less someone consumes, the less tax she pays, and the more she is *able* to save. Because people differ enormously in the proportions of their incomes they save, this effect is important. It has been investigated carefully by the economists Laurence Seidman and Ken Lewis, who estimate that horizontal redistribution alone would increase aggregate U.S. savings by about 11 percent—and this in response to the relatively modest degree of progressivity in current USA tax proposals.[7]

An even more important deficiency of existing estimates of how consumption taxation would affect savings is that they ignore the effect of community consumption standards on savings rates. This is by far the most important single channel through which a progressive consumption tax would stimulate savings. As discussed earlier, even though the direct effect of the tax might be to reduce any one family's consumption only slightly, this would initiate a self-reinforcing sequence of indirect effects. For example, when others consume less, the amount that we consume would decline still further, and our responses would then influence others, and so on. Once these multiplier effects are taken into account, the effect of even a very small initial change in savings rates is likely to be substantial.

Some economists have argued that our experiments with tax-free savings in the past—such as the Individual Retirement Accounts (IRAs) of the 1980s, which enabled U.S. taxpayers to shelter up to $2,000 of savings from tax each year—had little appreciable impact on savings. For example, some authors claim that these exemptions merely shifted the form in which people saved, not the total amounts.[8] Others concede that the programs had at least a modest positive impact on total savings.[9] No one, however, claims that IRAs and other similar exemptions had a major effect on savings. And so, as the conventional wisdom has it, the effect on total savings of switching from the current income tax to a consumption tax is likely to be relatively small.

But skepticism based on past reactions to IRAs is also unpersuasive. For one thing, IRAs and other similar exemptions are simply very different from an unlimited savings exemption. The people who do most of the saving in this country save considerably more than $2,000 in any tax year, which means that the exemptions provided by IRAs did not really change the incentives these individuals faced.

Another important difference is that an unlimited savings exemption, unlike an IRA, does not impose hefty penalties on savings withdrawn before retirement. Many people were understandably reluctant to utilize IRAs more fully out of fear that financial emergencies might force them to draw down their savings before retirement. Under a consumption tax, this fear simply does not arise. Savings could be withdrawn at any time with no penalty beyond the tax on the additional consumption financed by the withdrawals.

For the consumption tax to achieve a substantial impact on savings, its rates must be steeply progressive. We know that even the wealthy adjust their consumption in response to the effective prices they face, as evidenced by the fact that when extremely wealthy families move to cities like Manhattan, they buy considerably smaller houses than the ones they left behind in cities with lower land prices. Because of the importance of demonstration effects in consumption, when the wealthy respond to the new incentives by spending less and saving more, those just below them on the income ladder will do likewise. And so, in turn, will the people just below them. In short, we have every reason to expect that the progressive consumption tax can provide the necessary leverage to achieve a manyfold increase in the net savings rate.

The Consumption Mix

The second reason a progressive consumption tax would stimulate economic growth involves the wasteful consumption patterns that have been our focus in this book. If a steeply progressive consumption tax encouraged a reversal in the recent trend toward longer hours, then trickle-down theory, which measures national well-being by per-capita income, would regard that as bad outcome. If the evidence we have seen on the determinants of life satisfaction is valid, however, this conclusion would simply not be justified. On the contrary, if the tax were to induce a switch from more-conspicuous to less-conspicuous forms of consumption, the expected outcome would be an increase in overall well-being, not a decrease. This might not show up as an increase in per-capita income as conventionally measured, but it would nonetheless constitute a real increase in the value of what we produce. (More on this measurement issue later.)

Occupational Choice in a Winner-Take-All Economy

A third way in which higher tax rates at the top would actually stimulate the economy stems from a relationship largely ignored by trickle-down theorists—namely, the effect of tax policy on occupational choice. Economic orthodoxy asserts that free-market incentives allocate talent across different occupations in socially beneficial ways. This assertion rests on the assumption that an individual's reward in any occupation depends on absolute performance. As discussed in chapter 3, however, the modern economy is increasingly permeated by winner-take-all markets, in which small differences in relative performance translate into large differences in reward.

The incentive structure inherent in these markets calls into question our conventional beliefs about the social attractiveness of career choices driven purely by market incentives. When rewards in different occupations depend only on absolute performance, Adam Smith's invisible hand performs reasonably well. But when rewards in some occupations depend strongly on relative performance, career choices that are smart for one are often dumb for all. And this observation suggests that higher taxes on top earners would alter the distribution of talent across occupations in ways that would benefit everyone.

Young people in increasing numbers now pursue top positions in law, finance, consulting, and other overcrowded arenas, in the process forsaking careers in engineering, manufacturing, civil service, teaching, and other occupations in which an infusion of additional talent would yield great benefits. One study estimated, for example, that whereas doubling enrollments in engineering would cause the growth rate of national income to rise by half a percentage point, doubling enrollments in law would actually cause a decline of three-tenths of a point.[10] Yet the number of new lawyers admitted to the bar each year more than doubled between 1970 and 1990, a period during which SAT scores of entering public school teachers declined significantly.[11] The problem, in short, is that winner-take-all markets attract a glut of contestants even as many other important labor markets go begging for talent.

One might hope that such imbalances would fade as wages are bid up in underserved markets and driven down in overcrowded ones, and indeed the number of law school applicants has recently declined. For two reasons, however, such adjustments are destined to fall short, even in the long run.

First, there is an informational problem. An intelligent decision about whether to pit one's own skills against a largely unknown field of contestants for a superstar position obviously requires a well-informed estimate of the odds of winning. Yet people's assessments about these odds are notoriously inaccurate. Survey evidence consistently shows, for example, that more than 90 percent of us think we are better than average drivers; and that more than 90 percent of workers consider themselves more productive than their average colleagues.

Psychologists call this the Lake Wobegon Effect, and its importance for present purposes is that it leads people to overestimate their odds of landing a superstar position. Indeed, overconfidence is likely to be especially strong in the realm of career choice because, in addition to the usual motivational biases that support it, the biggest winners are so conspicuous. The seven-figure NBA stars appear on television several times each week, whereas the many thousands who fail to make the league never attract a moment's notice. When people overestimate their chances of winning, the number who forsake productive occupations in traditional markets to compete in winner-take-all markets will be larger than what could be justified on traditional cost-benefit grounds.

The second reason for persistent overcrowding in winner-take-all markets is one of the structural incentive problems we encountered in chapter 10—namely, the tragedy of the commons. As discussed, this problem accounts for overfishing of coastal waters, overgrazing of common pasturelands, and overcutting of public forests. It also helps explain why we see too many prospectors for gold, a problem closely analogous to the problem at hand. Although the presence of additional prospectors may significantly increase the total amount of gold found in the initial stages of exploiting a newly discovered goldfield, beyond some point it contributes very little to the total find. Thus the gold found by a newcomer to a crowded goldfield is largely gold that otherwise would have been found by others.

Consider a man who must choose whether to work in a factory for $10,000 a year or to become a prospector for gold. If the two activities are equally attractive apart from the matter of pay, he will become a prospector only if he expects to find at least $10,000 worth of gold a year. Suppose he expects to find $11,000 in gold, and that $9,000 of that gold would have been found by others if he had gone to work in the factory. It will then be worth his while to go prospecting, even though his presence in the goldfield will increase the total amount of gold found by only $2,000. Society's total income would have been $8,000 higher had he gone to work in the factory.

Similarly misleading incentives confront potential contestants in winner-take-all markets. Thus, beyond some point, an increase in the number of aspiring mergers-and-acquisitions lawyers produces much less than a proportional increase in the commissions to be had from such transactions. One law student's good fortune in landing a position in a leading Wall Street firm is largely offset by her rival's failure to land that same position.

The incentive gap that leads to the market failure here is similar to the one that caused trouble for gold prospectors: Just as individual prospectors take no account of the fact that most of the gold they might find would otherwise be found by others, so also do aspiring superstars tend to ignore the fact that their presence makes other contestants less likely to win.

In addition to causing a misallocation of talent, the winner-take-all payoff structure encourages another form of waste in that it invites—indeed, virtually compels—competitors to take costly steps to enhance their prospects of winning. As we saw earlier, consumption of anabolic steroids by professional athletes entails potentially serious risks, yet adds virtually nothing to the value of the entertainment provided. National Football League fans have little reason to prefer that opposing linemen average 300 pounds rather than 250. Yet the advantage of larger players can be decisive for any team. And so, in the absence of effective drug testing, widespread ingestion of steroids with all their attendant health risks is inevitable. Winner-take-all markets spawn a host of similar spending arms races that augment the losses stemming from overcrowding.

Society's highest incomes accrue to the top performers in winner-take-all markets, which persistently attract too many contestants. To the extent that economic incentives matter at all (and it is the cornerstone of trickle-down theory that they do), higher taxes on top earners would lead fewer people to compete for limited slots at the top. Moreover, the ones most likely to drop out would be those whose odds of making it into the winner's circle were smallest to begin with. Thus the value of what gets produced in winner-take-all markets would not be much reduced if higher taxes were levied on winners' incomes; and any reductions that did occur would tend to be more than offset by increased output in traditional markets.

What is more, higher taxes on the highest incomes would blunt the incentives for contestants to ingest steroids and engage in other costly battles for top positions. The increasing prevalence of winner-take-all markets thus suggests another way in which a more progressive tax structure would help bring about not only greater equality but also higher economic growth.

OTHER LINKS BETWEEN GROWTH AND INEQUALITY

There are still other reasons to question the fundamental premise of trickle-down economics. One involves the extent to which the productivity of any given member of a team depends on the productive contributions of its other members. Thus the amount by which the efforts of skilled engineers or managers augment national income will be many times greater in an economy with a highly skilled workforce than in one whose workers are poorly trained. Similarly, a doctor in a poor country will typically earn far less than one who performs the very same mix of services in a wealthy country. Those at the top of the productivity ladder have good reasons for wanting to work with others of the highest possible caliber. Yet beyond some point, income inequality may prevent many of those near the bottom of the income ladder from developing their skills and abilities to the fullest. And this works not just to their own disadvantage but also to the disadvantage of those at the top.

The resulting losses will be most pronounced in settings in which many live in absolute poverty. In these settings, after all, further increases in inequality will compromise parents' ability to feed, house, and clothe their children, to say nothing of their ability to invest adequately in their education. Yet these costs are by no means confined to the realm of absolute poverty. For example, as Richard Wilkinson, Michael Marmot, and others have shown, there is a surprisingly strong positive link between the degree of income inequality and the incidence of a variety of stress-related illnesses, even in the wealthiest countries (see chapter 9). These illnesses burden not just the people directly afflicted by them. Often they result in medical services provided at public expense, which means an additional tax burden for healthy people. And to the extent that many illnesses prevent people from achieving their full productive potential, healthy people will also miss many of the indirect benefits that spring from working with more productive colleagues.

Here again we must bear in mind that small changes in initial conditions often cause major changes in final outcomes. As Philip Cook and I have argued elsewhere, even small events are important in the labor market because the process of normal career development is much like a succession of elimination tournaments in sports.[12] Before moving on to the next stage, one must perform well at the current stage. And to have reached the current stage, one must have performed well at the immediately prior stage, and so on. Failure to succeed at one stage, for whatever reason, often makes it impossible to get the additional training, experience, and other resources needed to move on. What is more, failure at any stage can result, as in sports, from even the slimmest performance deficit. The upshot is that although two people start out in life equally well positioned to succeed, their careers may end up following dramatically different trajectories. Small initial increases in income inequality need not generate large deficits in education, health, or other capabilities to have large and widespread depressing effects on productivity.

To the extent that greater income inequality makes it more difficult for some people to capitalize on legitimate career opportunities, it also increases the attractiveness of pursuing options beyond the law. Or at any rate, such is the prediction of any theory in which incentives matter. These theories predict that if a lack of legitimate opportunities drives people to crime, the crimes of choice will be crimes of property—burglary, robbery, drug dealing, and so on. Although a significant link between poverty and crimes of property has been found in many studies,[13] in many others this link is not significant.[14] There does, however, appear to be a consistent and strong link between poverty and violent crimes.[15] These findings suggest that whereas some may respond in narrowly self-interested ways to diminished legitimate opportunities, others may simply lash out in frustration.

In either event, the negative implications for economic growth are all too clear. Some 4 million fearful Americans now sequester themselves in gated communities, more than twice as many as a decade earlier.[16] Total U.S. spending on private security products and services topped $57 billion in 1996, an all-time high and a 46 percent increase over 1991.[17] According to the U.S. Department of Justice, the private security industry now employs some 1.5 million persons, more than two and one-half times the number in public law enforcement.[18]

To the extent that people are busy either committing crimes or trying to avoid being victims of them, they are diverted from producing legitimate goods and services. Increases in criminal activity thus reduce the rate of economic growth as conventionally measured by changes in per-capita income. But this measure may substantially understate the true impact of crime on growth, for many of the extra expenses incurred in the process of committing or avoiding crimes—spending for guns, burglary tools, gated communities, locks, burglar alarms, security guards, local police, and so on—count as increases in national income under our current accounting conventions. As others have suggested, a more accurate picture of economic growth would require the exclusion of such expenditures.[19] An accounting system modified along these lines would further emphasize the positive links between equality and economic growth.

THE CONCEPT OF WHOLE INCOME

Another important flaw in using per-capita income as a measure of economic growth and well-being is that it fails to assign any value to leisure. If the exhortations of the voluntary simplicity movement or the incentives implicit in a steeply progressive consumption tax led everyone to work, say, 10 percent fewer hours, the result, in the short run at least, would be a 10 percent reduction in per-capita income. But if the value of the extra leisure were greater than the value of the wages thus forgone, it would clearly be a mistake to interpret this as a signal of economic decline. Per-capita income is simply not a good measure of economic well-being.

Because per-capita income is typically the most convenient measure at hand, it has disproportionate influence on our sense of how well the economy is doing, and its maximization often becomes a social goal unto itself. It might thus be easier for us to exchange goods for additional leisure if we modified our traditional accounting procedures to track not just incomes earned in the marketplace, but also an augmented measure we may call "whole income."[20] Any individual's annual whole income is simply her hourly wage rate times 2,000 hours, or the amount that she would earn *if* she worked full time all year. On this measure, two people with the same wage rate would thus have the same whole incomes, even if one chose to work full time while the other chose to work only part time. Keeping our accounts in this way would make it less likely that we would misinterpret a voluntary, across-the-board move to shorter hours as a signal of economic decline. And on the evidence we have seen, this would be a completely justifiable step—because human well-being depends not just on the quantity of goods we consume but also on the time we have available to do as we please.

———

To recapitulate briefly, there is little evidence that higher tax rates on top earners would produce significant reductions in economic growth as conventionally measured, and even less evidence that any such reductions should be interpreted as a signal of economic decline. This raises an obvious question: If the fundamental premise of trickle-down economics is as deeply flawed as I claim, why is it so widely accepted?

As I noted at the beginning of this chapter, much of the appeal of this premise derives from its close association with the belief that incentives matter. Incentives *do* matter, a fact that appears to have escaped the attention of many social-policy planners during the last several decades. But we must be clear about *which* incentives matter.

Trickle-down economics assumes that absolute rewards are the incentives that really count. On the best available evidence, however, relative rewards matter just as much, if not far more.

Since this evidence has been available for quite some time, it would be puzzling indeed if there had not been at least some form of more systematic challenge to the fundamental premise of trickle-down economics. In fact, just such a challenge has been gaining momentum over the last several years. Scholars in this movement have examined the relationship between economic growth and inequality both within and across countries. And in every instance their findings have been squarely at odds with the predictions of trickle-down theory.

Growth and Inequality Across Nations

A burgeoning empirical literature has found a negative correlation between various measures of income inequality and economic growth in cross-national data. For example, using World Bank and OECD data for a sample of industrial nations, the economists Andrew Glyn and David Miliband examined the relationship between income inequality and economic growth. (They measured income equality by the ratio of the income of the top 20 percent to the income of the bottom 20 percent for each country in 1980 and they measured economic growth by the annual percentage growth rate in labor productivity between 1979 and 1990).[21] Their findings, which are shown in the figure below, reveal a significant negative association between income inequality and growth.

In another study, the economists Alberto Alesina and D. Roderick found that national income growth rates in 65 countries were negatively related to the share of national income going to the top 5 percent and top 20 percent of earners; and that, by contrast, larger shares for low- and middle-income groups were associated with higher rates of growth.[22] Essentially the same pattern has been confirmed in several other independent studies.[23]

Of course, the mere fact that inequality and growth are negatively correlated in cross-national data does not imply that greater inequality

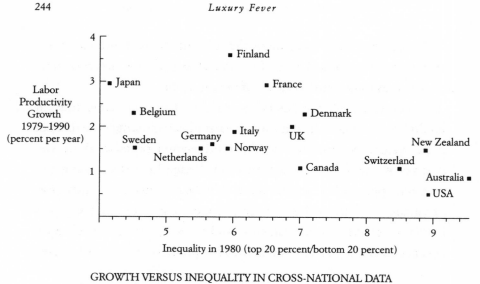

GROWTH VERSUS INEQUALITY IN CROSS-NATIONAL DATA

Source: Glyn and Miliband, 1994, p. 3.

is necessarily a cause of slower growth. A multitude of other factors that affect growth rates differ sharply across nations, and if some of the most important of these are positively correlated with income inequality, that might explain the pattern. One way to check for this possibility is to see whether the negative relationship between inequality and growth holds up when we examine these two variables within countries over time.

Growth and Inequality Over Time

Several recent studies have found that the correlation over time between inequality and economic growth is also negative. For example, as the economists Don Corry and Andrew Glyn note in their recent survey, the postwar experience in most industrial countries may be partitioned neatly into two periods for the purpose of describing variations in economic growth and income inequality.[24] The first, from roughly the end of World War II until about 1973, has been called the golden age of economic growth. National income growth during that period averaged 5 percent and more in many developed countries. By contrast, the growth rates of national income in the OECD countries have been only about half as large during the post-

1973 period. Corry and Glyn also note that by virtually any measure, income inequality during the golden age was low by historical standards and in most countries was falling throughout the period. They go on to point out that the degree of income inequality in most countries has risen significantly since 1974, although the change began at different times in different countries. As in the cross-national data, higher growth rates are associated not with higher income inequality, as predicted by trickle-down theory, but with lower inequality.

Here again, however, the observed negative correlation does not necessarily imply that growing inequality is the cause of slower growth. As before, it could be that other factors positively correlated with inequality are the real causal agents. Yet it seems unlikely that the same unobserved causal agents that might have explained the pattern in cross-national data could also have been at work in the time-series data. It *could* have happened that way. But now we need two coincidences, not just one, to get inequality off the hook.

THE FREE MARKETEER'S COMPLAINT

Most free marketeers think that economic growth is a good thing, and all but a lunatic fringe will concede that we need a government and therefore need to collect taxes. Yet many will object, in principle, to the deliberate use of tax policy to stimulate economic growth. Why, they will ask, is the choice between present and future consumption any different from the choice between apples and oranges? As the free marketeer sees it, the government has no more business regulating one choice than the other.

Those in the thrall of invisible-hand theory see America's recent low-growth trajectory as the outcome of decisions by individual consumers who, having rationally weighed the relative merits of present and future consumption, simply opted to emphasize the former. To second-guess these decisions, they say, is the height of bureaucratic hubris. How can the government know better than the people themselves how best to resolve this trade-off?

Free marketeers are by no means the only ones troubled by the specter of meddlesome social engineers. Yet collective efforts to stimulate savings can be justified on a variety of grounds that do not entail second-guessing consumers. At the most basic level, for example, we may observe that the government already has in place a number of policies whose side effects are to reduce the amounts that rational consumers would otherwise choose to save. For instance, people who believe they can still count on Social Security to replace a significant fraction of their earnings during retirement are rational to save considerably less than they would in the absence of this program. Yet, as noted earlier, Social Security is not a true savings program at all, but rather a transfer from workers to retirees. It generates none of the growth that comes from real savings.

Other parts of the social safety net, such as Medicare, Medicaid, and unemployment insurance, have a similar effect. Many people would save more if not for the protections these programs provide against unforeseen financial emergencies. Some, though by no means all, free marketeers would prefer that these social programs simply not exist. But they do exist, and they will continue to cause people to save less than they would in a completely unrestricted environment. Collective efforts to stimulate additional savings can thus be seen not as an attempt to second-guess consumers but as a way for them to achieve savings levels closer to the ones they would have chosen under truly free-market conditions.

Alternatively, one might argue, as I have throughout this book, that the savings decisions that look best to each individual are not the ones that best promote our collective interests. As we have seen, it is perfectly rational for a job seeker to save less in order to upgrade his professional wardrobe, or for a parent to save less in order to buy a house in a better school district. Yet when all follow these incentives, the hoped-for results do not materialize, despite the savings deficit.

A related possibility is that the growth rate of an economy has important elements in common with other public goods like national defense. Private firms are not well suited to provide national defense services because even people who refuse to pay for these services can still expect to benefit from them. If any one citizen is to be protected from a foreign invasion, all must be. Recognizing the difficulty posed by the inability to exclude nonpayers, even free marketeers acknowledge the legitimacy of taxing citizens to pay for national defense services and other public goods. If Benjamin Friedman is right that democratic values and social harmony are more easily maintained in a high-growth environment (see chapter 7), then a high rate of growth is also a public good, and tax policy is a legitimate tool for promoting it.

Laurence Seidman has suggested yet another respect in which high national growth rates may constitute a public good.[25] He notes that citizens of a country that occupies a high rank among the community of nations enjoy many advantages similar to those that accrue to individuals of high rank among their peers. Political autonomy, for example, is closely linked to relative military capability, which in turn depends closely on relative economic strength. Similarly, the ability to maintain a competitive position in many global markets depends on the ability to expand the frontiers of scientific research, and this ability as well depends on relative wealth. Many people may also enjoy a measure of psychological comfort in knowing that their nation's standard of living is second to none.

The higher growth rates made possible by higher savings rates promote all these advantages. Yet no individual's savings decisions have any significant impact on national growth rates. As a group, we might value the improved social climate or higher national rank made possible by a higher savings rate much more than enough to compensate for giving up some current consumption. As individuals, however, we cannot affect this trade-off.

In such situations, it simply makes no sense to complain that progrowth policies are an instance of meddlesome social engineers trying to impose their will on a resisting public. Just as we want government to levy taxes to support the advantages that stem from an effective national defense capability, so too might we want government to employ tax policy in pursuit of the public benefits that accompany rapid economic growth.

HOMO REALISTICUS

Collective action to stimulate higher savings would be justified even if everyone had the formidable cognitive skills and self-discipline that free marketeers ascribe to the *homo economicus* stereotype. But the world we live in is of course very different from the arid landscape assumed in orthodox economic theory. The prototypical actor in our world is not *homo economicus* but a far different animal, someone we may call *homo realisticus*. By comparison to *homo economicus,* he is a little short on cognitive processing power and noticeably deficient when it comes to self-discipline. And therein, as we have seen, lies still another reason that our saving rate falls short of the theoretical ideal.

It is a complex matter indeed to formulate a savings plan that is optimal for any individual's particular circumstances. And even if someone could formulate such a plan, she would still face the formidable problem of having to execute it. The difficulty is that the rewards from savings come only in the future, whereas the lure of many forms of consumption is both immediate and powerful. Many a well-intentioned savings plan has foundered on the shoals of temptation. The implication is that by making the most conspicuous forms of consumption less attractive, a steeply progressive consumption tax would also make it easier for many of us to save at the rates we feel we should.

If the temptation to consume too much were the only reason we save too little, it might be difficult to justify collective action to restrict consumption. Individuals are free, after all, to take steps of their own that can help ameliorate self-control problems. Many people, for example, enroll in payroll-deduction savings plans, which automatically divert a part of their earnings into savings, thereby restricting the amounts they are free to spend.

Yet the temptation problem is by no means the only reason for taking collective action to promote greater savings. As we have seen, a steeply progressive consumption tax can be defended on numerous other plausible grounds. Still, it bears noting that one side effect of such a tax would be to help many consumers in their personal struggles to achieve their own savings goals. If this effect, by itself, would not justify the move to a progressive consumption tax, it is a positive effect nonetheless.

Although the fundamental premise of trickle-down economics is widely and firmly held, there appears to be little theoretical or empirical support for it. On the contrary, there are coherent theoretical reasons for expecting that higher tax rates on top earners would lead to higher, not lower, rates of economic growth. If levied on consumption rather than income, they would stimulate additional savings. A steeply progressive consumption tax would also provide powerful incentives to curb wasteful consumption patterns. And this tax would help steer talent away from overcrowded superstar markets toward occupations that sorely need it. Such a tax might also stimulate growth by lessening the disparities in consumption that have been growing in recent decades, thus enabling poorer families to better educate and care for their children; or by enabling these families to enjoy more robust physical and psychological health; or by making it less likely that they would commit crimes.

Whatever combination of these theoretical possibilities might actually be at work, this much is clear: The observed patterns in the data are flatly inconsistent with the fundamental premise of trickle-down theory. In both cross-national data and time-series data, greater inequality of reward is associated with lower, not higher, rates of economic growth. The fundamental premise of trickle-down economics simply provides no intelligible basis for rejecting the progressive consumption tax. Nor, as we have seen, does the claim that private consumption decisions are not a legitimate concern of public policy.

A steeply progressive consumption tax can help free us from the grip of luxury fever. In the least coercive possible way, such a tax, phased in gradually, would cause an across-the-board reduction in the rate of growth of expenditures on conspicuous consumption. Because the satisfaction people derive from such expenditures is largely context-dependent, this would not be a painful step. What is more, it is a step that would free up literally trillions of dollars of resources that could be put to better uses. We must not be discouraged from taking this step by the false belief that a more progressive tax structure entails slower economic growth.

CHAPTER 16

WE CAN'T AFFORD IT?

O ur focus thus far has been on the profound waste inherent in our current spending patterns, not just in the eyes of those with pressing unmet needs, but even for those with the most to spend. But where there is waste, there is also opportunity. Up and down the income ladder, there exist promising alternative ways in which we could be spending our time and money. The evidence we have seen suggests that even the top earners would lead longer and more satisfying lives if everyone spent less on conspicuous consumption and more on various forms of inconspicuous consumption.

Although I have focused primarily on the attractions of alternative consumption opportunities in the private sphere—more time with families and friends; greater workplace autonomy; a schedule that allows more time for exercise, sleep, and other restorative activities—we have also missed out on important opportunities in the public sphere. Apart from the rapid growth in entitlement programs for the elderly in recent decades, we have been busily slashing expenditures on public goods and services of all sorts. But although many of the programs cut were clearly wasteful, many others delivered good value for our money. And the programs hardest hit have been ones that serve our poorest citizens.

More striking than these changes themselves has been the fact that they have generated so little critical scrutiny. Oh, a small cadre of die-hard social activists has bemoaned each cutback in the social safety net. Yet, for the most part, mainstream political discourse in the United States has taken the need for widespread budget slashing to be self-evident.

Indeed, not even the most committed liberals disputed the fact that *something* had to be done to curb the recent explosive growth in our national debt. Whereas the total U.S. federal government debt stood at roughly $1 trillion when Ronald Reagan took office in 1981, in the ensuing years annual deficits averaging more than $200 billion have increased that total to more than $5 trillion. The interest on this debt now comes to more than $300 billion each year, much of it paid out to the citizens of other nations. As commentators from both sides of the political aisle have rightly emphasized, this burden threatens to make our children the first generation in American history with a lower standard of living than their parents. And this unhappy prospect was an important impetus behind the persistent budget cutting that, for the time being, has eliminated the federal budget deficit.

Yet history will not look kindly on the particular manner in which we pursued this goal. There are essentially two ways to eliminate a budget deficit: We can reduce the amount we spend, or we can increase the amount we collect in taxes. Near the end of the Bush administration, budget legislation produced a slight upward revision in the top tax rates that had been cut so sharply in 1981 and 1986, and there was another slight increase in 1993. Even with these increases, however, the tax rates on top earners remain 25 percent below even their 1985 levels, and the bulk of our deficit-reduction efforts, including the 1997 budget accord, have emphasized spending reduction. Indeed, the 1997 budget accord actually calls for tax cuts totaling $127 billion by 2002, many of them targeted for upper-income families. For instance, families earning up to $110,000 will receive a $500 tax reduction for every dependent child. These tax cuts come on the heels of more than 25 years of unprecedentedly high rates of growth in the incomes received by top earners. And as noted, the budget cuts have fallen disproportionately on programs serving those who earn the least.

Among the few who have spoken out against this pattern, a common charge is that it can be understood only by reference to the greed and mean-spiritedness of those with the most influence over government. But although there may be persons of influence who fit this description, this explanation misses the essence of what has happened. Our current course is primarily the result not of greed or nastiness, but of false beliefs about the consequences of higher taxes.

If we were to eliminate budget deficits by higher taxes, the bulk of those taxes would have to be levied on middle- and upper-income taxpayers—since, after all, these people are the only ones with the *means* to pay higher taxes. Yet the consensus view of political leaders of the 1990s, liberals and conservatives alike, is that higher tax rates on top earners will stifle effort and risk-taking, and thus might actually exacerbate the budget deficit. So firmly entrenched is this belief that higher taxes on the wealthy were not even one of the options seriously discussed during the 1997 budget negotiations.

As we saw in chapter 15, however, higher tax rates on top earners—especially if levied on consumption rather than income—are not only consistent with robust economic performance, they are likely to promote it. We could have eliminated the budget deficit quite easily without paring even a single nickel from the expenditure column. The primary cost, had we followed this strategy, would have been a reduction in the rate of growth of luxury consumption spending.

Again, this is not to deny that many government programs should have been cut or eliminated. Yet, as even the staunchest conservatives freely concede, many other programs yield benefits that far exceed their costs. In today's sterile political discourse, however, we hear little about whether programs slated to be cut might be truly cost effective.

Instead, we apply budgetary pressure to *every* government program, good or bad, simply by chanting, "We can't afford it." Programs backed by powerful constituencies are naturally able to resist this pressure better than others. But not even programs strongly favored by high-income voters, such as public television and radio, have escaped the budget ax.

A century hence, those who read the history of our time will be puzzled about the arguments we have used in defense of cutting, or refusing to fund, so many clearly useful public programs. They will wonder, for example, why we failed to replace our deteriorating municipal water systems, thereby exposing millions of families to toxic levels of lead, manganese, and other heavy metals. They will not understand why we didn't adopt more stringent air-quality standards, which would have prevented millions of serious illnesses and many thousands of premature deaths; or why we didn't hire more beef inspectors in response to the growing threat from deadly E-coli 0157 bacteria. They will be puzzled by our having spent so little to maintain our streets, highways, and bridges. And it will not be obvious to them why, despite our considerable wealth, we failed to pay enough to attract the best and brightest teachers for our public schools.

In my own community, we are confronted each day with additional spending cutbacks that make life less pleasant for everyone: Our local public library, like libraries in countless other communities, cites budget cutbacks to explain why it is no longer open on Sundays. The department of public works cites fiscal distress to explain the growing litter on city streets. The school system sharply curtails its music and art programs, saying it no longer has the money to pay for them. The Youth Bureau cites budget cuts to explain why the municipal swimming pool now closes an hour earlier, even on summer's hottest days. And the police department offers the same explanation for why it no longer stations officers to control traffic flows during peak hours at especially busy crossroads.

At every level of government, our refusal to make cost-effective public investments is a widespread and growing problem. The almost 40 million Americans who currently lack health insurance are often forced to rely on costly emergency-room services when they fall ill, and the higher costs are passed along as higher taxes and insurance rates.[1] It would be better, and cheaper, to have federally funded health insurance for everyone. Summer recreation programs in the inner cities are relatively inexpensive and produce large reductions in crime.[2] These programs should be growing in number rather than shrinking. Funding for student loan programs, a critical component of our efforts to assure equality of educational opportunity, should be increasing rather than decreasing. Small and large, each of these government activities represents good value for our money. And yet we say we cannot afford them.

THE CHILDREN OF THE POOR

Far more troubling than our failure to make cost-effective investments in our public infrastructure has been our failure to provide decent opportunities for the children of our poorest citizens. In the first case, our descendants will look back and wonder how we could have been so stupid; but in the second they will ask how we could have been so callous.

Most of the children born in our inner-city neighborhoods live in squalid housing in which violence and drug abuse are rampant; they are often poorly nourished; and their parents—when they have parents—are often unable to provide any real nurturance or guidance. Many of these children are also worn down from a variety of chronic physical ailments. They suffer from astonishingly high rates of asthma, and it is common to see children with rotten teeth; infected gums; and festering, untreated sores.

Lacking a quiet, safe place to sleep at night, many poor children also suffer from chronic fatigue. A South Bronx woman tells of a neighbor's seven-month-old boy who had been attacked by rats in his crib on several different occasions: "The baby's fingers were all bloody. I think it was the third time that this baby was attacked. His mother's terrified but can't move out. The city put her in this building and she don't have any money to move somewhere else."[3] And rats are not the only thing that disrupts poor children's sleep. Their dwellings are swelteringly hot in summer and bitterly cold in winter. And fires occur so frequently that the threat of being burned to death weighs heavily on many of their minds.

But perhaps the most troubling handicap of many inner-city children is the significant neurological impairment they suffer from low-weight premature birth, exposure to drugs *in utero,* and widespread exposure to lead, both in their homes and in their schools. A rat's bite will heal, but much of this other damage is not reversible.

In view of the conditions in which many children of the poor have to live, one might have expected that as a society we would take special pains to compensate by investing heavily in their schools. Yet the conditions in many inner-city schools are not only no better than those experienced at home, they are often even worse. Thus, as Jonathan Kozol recounts in his 1995 book, *Amazing Grace,*

> At Morris High School barrels were filling up with rain in several rooms the last time I was there. Green fungus molds were growing in the corners of the room in which the guidance counselor met kids who were depressed. Many of these schools quite literally stink. Girls tell me they won't use the toilets. They rush home the minute school is over. If they need to use the bathroom sooner, they leave sooner. . . . At one junior high school in the South Bronx . . . only 15 teachers in a faculty of 54 were certified. The overcrowding of children in these schools compounds the chaos caused by staffing difficulties. At some schools . . . classes were taking place in settings like stair-landings, bathrooms, and coat closets, because the population of poor children was increasing but there was, according to the press, no money to build schools for them.[4]

Under the circumstances, it is hardly surprising that more than 80 percent of the children growing up in places like the South Bronx fail to graduate from high school.

Professor Laurence Mead, a political scientist at New York University, has said that "if poor people behaved rationally, they would seldom be poor for long in the first place."[5] On a moment's reflection, however, it seems clear that even the most rational, energetic, and talented persons growing up in environments like the South Bronx stand a pretty good chance of experiencing as adults the same grinding poverty they knew as children. Indeed, the wonder is that any ever manage to escape poverty at all. For people in such environments, we are foolish to expect that "behaving rationally" would have made much difference. And yet the focus of our current budget sessions is to cut further the few remaining programs that serve the poor. Not even the celebrated Earned Income Tax Credit has escaped attack.

THE EARNED INCOME TAX CREDIT

Proposed by President Richard Nixon in 1969, the Earned Income Tax Credit (EITC) was signed into law by President Gerald Ford in 1975.

Its purpose is to provide additional purchasing power to the more than 10 million American workers who live below the official poverty line. The program works by providing a credit that reduces the income tax bill of families whose earned incomes fall below a given threshold. Families whose incomes are sufficiently low to begin with actually receive a check—a negative tax payment—from the federal government. For example, the biweekly $471 paycheck received by Florence Shorter, a cook's assistant at a nursing home in Washington, D.C., includes a $40.60 rebate from the EITC.[6]

The EITC has long been popular among conservatives because it increases incentives for people to hold paying jobs. People who do not work simply do not receive the EITC. This program has also been popular among liberals for its ability to transfer additional resources to needy families. "The EITC is one of the most important tools we have to help parents build a better life for their children and prevent working families from slipping into poverty," said former Senator Bill Bradley, a strong supporter of the program. "This money is not used for fancy dinners or limo rides. It's rent money. It pays the electricity bills, or it buys clothing for the kids."[7] Even Ronald Reagan, no advocate of wasteful government spending, was a vocal proponent of the EITC.

Yet budget proposals submitted in both the House and Senate in 1995 called for sharp reductions in EITC spending—$43 billion over seven years in the Senate version and $23 billion in the House version. Only the budget impasses of the ensuing years kept these large cuts from being implemented. Because the EITC enables poor families to achieve a higher living standard by working than by going on welfare, it is not only a humane policy but also a good investment. Yet our elected representatives seem to be telling us that we cannot afford it.

WELFARE REFORM

Although the dismal lives of many of the nation's poor are the result of circumstances they are largely powerless to control, our national policy for dealing with the poor has increasingly become one of simply exhorting them to get their act together. Rather than mount any serious

"Otis, shout at that man to pull himself together."

attempt to provide better opportunities for our neediest fellow citizens, we have declared that the conditions of their lives are no longer a matter of public concern. Thus, in 1996, Congress enacted welfare "reform" legislation making families ineligible for more than two years of support from the welfare system.

At least some of the people who supported this legislation did so in the sincere belief that it would provide stronger incentives for poor people to find jobs and thus help to eliminate a "culture of dependency." Yet its almost certain short-term effect will be to make conditions even more miserable for millions of existing families. Because many of the poor have little education or experience and lack even rudimentary work habits, private employers have been understandably reluctant to shop for new workers in communities like the South Bronx. Already there are many people in these communities who desperately want jobs yet cannot find them. Dumping millions of former welfare recipients into this unemployed pool is not likely to improve matters much.

My point is not that the existing welfare system has not encouraged dysfunctional patterns of behavior. Nor should liberals imagine that poverty in the inner cities could be permanently eliminated if we only wrote bigger welfare checks. As the social science community has amply demonstrated, our current system often undermines incentives, in many cases causing problems far more serious than the ones it solves.

In the end, steady employment offers the only real hope for lifting families permanently out of poverty. Yet there is little serious discussion, either in government or academic circles, about how to create employment opportunities for the poor. It is unrealistic to expect substantial increases in inner-city workers hired by private companies. And in the face of the almost universal presumption that government spending simply cannot grow, no one seriously proposes public-sponsored employment for the poor.

AN ALTERNATIVE APPROACH

The irony is that despite our ceaseless hand-wringing about budget deficits, we have ample resources to assure that all our children receive a decent start in life. As we approach the millennium, the United States remains by far the richest nation on earth. Yet we are currently squandering much of our wealth on fruitless mine-is-bigger consumption arms races. If we wish to use these resources in other more fruitful or humane ways, we are free to do so. That important problems must remain unaddressed because we lack the resources to deal with them is simply a false belief. Once loosed from its shackles, we will quickly discover that the problem of how to provide better opportunities to our neediest citizens is less daunting than it had appeared.

The first step is to understand clearly why our historical mix of social-welfare programs failed so miserably. The fundamental difficulty confronting any social-support system is how to provide adequate levels of assistance for the people who truly need it, without at the same time encouraging others to quit work and go on the dole. Our current system failed because it failed to resolve this difficulty.

To discourage able-bodied people from seeking public support, the current system has employed a two-pronged strategy. One is simply to have offered an extremely low level of support. Contrary to the florid political rhetoric of the right wing, there have never been many welfare queens driving Cadillacs. In most jurisdictions, the amount of support available remains well below even the most minimal estimate of what it takes to escape from poverty. To offer more, it was feared, would have been to encourage indolence.

The second prong in the current system's strategy to discourage goldbricking is to have erected formidable bureaucratic hurdles between the system and its potential client pool. To pursue eligibility for public assistance in most jurisdictions, the poor must stand in line for hours and cut through layers of red tape that even many experienced attorneys would find daunting. And welfare assistance often comes in forms that many experience as stigmatizing. For instance, many recipients describe contemptuous remarks by other shoppers who see them paying for their groceries with food coupons.

Although both low support levels and complex bureaucratic procedures have undoubtedly deterred many people from seeking public support over the years, the system has nonetheless had pernicious effects on incentives. Contrary to the political rhetoric of the far left, people really do weigh the costs and benefits of their alternative courses of action; and when rewards change, they often change their behavior accordingly. One problem is that the welfare system confronts many participants with effective tax rates that make taking a paying job totally counterproductive. Benefit payments are often administered by separate agencies—food stamps from one group, housing subsidies from another, energy stamps from another, and so on—with payments typically reduced by a significant proportion for each additional dollar the recipient earns from a job. Thus a participant in four separate programs might lose 50 cents worth of benefits from each program for every additional dollar she earns—an effective marginal tax rate of 200 percent!

What is more, when a welfare recipient accepts a low-wage job, she often loses her Medicaid eligibility, and her children may no longer be eligible for Head Start or school lunch subsidies. Under these circumstances, working simply doesn't pay. In middle-class neighborhoods, the rational pursuit of self-interest may well be sufficient to inoculate most people against poverty. But responding rationally to the existing incentive structure has no such effect in many inner-city neighborhoods. As miserable as the standard of living of welfare recipients may be in these neighborhoods, the alternatives are typically even worse.

The problem with the current system, in a nutshell, is that it is unable to provide adequate levels of support for the people who really need it without at the same time destroying others' incentives to fend for themselves. There is a disarmingly simple solution to this problem. Instead of writing checks to people who are sufficiently poor and willing to jump over enough bureaucratic hurdles, we can issue a paycheck to anyone willing to perform a public-service job. Offering pay in exchange for work would eliminate once and for all any worry that people might quit work to live lives of leisure at taxpayer expense.

Although private employers do not find it profitable to hire many of today's poor, there are nonetheless many useful tasks that people with little training or experience can perform. With proper supervision, for example, they can plant new shrubs and flower gardens in our public spaces; they can help with new landscaping along our highways; they can paint government buildings; they can recycle newspapers and aluminum cans; they can remove graffiti from buildings and highway overpasses; they can fill potholes in our city streets; they can replace burned out streetlamps; they can assist in reforestation and erosion-control projects; they can drive vans and buses to transport the elderly and the disabled; and so on.

Unlike the current welfare system, whose budgets provide no useful services to communities that desperately need them, public-service jobs would add real value to our communities. At the same time, these jobs would put purchasing power in the hands of the people for whom support is most likely to make a difference. Even more important, people with useful jobs become full-fledged participants in the economy. And when that happens, the entire environment is transformed. As the sociologist William Julius Wilson has emphasized, neglected children and substandard schools are rare in communities in which most people hold gainful employment.[8]

The advantages of public employment over welfare payments have been noted many times in the past. Serious proposals have not gone forward, however, because of the preconception that we simply cannot afford them. And indeed, a large-scale program of public-service employment would not be cheap. Yet we are an extraordinarily rich country, and one with a substantial measure of economic slack. In time, we could recover literally trillions of dollars annually simply by curbing the growth rate of spending on luxury goods.

Can enough resources be diverted from luxury consumption growth to assure employment for all at a living wage? If the number of jobs we had to support were no greater than the current number of chronically unemployed persons in the American economy, the answer would surely be yes. The burden of paying for the program would become significantly greater, however, if public-service jobs attracted large numbers of people away from existing jobs in the private sector. Unfortunately, it appears that entry-level government job postings almost always do, in fact, attract enormous numbers of applicants who already hold low-wage private jobs.

But even this problem, it turns out, has a relatively simple fix. One reason that entry-level government jobs tend to attract so many applicants is that these jobs usually pay higher wages than typical private jobs for unskilled workers. The first step in keeping the program affordable is thus to post a wage for the public-service jobs that is substantially below the minimum wage for private-sector jobs. For example, if entry-level jobs in the private sector pay a salary of $10,000 a year, the salary in public-service jobs could be set at only $8,000.

A subminimum wage, however, would not only hold down the number of private-sector workers who want to switch to public-service jobs, it would also prevent holders of public-service jobs from escaping the clutches of poverty. To avoid this outcome, we need a second step—a small monetary allowance paid out to every person, irrespective of employment status. By itself, this allowance must be far too small to live on—say, $2,000 per year per person—lest it encourage people to give up jobs to go on the dole. But when combined with the salary from a public-service job, a monetary supplement of that size would push holders of these jobs above the poverty line.

For example, a family of four headed by someone with a public-service job paying $8,000 would have a total spendable income of $16,000 a year, or just enough to lift it from poverty. Because the monetary supplement is independent of employment status, that same family with an earner in a private job paying $10,000 would have a spendable income of $18,000. This income difference would provide an incentive for public-job holders to move into private jobs as quickly as they could, thereby holding down the expense of extending the job guarantee.

Although this simple jobs-plus-supplement approach would be costly, it is well within our means. Completely apart from our moral responsibility to provide the best possible opportunities to our neediest families, a well-implemented public-service employment program would deliver high value for our dollars. Notwithstanding the prospect that federal welfare-reform legislation will reduce the number of people in our inner cities who are officially eligible for support from the government, these bleak environments will continue to produce large numbers who are ill-equipped to make it on their own. And the fact that they may not be eligible for welfare payments does not mean that they will cease to be costly to society.

To believe otherwise is to make the same mistake we made by imagining that we could save money by having almost 40 million people living without health insurance. Insured or not, these people still get injured and sick, and their medical costs—often inflated by inefficient modes of care—are almost always passed on to the rest of society. In the same manner, lower levels of welfare support are likely to translate into higher costs for society, especially in the short run.

Thus, as poverty, drug abuse, and hopelessness have pervaded the inner cities, we have seen explosive growth in the number of people behind bars. The number of inmates in New York City's Riker's Island facility, which stood at 6,000 in 1982, is now more than 20,000. The city currently spends almost $60,000 a year on each adult inmate, and $70,000 on each juvenile—some 10 times the amount it spends per pupil in its public schools. And despite its current mood, Congress appears unlikely to forever turn its back on the neurologically impaired children of the drug epidemic. As we saw in chapter 4, the enormous medical costs these children experience shortly after their births are often just the tip of the iceberg.

Shifting to a program of guaranteed public-service employment would also eliminate a variety of other costs we now incur in our often clumsy and ill-advised efforts to ease the burdens of the poor. During the energy crises of the 1970s, for example, concern for the well-being of the poor led to the imposition of gasoline price controls, and a resulting need to ration short supplies. The lines of cars queued up for gas at many urban stations stretched for several blocks, each car belching fumes and wasting fuel as it inched toward the pumps. Far better for all would have been allowing gasoline prices to rise to their market-clearing levels, and then increasing the monetary supplement to ease the burden on the poor.

Rent controls and subsidized public housing are similarly clumsy and wasteful ways of trying to deliver services that the poor could better purchase for themselves in the open market, if only they had more income. To ask whether we can afford to switch to a public-service employment approach is simply to ask the wrong question. Our current system is not only enormously expensive, but also largely counterproductive. The far more pertinent question is whether we can afford *not* to switch.

Many self-styled advocates for the poor have argued against public-service employment on the grounds that it is akin to slavery. By requiring people to work for a paycheck, they say, the government robs them of their dignity. But how, exactly, does getting paid to perform useful tasks on behalf of the community rob people of their dignity? No one would be *required* to perform a public-service job. It is merely an opportunity, and a far better one than the poor now confront.

Some who object to public-service employment believe that the poor should be given a generous cash stipend with no strings attached. But that is simply not one of our options. The practical alternatives before us are for the poor to continue to jump through hoops in return for assistance that scarcely alleviates their misery—our current system—or for them to earn a living wage by performing useful work for the community. From the perspective of both rich and poor, the latter alternative is clearly better; and those who oppose it become, in effect, advocates for the status quo.

Jobs not only provide incomes but they also help integrate people into their communities. By comparison to persons who have been unemployed for protracted periods, people with jobs enjoy significantly greater self-esteem and psychological well-being. Serious depression is a common condition among the long-term unemployed. Among unemployed males in the United Kingdom, for example, almost 1 in 20 attempt suicide in any given year.[9]

The grave human costs associated with joblessness can be almost completely avoided. There are important tasks that need to be done, and we have ample resources to hire people who are currently idle to perform them. For this to happen, the only sacrifice we need make is to accept a temporary reduction in the growth rate of our spending on conspicuous consumption.

With the resources thus saved, public-service employees could be engaged to produce many forms of inconspicuous consumption that would otherwise be in short supply. And as they gain experience performing entry-level tasks, many will prove capable of moving on to more demanding ones. Some could help repair worn-out roads and bridges. Some could help replace antiquated water-supply systems or become peer counselors in drug treatment programs or take jobs as supervisors in recreation centers. It is difficult to imagine a more harmonious confluence of need and opportunity.

CHAPTER 17

CASH ON THE TABLE

The summer months always seem to slip by quickly in Ithaca, and this year I never managed to replace my broken-down propane grill before the outdoor cooking season was over. That errand can easily wait until next spring, of course, but in the meantime a few problems surfaced with our kitchen stove that called for more immediate action. Both the stove's timer and its self-cleaning oven feature failed simultaneously—the culmination of a series of failures over the years—and my wife and I had earlier vowed that we would not invest any more money and hassle on this particular appliance. (I cannot help thinking, though, how strange it would have seemed, during my years living in Nepal, that someone might view such problems as urgent.)

So now we have a new kitchen stove. To my chagrin, it cost us more than four times as much as the one it replaced, and has two 15,000-BTU burners—the signature emblem of 1990s superfluity. Yet I immediately saw that it was fruitless to resist. After all, it *is* a nice stove; and it did cost significantly less than the corresponding Viking models that grace the kitchens of many of our friends—models that have four 15,000-BTU burners instead of two. I console myself with the thought that, in a few years, even base-model stoves will offer 15,000-BTU burners.

The increase in the amounts we spend on appliances is part of the broader change in spending patterns that has been occurring in America, Europe, and elsewhere. Our houses are bigger and our automobiles are faster and more luxuriously appointed than ever before. But to finance these purchases, we have been spending more time at the office and taking fewer vacations. We have less time for family and friends, and less time for sleep and exercise. Each year the number of Americans who undergo cosmetic surgery sets a new record, as does the number who file for personal bankruptcy. At a time when our spending on luxury goods is growing four times as fast as overall spending, our savings rate is at an all-time low. Our streets are dirty and congested. Our highways and bridges are in disrepair, placing countless lives in danger. And the misery in our inner cities continues unabated.

NO EXPLANATIONS, WRONG EXPLANATIONS

Ideas matter. How we think about our current spending patterns—or, indeed, whether we even notice them at all—depends strongly on our theoretical preconceptions. Members of my own economics profession, for example, have had almost nothing to say about these patterns. Armed with Adam Smith's invisible-hand theory—the notion that the individual pursuit of self-interest in the open marketplace results in the greatest good for all—many economists simply do not see anything amiss. Because orthodox economic theory asserts that free-market exchange satisfies human needs and wants to the maximum possible extent, these economists are disinclined to scrutinize our spending patterns in evaluative terms. To the extent that they pay any attention to these patterns at all, it is merely to use them as data for inferring what people's preferences must be. Thus, if we have squalid cities and expensive private cars, many free-market economists conclude that this must be what we really want.

Modern conservatives take their inspiration from the laissez-faire economic theories of the eighteenth century. And since these intellectual underpinnings tell them that nothing is wrong with our current consumption patterns, it is no surprise that they seldom propose government interventions aimed at changing things. On the contrary, the free-marketeer's rallying cry has been further cuts in taxes. After all, they reason, if the results of individual consumption decisions are presumptively benign, then more of the same should be even better.

If the preconceptions of free-market conservatives blind them to the possibility that anything might be amiss, many liberals seem to suffer from the opposite problem. Armed with their theories of exploitation and market power, they see almost no redeeming features in our current spending patterns. In their eyes, consumers and workers are hapless victims. Ill-informed and poorly disciplined, they are simply no match for the sophisticated manipulations of Madison Avenue, or for the raw power of wealthy employers. Inequality is seen as the exclusive result of class and privilege, great fortunes the result of ill-gotten market power.

The left's preferred alternative to capitalism's unbridled free-for-all was once something like the collectively managed economies of the former Soviet Union, but events were of course to reject that vision decisively. More recently, progressives have been treading water, carping here and there about the specifics of conservative proposals, but unable to offer a coherent vision of their own.

The left's current favored remedy is regulation—often detailed, intrusive, prescriptive regulation of what people and corporations can do—and if that doesn't work, then even heavier doses of the same. In Europe, where the left's ideas have traditionally held greater sway than in the United States, these views have led to far more extensive regulation than we see here. Yet there is prescriptive regulation aplenty even in this country, and good reasons for fearing that it does more harm than good.

To their credit, social reformers on the left seem to have recognized that our current spending patterns are deeply problematic. But they miss the mark when they interpret these patterns as the result of the strong exploiting the weak. Indeed, on close examination, our current consumption patterns appear to have little to do with class privilege and abuse of monopoly power. It is true, of course, that the children of high-income families are more likely to have high incomes than the children of low-income families. Yet there is enormous disparity in incomes even when we control for parents' economic status. Given the way winner-take-all markets amplify even small differences in talent, the sad truth is that substantial inequality would remain even if everyone had an absolutely equal start in life.

As for the left's portrayal of us as hapless consumers, we may indeed often lack relevant information and self-discipline, yet the same can be said of the legislators and bureaucrats whom the left would entrust to regulate us. In any case, we are remarkably good, for the most part, at pursuing our own interests as individuals. Monopolies, or near monopolies, exist in many markets, but even the sole supplier of any good or service is held in check by the threat that a potential rival may enter. What is more, many of the ills that the left attributes to monopoly power—unsafe working conditions, long hours, low pay—appear to be attributes not of monopolies but of labor markets that employ primarily unskilled workers. Many of these markets are among the most bitterly competitive in the economy. The reason the unskilled feel pressure to choose relatively unsafe jobs is not that employers with market power exploit them, but rather that they desperately need more money. People who are employed by the most powerful firms typically fare much better. Microsoft is close to a monopoly in many important software markets, but it needs its talented programmers every bit as much as they need Microsoft.

Although we have seen a substantial body of evidence consistent with the claim that our current consumption patterns are profoundly wasteful, we are unlikely to reach consensus on ways of changing these patterns until we can agree on *why* they are wasteful. What is it, exactly, that makes the invisible hand go awry?

THE INVISIBLE HAND RECONSIDERED

I hasten to emphasize that, in posing the question in these terms, I do not mean to suggest that Adam Smith's invisible hand idea has had a negative impact on the course of human history. On the contrary, free-market economies all over the globe, whose institutions were inspired by it, have prospered to a degree that even Smith himself would have found difficult to imagine. Contrast theirs to the experience of the former Soviet Union and other collectively managed economies. Organized on the principle that government ownership and management of the means of production would best serve society's ends, these experiments have invariably proved dismal failures.

We must be careful, however, not to infer too much from this contrast. It tells us not that the economy-as-free-for-all is the best of all possible arrangements, but only that it works far better than the economy-as-bureaucratic-committee. As even the most ardent free-market economists have long recognized, the invisible hand cannot always be expected to deliver. In particular, the individual pursuit of self-interest will not result in the greatest good for all when each individual's well-being depends on the actions taken by others.

This qualification was once thought to justify collective action in only a limited number of arenas—most importantly, the regulation of environmental pollution. We now recognize, however, that the interdependencies among us are considerably more pervasive. For present purposes, chief among them are the ways in which the spending decisions of some individuals affect the frames of reference within which others make important choices.

Many important rewards in life—access to the best schools, to the most desirable mates, and even, in times of famine, to the food needed for survival—depend critically on how the choices we make compare to the choices made by others. The person who stays at the office two hours longer each day to be able to afford a house in a better school district probably has no conscious intention to make it more difficult for others to achieve the same goal. Yet that is an inescapable consequence of his action. The best response available to others may be to work longer hours as well, thereby to preserve their current positions. Yet the ineluctable mathematical logic of musical chairs assures that only 10 percent of all children can occupy top-decile school seats, no matter how many hours their parents work.

That many goods become more attractive to us when others also have them means that consumption spending has much in common

with a contagious illness. The explosive proliferation of sport-utility vehicles in American parking lots is simply unintelligible if we adopt the
orthodox view that each person's consumption choices have no impact
on the choices made by others. Economists who insist otherwise will
someday be categorized with physicians who failed to acknowledge the
germ theory of disease.

In a world in which context is often decisive, the $1,000 bottles of
wine drunk by the rich make the $100 bottles drunk by the near rich
seem no longer quite good enough, and so on down the income ladder.
Although the channels through which one person's spending influences another's are often psychological, far more tangible costs and
benefits are at stake as well, as when the 6,000-pound Range Rovers of
the rich lead many of the rest of us to seek shelter in sport-utility vehicles of our own. The fact that our current spending patterns have all
the trappings of a luxury fever is most parsimoniously explained by
noting that, in a very real sense, they *are* a luxury fever.

That unbridled competitive forces often do not lead to the greatest
good for all is neither a new idea nor a radical one. It was clearly evident in the writings of Charles Darwin, who saw that competition frequently creates fundamental conflicts between the interests of
individual animals and those of broader groups. Male elks would do
better if all had narrower racks of antlers, and peacocks would do better if all had shorter tailfeathers. Yet any individual who deviated from
the prevailing norm would be at a hopeless disadvantage. In precisely
similar ways, many spending decisions that are adaptive for the individual are maladaptive for society as a whole. Far from being a principle that applies in most circumstances, the invisible hand is valid only
in the special case in which each individual's rewards are completely independent of the choices made by others. In the rivalrous world we
live in, precious few examples spring to mind.

This is the bad news. The good news is that there exists a simple
remedy. If the problem is that conspicuous consumption is misleadingly
attractive, the most straightforward response is to make it less attractive
by taxing it. The same arguments that have persuaded economists that
effluent taxes are the best way to curb excessive pollution suggest that

consumption taxes are the best way to curb conspicuous consumption. Phased in gradually, a steeply progressive consumption tax would curb the current rapid growth of spending on larger houses and faster cars, in the process freeing up resources that can be put to much better uses. Such a tax would also be simple to administer. Indeed, a progressive levy on the difference between income and savings could be made far simpler than our current income tax.

Like all taxes, of course, the progressive consumption tax would limit our ability to pursue certain options. But unlike our current income tax, it would also increase our ability to pursue other options. Someone who would have spent $400,000 on the best available performance car in the year 2010 might no longer be able to afford that car. Because others would be similarly affected, however, the cheaper car he and others would choose instead would end up being just as thrilling. And since all savings would be exempt from tax, he and others could retire sooner if they chose to. By the same token, because the tax would reduce the growth in spending needed to meet community consumption standards, people could spend more time with family and friends, or more time exercising. What is more, by diverting resources from conspicuous consumption, we could restore our long neglected public infrastructure and repair our tattered social safety net.

Milton Friedman and many other free marketeers will object to higher taxes in any form, saying that no government bureaucrat ever spends people's money with the same care as they themselves spend it. The best society, in this view, is one in which the largest possible proportion of spending decisions are made at the individual level.

We have little reason to doubt Friedman's claim that most people know what pleases them better than bureaucrats do. But this claim simply does not imply that market incentives lead individuals to make choices that are best for all. Indeed, even Friedman concedes that at least some decisions are *not* best left in the hands of individuals— again, the most commonly cited examples being those with respect to activities that generate pollution. Yet ordinary consumption spending is often *precisely* analogous to activities that generate pollution. When some job seekers buy custom-tailored interview suits, they harm other job seekers in the same way that motorists harm others when they disconnect the catalytic converters on their cars. Yet in each case, the rational individual response to market incentives is to take these harmful actions. And we have no reason to believe that the stresses people experience in trying to keep up with escalating community consumption standards are any less damaging to their health and longevity than the soot and ozone in the air they breathe.

Traditional liberals continue to argue against Milton Friedman on paternalistic grounds. We need government's help, they say, to protect us from both exploitation and our own human frailties. But these are losing arguments. Even though most of us aren't the perfectly informed rational actors assumed in economic orthodoxy, we are reasonably good at discerning our interests and acting on them. To be sure, advertising influences human behavior, just as liberal social critics charge. And yet conspicuous consumption long predates Madison Avenue and the information age.

The problem is not that we fail to perceive our interests as individuals, or fail to pursue them with sufficient diligence. On the contrary, it is that we do so only too well. Given the kinds of economic decisions we face, actions that are smart for one are all too often dumb for all. Traditional liberals will continue to lose their arguments with Milton Friedman until they recognize that, as with excessive environmental pollution, the real source of our skewed consumption patterns is the gap between individual and group incentives.

WRONGHEADED ECONOMIC POLICIES

If the diagnosis of the problem is wrong, we should not be surprised when remedies based on that diagnosis fail. Such has been true for many of the remedies proposed by right and left, with results that have proved enormously costly in recent years.

The cornerstone of conservative economic policy since the early 1980s has been tax reduction. Motivated by the twin beliefs that lower tax rates would pay for themselves by spurring economic growth and that the results of individual spending decisions are invariably benign, conservative governments in both the United States and the United Kingdom implemented wholesale reductions in the tax rates facing top earners. The legacy of these steps, of course, has been a massive run-up in government debt and additional fuel for the luxury-consumption bonfire. Now, astonishingly, conservatives in the United States urge us to adopt the so-called flat tax, which would further reduce the tax rates on top earners by more than half.

Though no less well intentioned than the policies of the right, many of the economic policies favored by the left have also proved counterproductive. Trust-busting, for example, has been far more likely to penalize the developers of successful products than to result in lower prices or to eliminate imbalances in our consumption patterns.

Consider also the Byzantine regulations of private labor contracts in many European countries, which—in combination with generous levels of public assistance for people without work—have been an important factor behind persistent double-digit unemployment rates on the Continent. Labor regulations have made it so costly and complicated to hire workers, to employ them lawfully, and to fire them when necessary, that many employers have simply turned to outside contractors for products they used to make for themselves. In contrast to the static employment figures in many European markets, the relatively less regulated U.S. labor market has generated more than 14 million new jobs since 1993, a period during which the unemployment rate has been consistently near or below 5 percent.[1]

Confronted with these figures, many European government officials complain that whereas employment growth in the United States has consisted mainly of low-paying jobs, European regulations assure that all jobs are quality jobs. Even apart from the inaccuracy of this characterization of new U.S. jobs (many of which are in high-tech start-up firms that offer generous wages and benefits), the European response is curious. As Joseph Stiglitz, former chairman of the Council of Economic Advisors in the Clinton administration, described it, "They seem to be saying, 'we haven't created any new jobs, but if we had created any, they would have been good ones.' "[2]

RIGHT POLICIES FOR THE WRONG REASONS

Of course, failure to diagnose a problem correctly does not *guarantee* that a faulty remedy will be adopted. It merely makes that outcome more likely. There are at least several instances in which the remedies proposed by the left appear to have done some good despite having been adopted for essentially the wrong reasons. This is a fair characterization, for example, of certain workplace safety regulations and other regulations that limit work hours. Liberals defend these regulations on the grounds that they are needed to protect workers from being exploited by firms with market power. Yet, as noted, these regulations are most frequently binding in labor markets that, by all objective measures, would be considered highly competitive. If workers in these industries work too many hours, or are subject to unacceptably dangerous conditions, it is not because they are at the mercy of employers with market power.

As we have seen, however, there are other reasons that might lead people to work too many hours or to take too many safety risks. Both steps, after all, offer a means to get ahead. Yet when all work longer hours or take greater risks, the resulting increments in absolute pay leave relative position unchanged. If laws that limit working hours and exposure to health and safety risks improve matters, it is because they counteract this discrepancy between individual and group incentives.

Concerning the regulation of vacation time, the evidence suggests that Europeans have come closer to striking the right balance than Americans have. In the United States, where labor law leaves the length of vacation time entirely up to employers and workers, entry-level jobs seldom offer more than 10 days of vacation a year, and one-week vacations are common. By contrast, the labor laws of many European countries call for four weeks or more of vacation each year for entry-level workers. Given the evident lack of utility from across-the-board increases in consumption financed by the extra weeks of work, a case can be made for moving toward the European model.

OUR CURRENT TRAJECTORY

Although it is always difficult to change the status quo, continuing on our current course is hardly an appetizing prospect. The forces that have produced rapidly growing income inequality in recent decades show no signs of abating. Thus, as communications networks continue to improve, as shipping costs continue to decline, and as global competition continues to intensify, well-positioned players in winner-take-all markets will take home ever increasing slices of the global economic pie. And as the winners continue to grow richer, they will naturally spend much of their newfound wealth on larger houses, more luxurious automobiles, and a variety of other conspicuous-consumption items. The gas grills advertised in the upmarket catalogs mailed out a decade hence will sell not for $5,000 but $10,000. Instead of two ancillary range-top burners, they will have three or four, each capable of churning out not 15,000 BTUs but 20,000. Chief executives will have to signal their wealth and position by building houses with not 50,000 square feet of living space but 100,000; by buying cars that cost not $100,000 but $200,000; wristwatches that cost not $25,000 but $50,000; and so on.

These new higher levels of spending will cause continued escalation in the community consumption standards that others feel compelled to meet. Overdue debt and personal bankruptcies will continue to rise. Investment in our public infrastructure will fall even farther behind. And the already miserable standard of living in our inner cities will continue to deteriorate. When we complain, our elected leaders will tell us that budget deficits—having soared to new record levels because of baby boomer retirements—make them powerless to act. Yet we continue to accumulate luxury goods as if we had money to burn.

How absurd. With national income in the United States now more than $8 trillion a year—an average of almost $30,000 for every man, woman, and child—it is ludicrous to pretend that we cannot afford to repair our infrastructure and provide better opportunities for the poor, or that we cannot afford more time for our families and friends. These goals and more are within easy reach. The only required sacrifice is a temporary reduction in our rate of growth in spending on luxury consumption. If we opt to remain on our current course, we will be saying, in effect, that continued growth in luxury consumption is our overriding social goal.

Our alternative is to change our current course by adopting a progressive consumption tax, which, by temporarily holding future expenditures on luxury products at roughly their current levels, will free up resources to meet much more pressing needs. Defenders of the status quo will object that making this move would deprive the people of the right to decide for themselves how best to spend their own money. But this makes no more sense than objecting that a tax on pollution deprives polluters of the right to decide for themselves how much toxic waste to dump into the environment. In both cases, individual choices have negative consequences for others, and there are clear reasons for believing that we will get better results if we change our incentives. In both cases, moreover, it is not an alien government that takes this action, as defenders of the status quo are wont to say. Rather, the same logic that leads us to instruct our elected representatives to alter incentives regarding pollution also provides a reason to instruct them to alter our incentives regarding consumption spending.

By adopting a progressive consumption tax, we would not cause the federal bureaucracy to become more bloated. Nor would we force ourselves to engage in painful acts of self-denial. Nor would we interfere with incentives to create new wealth, properly measured. And nor, finally, would we have to compromise any of our cherished economic and political freedoms. A progressive consumption tax would merely render further growth in luxury consumption less attractive relative to alternative ways of spending our time and money.

On what grounds, then, might we defend a decision to remain on our current trajectory? How might we explain to our grandchildren why we pursued further embellishments of our outdoor cooking appliances at the expense of safer highways and cleaner air? Or why we found continued escalation in the amounts spent on Patek Philippe wristwatches and Hermés handbags more important than cleaner drinking water and safer food? Or why we thought we could not afford to provide better opportunities for inner-city children?

CASH ON THE TABLE

Cash on the table is the economist's familiar metaphor for situations in which people seem to be passing up opportunities for gain. In the United States alone, we leave several trillion dollars on the table each year as a result of the waste inherent in our current consumption patterns. Much of this waste can be curbed by a disarmingly simple policy change—in essence, a one-line amendment that exempts savings from the federal income tax. Adoption of this change would free up resources that would greatly enhance our ability to pursue our respective visions of the good life.

The only intelligible reason for having stuck with our current spending patterns for so long is that we haven't clearly understood their sources and how painless it would be to change them. But we now have all the evidence we could reasonably demand on these points. With a prodigious amount of cash on the table and a host of good ways to use it, we stand poised to seize by far the most exciting economic and social policy opportunity of the modern era.

Will it happen any time soon? As a much younger man, I would have thought surely yes—expecting that once the relevant evidence had even the most minimal opportunity to circulate, legislators would rush to act. As I have long since discovered, however, things rarely play out this simply.

Imagine that as a member of Congress, you are persuaded of the merits of the progressive consumption tax and are considering sponsoring a bill to enact it. In an era in which political positions must be communicated in 10-second television sound bites, you can anticipate that few of your constituents will ever get to hear the *reasons* for your position. But you can be sure that, if you do go forward, your next challenger will spare no expense to remind voters that you are an advocate of higher taxes. You also know that, despite your best efforts to explain why a consumption tax is different from an income tax, this charge will cost you, for in the minds of many voters, support for higher taxes has come to symbolize advocacy of government waste.

Faced with these realities, it is easy to see how your most prudent course might be to try to solidify your political base for a few more years before moving forward with your proposal. And because the same incentives will also confront other potential backers of the progressive consumption tax, it seems clear that this tax will prove difficult even to *talk* about publicly, much less to advocate.

If optimism about the short-run prospects for the progressive consumption tax is unwarranted, it is also a mistake to be too pessimistic. Indeed, we may hope that the historical tendency for good ideas to triumph over bad ones in the long run will continue. Sometimes change comes only at the initiative of actors whose positions on sensitive issues are so clear in the public's mind as to run no possible risk of misinterpretation. For instance, among postwar American presidents, only Richard Nixon, the lifelong communist basher, was in a position to reopen diplomatic relations with China; and among Israel's leaders, only Menachem Begin, the hawk among hawks, could have launched peace talks with the Palestinians. By the same token, the political champions of the progressive consumption tax may be most likely to emerge from the ranks of lifelong vocal opponents of wasteful government spending.

MONEY FOR NOTHING

Whatever its political future, the progressive consumption tax is, on the best available evidence, a compellingly good idea—one that will free up literally trillions of dollars each year to spend in ways that will create lasting improvements in the quality of our lives. This is money for nothing, in the sense that we can get it without having to sacrifice anything of enduring value. If the evidence we have seen is correct, we will almost certainly adopt the progressive consumption tax sooner or later. Yet the realities of political discourse make this more likely to happen later rather than sooner. In the meantime, our current incentives assure that we will keep on spending more and more money for nothing.

ENDNOTES

Chapter 1. Money Well Spent

1. Strauss, 1997, p. 7A.
2. Ibid.
3. Wallis, 1997, p. 17.
4. Campbell, 1981, p. 68.
5. Takahashi, 1997, p. A6.
6. Ibid.

Chapter 2. The Luxury Spending Boom

1. Cantrell, 1996, p. 290.
2. Ibid.
3. Starr, 1995, p. 7B.
4. Cantrell, 1996.
5. Veblen, 1899, p. 74.
6. Klepper and Gunther, 1996.
7. Spayd, 1996, p. C1.
8. Whitaker, 1997, p. 10F.
9. Canedy, 1996, p. D6.
10. Kuczynski, 1998, p. 3.
11. Keates, 1997, p. B1.
12. Ibid.
13. Ibid.
14. Ibid. p. B10.
15. Pressler, 1997, p. H1.
16. Kuczynski, 1998, p. 3.
17. Pressler, 1997, p. H1.
18. Carrier, 1998, p. D1.

19. Ibid.
20. Canedy, 1996.
21. Shnayerson, 1997, p. 190.
22. Ibid.
23. Ibid., p. 188.
24. Ibid.
25. Heath, 1997, p. 38.
26. Shnayerson, 1997, p. 194.
27. Ibid.
28. Heath, 1997, p. 37.
29. Canedy, 1996, p. A1.
30. Keates, 1997, p. B10.
31. Heath, 1997, p. 37.
32. Suris, 1996, p. B1.
33. Associated Press, 1998, p.CN3.
34. Lienert, 1998, p. W3.
35. Healey and Eldridge, 1996, p. B1.
36. Henderson, 1998, p. B1.
37. Ibid.
38. Brooke, 1996, p. A10.
39. Fatsis, 1997, p. B10.
40. Ibid.
41. Ibid.
42. Ibid., p. B10.
43. Brown, 1996, p. 39.
44. Molpus, 1997.
45. Harte, 1997, p. G2.
46. West, 1998, p. B1.
47. Ibid.
48. Ibid.
49. Ibid., p. B6.
50. Paik, 1998, p. W.10.
51. Moonan, 1998, p. E37.
52. Sharpe, 1996, p. B1.
53. Ibid., p. B1.
54. Ibid.
55. Daspin, 1997, p. B10.
56. Ibid.
57. Ibid.
58. Shnayerson, 1997, p. 200.
59. Carrier, 1998, p. D1.
60. Ibid.
61. Ibid.
62. Hardy, 1996, p. A12.
63. Ibid.
64. Uchitelle, 1997, p. A1.

65. Carrier, 1998, p. D1.
66. Bird, 1996, p. B4.
67. Snead, 1996, p. D2.
68. *The Economist,* January 11, 1992, p. 25.
69. Snead, 1996.
70. Ibid.
71. Ibid.
72. Ibid., p. D2.
73. Berton, 1997, p. B1.
74. Ibid.
75. Snead, 1996, p. D2.
76. Fletcher, 1997, p. B8.
77. Ibid.
78. Ibid.
79. Paik, 1996, p. B1.
80. Ibid, p. B14.
81. Hardy, 1996, p. A1.
82. Ibid.
83. Quoted by Hardy, 1996.
84. Brown, 1996, p. 39.
85. Ibid.
86. Hardy, 1997, p. A1.
87. Peers, 1997, p. B8.
88. Meltzer, 1997, p. 32.
89. Ibid.
90. Ibid.
91. Hardy, 1997, p. A1.
92. Ibid.
93. Ibid.
94. Hardy, 1997, p. A1.
95. Hubbard, 1997, p. 5.
96. Buzz Online, 1996.
97. Associated Press, 1997, p. 6B
98. Ibid.
99. Pacenti, 1996, p. 6.
100. Ibid.
101. Shnayerson, 1997, p. 188.
102. Canute, 1997, p. 54.
103. Brooks, 1996, p. D1.
104. Ibid.
105. Ibid.
106. Ibid.
107. Pitt, 1991, p. 83.
108. See for example, Chanda, 1997; Faruqi, 1997; Lucier, 1997; Moin, 1998; and Singer, 1998.
109. Galuszka, 1993, p. 40.

Chapter 3. Why Now?

1. Heath, 1997, p. 33.
2. Krugman, 1992.
3. Frank and Cook, 1995, p. 88.
4. Burtless, 1996b.
5. Hacker, 1995.
6. Bates, 1997, p. D4.
7. Shnayerson, 1997, p. 188.
8. Heath, 1997, p. 33.
9. West, 1998, p. B6.
10. Hardy, 1996, p. A12.
11. Peers, 1997, p. B8.
12. Gabriel, 1997, p. B8.
13. Truell, 1997, p. D1.
14. Shnayerson, 1997, p. 182.
15. Truell, 1997, p. D1.
16. Ibid.
17. McGeehan, 1997, p. A6.
18. Gabriel, 1997.
19. Berton, 1997, p. B1.
20. Frank and Cook, 1995.
21. LeBlanc, 1995.
22. Frank and Cook, 1995, p. 70.
23. Bertrand, 1997; Gokhal et al., 1995.
24. Crystal, 1991.
25. *The Economist,* November 5, 1994, p. 19.
26. *The Guardian,* November 25, 1996, p. 12.
27. *The Economist,* November 5, 1994, p. 19.
28. Perez-Pena, 1997, p. A1.
29. *The Economist,* December 20, 1997, p. 28.

Chapter 4. The Price of Luxury

1. Berner, 1997, p. A2.
2. *Business Wire,* 1997.
3. Ibid.
4. Ibid.
5. Canner, et al., 1995, p. 323.
6. Hays, 1996, p. B1.
7. Simmons, 1995, pp. 207, 208.
8. Hays, 1996, p. B1.
9. Ibid., p. B6.
10. Koss-Feder, 1997, Sec. 3, p. 10.
11. Selz, 1997, p. A1.

12. Ibid.
13. Ibid.
14. DeMarrais, 1997, p. B1.
15. Hays, 1996.
16. Cobb, Halstead, and Rowe, 1995.
17. Crossen, 1996, R4.
18. Selz, 1997.
19. Hays, 1996, p. B6.
20. Ibid.
21. Ibid.
22. Barker, 1997, p. D1.
23. Schlesinger, 1998, p. A1.
24. *Business Wire,* 1997.
25. Barker-Benfield, 1997, p. D1.
26. Cross, 1993.
27. Linder, 1970, p. 143.
28. Schor, 1991, p. 29.
29. Quoted by Mueller, 1997, p. 6.
30. Dauten, 1997, p. 11.
31. Reported by Shellenbarger, 1998, p. B1.
32. See Juster and Stafford, 1990; and Roberts and Rupert, 1995.
33. Wallich, 1994.
34. Wuthnow, 1996, p. 22.
35. Reported by Wuthnow, 1996, Chapter 1, n.8.
36. Hugick and Leonard, 1991, p. 10.
37. Reported by Shellenbarger, 1997, p. D3.
38. Ibid., p. D3.
39. Green, 1996, p. 8A.
40. Gallup Poll, quoted by Wuthnow, ch. 1, n. 15.
41. Troufexis, 1990, p. 78.
42. Maas, 1998.
43. Reported by Alston, 1997, p. A22.
44. Hochschild, 1997. See also Leete and Schor, 1994.
45. Hugick and Leonard, 1991, p. 10.
46. Reported by Ward, 1997, p. 12.
47. Ibid.
48. Reported by Schellhardt, 1996, p. B1.
49. Ibid.
50. Ibid.
51. Shellenbarger, 1997, p. B1.
52. Carrns, 1997, p. B1.
53. Ibid.
54. Pacelle, 1996, p. B1.
55. Ibid.

56. Ibid.
57. Quoted by Masters et al., 1998.
58. Cohen et al., 1996, p. 1.
59. Bryce-Smith, 1986.
60. Bryce-Smith, 1983.
61. Hester, 1996.
62. For a survey of the relevant literature, see Masters et al., 1998.
63. Ibid.
64. Gottschalk et al., 1991; Brody et al., 1994.
65. Fairhall and Neal, 1943.
66 Donaldson et al., 1981; Masters et al., 1993.
67. Pope, 1989.
68. Consumers Union, 1997.
69. Ibid.
70. Ibid.
71. Ibid.
72. Lobsenz, 1997.
73. Myers, 1997.
74. Manning, 1997, p. 1A.
75. Quoted by Manning, 1997, p. 1A.
76. Bor, 1997, p. 1A.
77. Marwick, 1997, p. 1341.
78. Gerth and Weiner, 1997, p. A10.
79. Ibid., p. A1.
80. Harty, 1996, p. 47.
81. Ibid.
82. Loeb and Page, 1997.
83. Bok, 1993.
84. Loeb and Page, 1997.
85. Steinberg, 1997, p. A40.
86. Simmons, 1997, p. A1.
87. Sjostrom, 1997, p. 1.
88. Van Voorst, 1992, p. 64.
89. DOT, 1991, quoted by Smith and Bush, 1997.
90. Quoted by Sjostrom, 1997.
91. Ibid.
92. PR Newswire, 1997.
93. McGuire, 1997, p. A3.
94. Wheeler, 1997, p. 1A.
95. Ibid.
96. Ibid.
97. Rice et al., 1991.
98. Copple, 1997.
99. Ibid.
100. Ibid.

101. Ibid.
102. Cited by Copple, 1997.

Chapter 5. Does Money Buy Happiness?

1. Nozick, 1974, p. 42.
2. Ibid., p. 43.
3. Cobb, Halstead, and Rowe, 1995.
4. Galbraith, 1967.
5. Bradburn, 1969; Diener and Emmons, 1985.
6. Hoebel, 1998.
7. Diener and Emmons, 1985.
8. Diener and Lucas, 1998.
9. Kahneman, 1998.
10. See Easterlin, 1974.
11. Goleman, 1996, p. C3.
12. Davidson, 1992.
13. Reported by Goleman, 1996.
14. For surveys of this evidence see Frank, 1985b, chapter 2; and Clark and Oswald, 1996.
15. Myers, 1993.
16. Bradburn, 1969.
17. Diener and Lucas, 1998.
18. Bradburn and Caplovitz, 1965.
19. Myers and Diener, 1995, p. 11.
20. Seidlitz and Diener, 1993.
21. Headey and Wearing, 1992; and Sandvik et al., 1993.
22. Diener and Lucas, 1998.
23. Diener and Diener, 1995.
24. Ibid.
25. Smolensky, 1965.
26. Rainwater, 1990.
27. Kapteyn and van Praag, 1976. See also Duncan, 1975–76.
28. Galbraith, 1958, p. 1.

Chapter 6. Gains That Endure

1. Townsend, 1979.
2. Loewenstein and Frederick, 1998.
3. Bulman and Wortman, 1977.
4. Cameron, 1972; Cameron, Titus, Kostin and Kostin, 1976.
5. Brickman, Coates, and Janoff-Bulman, 1978.
6. Myers, 1993, p.36.
7. For a survey, see Koslowsky et al., 1995.
8. Glass, et al., 1977.

9. Ibid.
10. Weinstein, 1982.
11. Glass, 1977.
12. Ibid., figures 5 and 6.
13. Long and Perry, 1985.
14. Ragland et al., 1987; Pikus and Tarranikova, 1975; and Evans et al., 1987.
15. Evans et al., 1987.
16. Evans and Carrere, 1991.
17. Evans, 1994.
18. Glass and Singer, 1972; Sherrod, 1974.
19. Stokols et al., 1978.
20. Ibid., table 3.
21. DeLongis et al., 1988; and Stokols et al., 1978.
22. Koslowsky et al., 1995, chapter 4.
23. Koslowsky et al., 1995.
24. Taylor and Pocock, 1972; Koslowsky and Krausz, 1993.
25. European Foundation for the Improvement of Living and Working Conditions, 1984.
26. Clark, 1994, p. 387.
27. Ibid.
28. For a survey, see Plante and Rodin, 1990.
29. Fontane, 1996.
30. Blair, 1989.
31. Palmer, 1995.
32. Greist et al., 1979.
33. Lichtman and Poser, 1983.
34. Palmer, 1995.
35. Sharp, 1996, p. 4M.
36. Argyle, 1998.
37. Burt, 1986.
38. Perkins, 1991.
39. Manning and Fullerton, 1988.
40. Colon et al., 1991.
41. Berkman and Syme, 1979.
42. House et al., 1982.
43. Argyle, 1996.
44. Rubenstein, 1980.
45. Ibid.
46. Weiss, 1991, p. 141.
47. Ibid.
48. For a survey, see Warr, 1998; see also Agho et al., 1993; Fried, 1991; Kelloway and Barling, 1991; Spector and O'Connell, 1994; Spector et al., 1988; Wall et al. 1996; and Xie and Johns, 1995.
49. Deci, 1971.
50. Campion and McClelland, 1993; and Warr, 1990.

51. Agho et al., 1993; Fried, 1991; Kelloway and Barling, 1991; Warr, 1990; and Xie and Johns, 1995.

Chapter 7. Our Forgotten Future

1. Lowenstein, 1995.
2. Net savings for a given period is calculated as the total amount saved by households, firms, and government in that period minus an estimate of the amount by which the value of existing capital depreciated during the period.
3. Wuthnow, 1996, chapter 1, n. 6.
4. Cantor and Yuengart, 1994.
5. Joint Economic Committee, 1988.
6. U.S. Bureau of the Census, 1996, p. 856.
7. See Shin, 1980; and Frank and Hutchens, 1993.
8. Tierney, 1997, p. 47.
9. Energy and Environmental Analysis, Inc., 1997.
10. Friedman, 1999, chapter one.
11. Thaler, 1980.
12. Thaler, 1982, pp. 178–79.
13. Ibid., p. 179.
14. Ibid.
15. Friedman, 1999, chapter 5.

Chapter 8. Excellent, Relatively Speaking

1. Campbell, 1981.
2. Diener, Sandvik, Seidlitz, and Diener, 1993, p. 214.
3. Quoted by Myers, 1993, p. 47.
4. Lykken and Tellegen, 1996.
5. Tellegen et al., 1988.
6. Noonan, 1997.
7. Neumark and Postlewaite, 1998.
8. Ibid., table 3.
9. See Guth et al., 1982.
10. Kahneman et al., 1986, table 1.
11. See especially Kahn and Murnighan, 1993, for evidence in favor of this interpretation.
12. See, for example, Kahneman et al., 1986; Fehr et al., 1993; Fehr and Kirchsteiger, 1994; Babcock et al., 1996; Rees, 1993; Frey and Bohnet, 1995; and Guth et al., 1993. For an excellent summary of recent economics research demonstrating the existence of concerns about relative position, see Zizzo, 1997.
13. For a more complete development of the argument to follow, see my 1985 book.
14. Ball et al., 1994, 1996.
15. Koford and Tshoegl, 1998.

16. Zahavi, 1995.
17. Frank, 1985b, chapter 8.
18. Frank, 1985b, chapter 8. See also Frank, 1985a.
19. Dynan et al., 1996; Carroll, 1998.
20. In particular, it is inconsistent with the permanent income hypothesis (Friedman, 1957) and the life-cycle hypothesis (Modigliani and Brumberg, 1955).
21. See Duesenberry, 1949, Kosicki, 1987.

Chapter 9. *Why Context and Position Are So Important*

1. McEwan, 1997, p. 73.
2. More precisely, Darwin's twentieth-century interpreters say that each organism's genes create a brain that identifies and motivates behaviors that maximize the likelihood that copies of themselves will make it into future generations. See, for example, Dawkins, 1976; Barkow, Cosmides, and Tooby, 1992; and Pinker, 1997.
3. Cosmides and Tooby, 1987.
4. For an accessible account, see Damasio, 1994.
5. Ibid, pp. 193, 194.
6. For an extended discussion of this point, see my 1988 book.
7. Damasio, 1994., p.172.
8. See, for example, Solnick and Hemenway, 1998.
9. Helson, 1964.
10. Strack et al., 1990.
11. Sen, 1981, chapter 1.
12. Smith, 1952 (1776), p. 383.
13. Hirsch, 1976; Sen, 1983, 1987.
14. Layard, 1980, p. 741.
15. Dawkins, 1976.
16. Wright, 1994.
17. Ibid.
18. Elias, August 19, 1997.
19. Diener and Lucas, 1998.
20. Quoted by Kuczynski, 1998, p. 3.
21. See McGuire, Raleigh, and Brammer, 1982.
22. Ibid.
23. Raleigh et al., 1986.
24. McGuire, personal communication.
25. Madsen, 1994.
26. Coppen, 1973; see also the summary discussion in Barchas and Usdin, 1973.
27. Coccaro, 1995.
28. See, for example, Mazur, 1983; Mazur and Lamb, 1980; and Elias, 1981.
29. See Rose, Bernstein, and Gordon, 1975.
30. Wilkinson, 1994, p. 27.
31. Wilkinson, 1986, 1990.
32. Marmot et al., 1984.
33. Wilkinson, 1994, pp. 31, 32.
34. Marmot, 1995, surveys the results of the two major Whitehall Studies.

35. Marmot et al., 1978.
36. Marmot et al., 1991.
37. Wilkinson, 1996.
38. Marmot, 1997.

Chapter 10. Smart for One, Dumb for All

1. For an engaging and lucid account of these exceptions, see Cronin, 1991.
2. Cronin, 1991.
3. Hamilton and Zook, 1982
4. Noonan, 1997.
5. Windsor and Dumitru, 1988.
6. See Frank and Cook, 1995, chapter 8.
7. Bauder, 1997, p. C1.
8. Hardin, 1968.

Chapter 11. Understanding Conspicuous Consumption

1. Landers, Rebitzer, and Taylor, 1996.
2. Solnick and Hemenway, 1998.
3. Eherenberg and Schuman, 1982; Roche et al., 1996.
4. See Frank, 1985b, chapters 7 and 8.
5. Smith, *Wealth of Nations,* Book IV, chapter 2.

Chapter 12. Self-Help

1. *The Standard Directory of Advertisers,* various volumes.
2. See Bandura, Ross, and Ross, 1963.
3. Reported in Cannon, 1993.
4. Tversky and Kahneman, in Kahneman, Slovic, and Tversky, 1982.
5. For a discussion, see Loewenstein and Schkade, 1998.
6. See Shin, 1980; and Frank and Hutchens, 1993.
7. Ainslie, 1992, chapter 3.
8. Pattison, Sobell, and Sobell, 1977.
9. Schelling, 1980.
10. Thaler and Shefrin, 1981.
11. Fergus, April 6, 1997.
12. Thynne, Feb. 2, 1997.
13. Fergus, April 6, 1997.
14. Andrews, 1997.
15. Fergus, April 13, 1997.
16. Goldstein, 1997, p. B2.
17. Continelli, 1997, p. 1F.
18. McCarty, 1997.
19. Goldstein, 1997, p. B2.

Chapter 13. Other Failed Remedies

1. Scott, 1973, p. 74, quoted by Hunt, 1996, p. 19.
2. Hunt, 1996, p. 23.
3. Ibid., p. 24.
4. Ibid., p. 353.
5. Othman, 1997, p. 7.
6. Ibid.
7. Vincent, 1969, p. 47.
8. Knaff, 1997, p. E2.
9. Kessler, 1997, p. E1.
10. Hunt, 1996, p. 353.
11. Smith, 1952 (1776), p. 150.
12. Hunt, 1996, p. 357.
13. On this point see Elster, 1989.
14. Segal, 1996, pp. 20ff.
15. Putnam, 1995.
16. Coffield, 1970, p. 24.
17. U.S. House of Representatives, Committee on Ways and Means, 1918.
18. Cnossen, 1977, p. 134.
19. Smith, 1952 (1776), p. 370.
20. Ibid., p. 316.
21. DiRe, 1991.
22. Berry, 1994, p. 214.

Chapter 14. Luxury Without Apology

1. For an excellent survey, see Dorris, 1996.
2. Carroll, 1998.
3. Hobbes, 1651, chapter 30, *Leviathan,* quoted by Seidman, 1997, p. 12.
4. Kaldor, 1955, pp. 11–13.
5. Fisher and Fisher, 1942, pp. 3–6, quoted by Seidman, 1997, p. 14.
6. Ibid., quoted by Seidman, 1997, p. 12.
7. For an excellent review, see Seidman, 1997.
8. Indeed, Friedman is the author of an eloquent paper in which he urged the government to finance swollen World War II budgets with a progressive consumption tax. (Friedman, 1943.)
9. Seidman, 1997.

Chapter 15. Equity Versus Efficiency: The Great Trade-Off?

1. Greenspan, 1997, p. A1.
2. Higgins, 1992, p. 38.
3. See Ehrenberg and Smith, 1994, p. 33.
4. See, for example, Feldstein, 1995.
5. See Auerbach and Slemrod, 1997; Hubbard and Skinner, 1996; Poterba et al., 1996; and Slemrod, 1990.

6. See especially Engen et al., 1996. The incentive effect, as conventionally measured, turns out to be small for a similar reason that tax increases seem not to have much effect on the number of hours people work. Because making savings exempt from tax is similar to increasing the effective reward someone gets from savings, it affects savings in two different ways. By increasing the reward from savings relative to the rewards from other activities, it provides an incentive to save more. At the same time, however, it also makes it possible to achieve a given savings objective by saving less. Empirical studies cannot reject the hypothesis that these two effects roughly offset one another. (See, for example, Elmendorf, 1996.)

7. Seidman and Lewis, 1996a, 1996b.

8. Engen, Gale, and Scholz, 1994.

9. Venti and Wise, 1990.

10. Murphy, Schleifer, and Vishny, 1991.

11. For a more complete discussion, see Frank and Cook, 1995.

12. Frank and Cook, 1995, chapter 5.

13. For a review, see Chiricos, 1987. See also Land et al., 1990.

14. Bursik and Grasmik, 1993.

15. See, for example, Curry and Spergel, 1988; and Taylor and Covington, 1988.

16. Blakely and Snyder, 1997.

17. Barron, 1997, p. 66.

18. Cited in Munk, 1994, p. 106

19. Cobb, Halstead, and Rowe, 1995.

20. This term was coined by the economist Robert Hall, 1972.

21. Glyn and Miliband, 1994.

22. Alesina and Rodrick, 1992.

23. Garrison and Lee, 1992; and Persson and Tabellini, 1992.

24. Corry and Glyn, 1994.

25. Seidman, 1997, chapter 2.

Chapter 16. We Can't Afford It?

1. Stewart, 1995.

2. Huston, 1996, p. 1.

3. Kozol, 1995, p. 114.

4. Ibid., pp. 151, 152, 155.

5. Quoted by Kozol, 1995, p. 21

6. Cooper, 1995.

7. Quoted by Cooper, 1995, p. 4.

8. Wilson, 1996.

9. Clark and Oswald, 1996.

Chapter 17. Cash on the Table

1. Raines, 1998.

2. Quoted by Pearlstein, 1997, p. A12.

REFERENCES

Aaron, Henry J., and William G. Gale. *Economic Effects of Fundamental Tax Reform,* Washington, DC: Brookings Institution, 1996.

Agho, Augustine O.; Charles W. Mueller; and James L. Price. "Determinants of Employee Job Satisfaction,"*Human Relations,* August, 1993: 1011–19.

Ainslie, George. *Picoeconomics,* New York: Cambridge University Press, 1992.

Alesina, Alberto, and Dani Rodrik. "Distribution, Political Conflict, and Economic Growth: A Simple Theory and Some Empirical Evidence," in *Political Economy, Growth, and Business Cycles,* ed. A. Cuckierman, Z. Hercowitz, and L. Leiderman, Cambridge: MIT Press, 1992: 23–50.

Alston, Chuck. "Comp Time's Time Has Come," *Wall Street Journal,* May 15, 1997: A22.

Andrews, Cecile. *The Circle of Simplicity: Return to the Good Life,* New York: Harper Collins, 1997.

Argyle, Michael. "Causes and Correlates of Happiness," in *Understanding Well-Being: Scientific Perspectives on Enjoyment and Suffering,* ed. Daniel Kahneman, Ed Diener, and Norbert Schwartz, New York: Russell Sage, 1998.

Argyle, Michael. *The Social Psychology of Leisure,* New York: Penguin, 1996.

Associated Press. "Americans Are Spending More on Cars," *Chicago Tribune,* March 15, 1998: CN3.

Associated Press. "Good Cigars Grow Hot," *Cincinnati Post,* February 27, 1997: 6B.

Auerbach, Alan, and Joel Slemrod. "The Economic Effects of the Tax Reform Act of 1986," *Journal of Economic Literature* XXXV, June 1997: 589–632.

Babcock, Linda; X. Wong; and George Loewenstein. "Choosing the Wrong Pond," Social Comparisons in Negotiations That Reflect a Self-Serving Bias," *Quarterly Journal of Economics* 106, 1996: 3–19.

Bagwell, Laurie Simon, and B. Douglas Bernheim. "Veblen Effects in a Theory of Conspicuous Consumption," *American Economic Review* 86, June 1996: 349–73.

Ball, Sheryl, and Catherine Eckel. "Status and Discrimination in Ultimatum Games: Stars Upon Thars," Virginia Polytechnic Institute Department of Economics, mimeographed, 1994.

Ball, Sheryl; Catherine Eckel; Philip Grossman; and William Zame. "Status in Markets," Department of Economics Working Paper, Virginia Polytechnic Institute, January 1996.

Bandura, A., D. Ross, and S. A. Ross. "Imitation of Film-Mediated Aggressive Models," *Journal of Abnormal and Social Psychology* 66, no. 1, 1963: 3–11.

Barchas, J., and E. Usdin, eds. *Serotonin and Behavior,* New York: Academic Press, 1973.

Barker-Benfield, Simon. "Booming Bankruptcies," *Florida Times-Union,* March 9, 1997: D1.

Barkow, J. H.; L. Cosmides; and J. Tooby, eds., *The Adapted Mind: Evolutionary Psychology and the Generation of Culture,* New York: Oxford University Press, 1992.

Barron, Kelly. "Your Money or Your Life," *Forbes,* November 17, 1997: 66.

Bates, James. "Company Town: Getting to the Bottom of Michael Eisner's $565-Million Payday," *Los Angeles Times,* December 4, 1997: D4.

Bauder, Don. "Banning Ads May Not Snuff Out Teen Smoking," *San Diego Union-Tribune,* July 12, 1997: C1.

Berkman, L. F., and S. L. Syme. "Social Networks, Host Resistance, and Mortality: A Nine-Year Followup of Alameda County Residents," *American Journal of Epidemiology,* 109, 1979: 186–204.

Berner, Robert. "Personal Savings Continue Steady Climb," *Wall Street Journal,* March 24, 1997: A2, A12.

Berry, Christopher. *The Idea of Luxury,* Cambridge: Cambridge University Press, 1994.

Berton, Lee. "A Rising Stock Market Also Lifts Faces, Noses, Tummies, and Necks," *Wall Street Journal,* February 24, 1997: B1.

Bertrand, Marianne. "From the Invisible Handshake to the Invisible Hand? How Product Market Competition Changes the Employment Relationship," Harvard University Department of Economics, mimeographed, 1997.

Bird, Laura. "Forget Ties; Catalogs Now Sell Mansions," *Wall Street Journal,* November 7, 1996:B1, B4.

Blair, S. N. "Physical Fitness and All-Cause Mortality: A Prospective Study of Healthy Men and Women," *Journal of the American Medical Association* 262, 1989: 2396–2401.

Blakely, Edward J., and Mary Gail Snyder. *Fortress America: Gated Communities in the United States,* Washington, DC: Brookings Press, 1997.

Blankman, Susan. "Money Does Buy Happiness Proves New Poll," *Business Wire,* January 22, 1998.

Bok, Derek. *The Cost of Talent,* New York: The Free Press, 1993.

Bor, Jonathan. "Scientists Delve into Dangers in Hamburger," *Baltimore Sun,* June 24, 1997: 1A.

Boskin, Michael, and E. Sheshinski. "Optimal Redistributive Taxation When Individual Welfare Depends on Relative Income," *Quarterly Journal of Economics* 92, 1978: 589–601.

Bosworth, Barry, and Gary Burtless. "Effects of Tax Reform on Labor Supply, Investment, and Saving," *Journal of Economic Perspectives* 6, Winter 1992: 3–25.

Boutcher, Stephen H., and Daniel M. Landers. "The Effects of Vigorous Exercise on Anxiety, Heart Rate, and Alpha Activity of Runners and Nonrunners," *Psychophysiology* 25, 1988: 696–702.

Bradburn, N., and D. Caplovitz. *Reports on Happiness,* Chicago: Aldine, 1965.

Bradburn, Norman. *The Structure of Psychological Well-Being,* Chicago: Aldine, 1969.

Bradford, David F. "The Case for a Personal Consumption Tax," in *What Should Be Taxed?,* ed. Joseph Pechman, Washington, DC: Brookings Institution, 1980: 75–113.

Breathnach, Sara Ban. *Simple Abundance,* New York: Warner Books, 1995.

Brickman, P. *Commitment, Conflict, and Caring,* Englewood Cliffs, NJ: Prentice Hall, 1987.

Brickman, P., and R. J. Bulman. "Pleasure and Pain in Social Comparison." in *Social Comparison Processes: Theoretical and Empirical Perspectives,* ed. J. M. Suls and R. L. Miller, Washington, DC: Hemisphere Publishing, 1977.

Brickman, P.; D. Coates; and R. Janoff-Bulman. "Lottery Winners and Accident Victims: Is Happiness Relative?" *Journal of Personality and Social Psychology* 36, August 1978: 917–27.

Brody, D., et al. "Blood Lead Levels in the U.S. Population," *Journal of the American Medical Association* 272, 1994: 277–83.

Brooke, James. "Tourists Win Cultural Shootout in Jackson Hole, Wyoming," *New York Times,* August 14, 1996: A10.

Brooks, Nancy Rivera. "Burning Ambition: Cigar Club Owners See Bright Future in Smoke-Filled Rooms," *Los Angeles Times,* October 25, 1996: D1.

Brown, Patricia Leigh. "Techno Dwellings for the Cyber-Egos of the Mega-Rich," *New York Times,* August 4, 1996: A1, A39.

Bryce-Smith, D. "Environmental Chemical Influences on Behaviour and Mentation," *Chem. Soc. Review* 15, 1986: 93–123.

Bryce-Smith, D. "Lead Induced Disorder of Mentation in Children," *Nutrition and Health* 1, 1983: 179–94.

Bulman, R. J., and C. B. Wortman. "Attributes of Blame and 'Coping' in the 'Real World': Severe Accident Victims React to Their Lot," *Journal of Personality and Social Psychology* 35, May 1977: 351–63.

Bursik, Robert, and Harold Grasmick. "Economic Deprivation and Neighborhood Crime," *Law and Society Review* 27, 1994: 263–83.

Burt, R. S. *Strangers, Friends, and Happiness,* GSS Technical Report No. 72, Chicago: National Opinion Research Center, University of Chicago, 1986.

Burtless, Gary. "Worsening American Income Inequality," *Brookings Review* 14, Spring 1996a: 26–31.

Burtless, Gary. "Trends in the Level and Distribution of U.S. Living Standards: 1973–1993," *Eastern Economic Journal* 22, Summer 1996b: 271–90.

Business Wire, "Credit Card Debt Reaches All-Time High Among Lower-Income Americans," Business Wire, Inc., March 24, 1997.

Buzz Online. May 1996: http://www.buzmag.com.

Cameron, P.; D. Titus; J. Kostin; and M. Kostin. *The Quality of American Life,* New York: Russell Sage, 1976.

Cameron, P. "Stereotypes about Generational Fun and Happiness Versus Self-Appraised Fun and Happiness," *The Gerontologist* 12, Summer 1972: 120–23.

Campbell, Angus. *The Sense of Well-Being in America,* New York: McGraw-Hill, 1981.

Campion, M., and C. McClelland. "Follow-up and Extension of the Interdisciplinary Costs and Benefits of Enlarged Jobs," *Journal of Applied Psychology* 78, 1993: 339–51.

Canedy, Dana. "In Retailing, Biggest Gains Come from Big Spenders," *New York Times,* December 12, 1996: A1, D6.

Canner, Glenn, Arthur Kennickell, and Charles Luckett. "Household Sector Borrowing and the Burden of Debt," *Federal Reserve Bulletin* 81, April 1995: 323–38.

Cannon, Carl. "Honey, I Warped the Kids: Television, Violence, and Children," *Mother Jones,* July 1993: 16ff.

Cantor, Nancy, and Catherine A. Sanderson. "Life Task Participation and Well-Being," in *Understanding Well-Being: Scientific Perspectives on Enjoyment and Suffering,* ed. Daniel Kahneman, Ed Diener, and Norbert Schwartz, New York: Russell Sage, 1998.

Cantor, Richard, and Andrew Yuengart. "The Baby-Boom Generation and Aggregate Savings," *Federal Reserve Bank of New York Quarterly Review,* June 22, 1994: 76ff.

Cantrell, John. "The Vanderbilts," *Town & Country,* October 1996: 290 ff.

Canute, James. "Cigars at Home in Dominican Republic," *The Financial Post* (Toronto), February 26, 1997: B1, B8.

Carey, Susan. "Why This Winter Travel Season Is Sizzling," *Wall Street Journal,* February 26, 1997: B1, B8.

Carrier, Jim. "Sailing the High-End Seas," *New York Times,* January 24, 1998: D1.

Carrns, Ann. "Office Workers Rub Elbows as More Workplaces Shrink," *Wall Street Journal,* May 7, 1997: B1, B10.

Carroll, Christopher D. "Why Do the Rich Save So Much?" in Joel Slemrod, ed., *Does Atlas Shrug: The Economic Consequences of Taxing the Rich,* New York: Oxford University Press, 1998.

Carson, Cary. ed. *Of Consuming Interests,* Williamsburg, VA: Colonial Williamsburg, 1997.

Caspersen, Erik, and Gilbert Metcalf. "Is a Value-Added Tax Regressive? Annual Versus Lifetime Incidence Measures," *National Tax Journal* XLVII, no. 4, 1994: 731–46.

Chanda, Abhik Kumar. "Indians Go on Spending Spree as Critics Cry Danger," *Agence France Presse,* February 6, 1997.

Chiricos, T. G "Rates of Crime and Unemployment: An Analysis of Aggregate Research Evidence, *Social Problems* 34, 1987: 187–212.

Clark, Andrew, and Andrew Oswald. "Satisfaction and Comparison Income," *Journal of Public Economics* 61, 1996: 359–81.

Clark, Charles S. "Traffic Congestion," *The CQ Researcher,* May 6, 1994: 387–404.

Cnossen, Sijbren. *Excise Systems: A Global Study of the Selective Taxation of Goods and Services,* Baltimore: Johns Hopkins University Press, 1977.

Cobb, Clifford; Ted Halstead; and Jonathan Rowe. "If the GDP Is Up, Why Is America Down?" *The Atlantic Monthly* 276, no. 4 October 1995: 59ff.

Coccaro, Emil F. "The Biology of Aggression," *Scientific American,* January–February, 1995: 38–47.

Coffield, James. *A Popular History of Taxation,* London: Longman, 1970.

Cohen, Brian A.; Richard Wiles; Erik Olson; and Chris Campbell. "Just Add Water," Report for Natural Resources Defense Fund, Environmental Working Group Online, http://www.ewg.org, May 1996.

Cole, H. L.; G. J. Mailath; and A. Postlewaite. "Social Norms, Savings Behavior, and Growth," *Journal of Political Economy* 100, 1992: 1092–1125.

Coleman, Mary, and John Pencavel. "Changes in the Work Hours of Male Employees, 1940–88," *Industrial and Labor Relations Review* 46, 1993: 262–83.

Colon, E.; A. Callies; M. Popkin; and P. McGlave. "Depressed Mood and Other Variables Related to Bone Marrow Transplantation Survival in Acute Leukemia," *Psychosomatics* 32, 1991: 420–25.

Condry, John. "Enemies of Exploration: Self-Initiated Versus Other-Initiated Learning," *Journal of Personality and Social Psychology* 35, 1977: 459–77.

Consumers Union. "Air Quality: Special Report," *Consumer Reports* 62, 1997: 36ff.

Continelli, Louise. "Cheap Thrills in an Era of Downsizing," *Buffalo News,* May 25, 1997: 1F.

Cooper, Mary H. "The Working Poor: Will Funding Cuts Make Their Future Grimmer?" *CQ Researcher,* November 3, 1995: 969–92.

Coppen, Alec. "Role of Serotonin in Affective Disorders," in *Serotonin and Behavior,* ed. J. Barchas and E. Usdin, New York: Academic Press, 1973.

Copple, James. "Prepared Testimony before the Senate Committee on Labor and Human Resources," *Federal News Service,* April 18, 1997.

Corry, Dan, and Andrew Glyn. "The Macroeconomics of Equality, Stability, and Growth," in *Paying for Inequality: The Economic Cost of Social Injustice,* ed. Andrew Glyn and David Miliband, London: Rivers Oram, 1994.

Cosmides, Leda, and John Tooby. "From Evolution to Behavior: Evolutionary Psychology as the Missing Link," in *The Latest on the Best: Essays on Evolution and Optimality,* ed. John Dupre, Cambridge: MIT Press, 1987.

Courant, Paul, and Edward M. Gramlich. "The Expenditure Tax: Has the Idea's Time Finally Come?" in *Tax Policy: New Directions and Possibilities,* Washington DC: Center for National Policy, 1984.

Cronin, Helena. *The Ant and the Peacock,* New York: Cambridge University Press, 1991.

Cross, Gary S. *Time and Money: The Making of Consumer Culture,* New York: Routledge, 1993.

Crossen, Cynthia. "Americans Have It All (But It Isn't Enough)," *Wall Street Journal,* September 20, 1996: R1, R4.

Crystal, Graef. *In Search of Excess,* New York: W. W. Norton, 1991.

Csikszentmihalyi, Mikhail. *Flow: The Psychology of Optimal Experience,* New York: Harper and Row, 1990.

Curry, G. D., and Irving Spergel. "Gang Homicide, Delinquency, and Community," *Criminology* 26, 1988: 381.

Damasio, Antonio R. *Decartes' Error: Emotion, Reason, and the Human Brain,* New York: G. P. Putnam and Sons, 1994.

Daspin, Eileen. "Hoarding Land as the New Weekend Hobby," *Wall Street Journal,* April 18, 1997: B10.

Dauten, Dale. "We Have No Time for Nothing, But Nothing Counts," *St. Louis Post-Dispatch,* August 4, 1997: 11.

Davidson, Richie J. "Anterior Cerebral Asymmetry and the Nature of Emotion," *Brain and Cognition* 6, 1992: 245–68.

Dawkins, Richard. *The Selfish Gene,* New York: Oxford University Press, 1976.

deCharms, R. *Personal Causation,* New York: Academic Press, 1969.

Deci, E. L., and R. M. Ryan. *Intrinsic Motivation and Self-Determination in Human Behavior,* New York: Plenum, 1985.

Deci, E. L.; N. H. Spiegel; R. M. Ryan; R. Koestner; and M. Kaufman. "The Effects of Performance Standards on Teaching Styles: The Behavior of Controlling Teachers," *Journal of Educational Psychology* 74, 1982: 853–59.

Deci, Edward L. "Effects of Externally Mediated Rewards on Intrinsic Motivation," *Journal of Personality and Social Psychology* 18, 1971: 105–15.

DeLongis, Anita; Susan Folkman; and Richard S. Lazarus. "The Impact of Daily Stress on Health and Mood: Psychological and Social Resources as Mediators," *Journal of Personality and Social Psychology* 4, 1988: 486–95.

DeMarrais, Kevin G. "Credit Study Downplays Fears," *Bergen Record,* March 13, 1997: B1.

Dember, William N.; Traci L. Galinsky; and Joel S. Warm. "The Role of Choice In Vigilance Performance," *Bulletin of the Psychonomic Society* 30, 1992: 201–4.

Diener, E., and R. A. Emmons. "The Independence of Positive and Negative Affect," *Journal of Personality and Social Psychology* 50, 1985: 1031–38.

Diener, Ed. "A Value Based Index for Measuring National Quality of Life," *Social Indicators Research* 36, 1995: 107–27.

Diener, Ed, and Carol Diener. "The Wealth of Nations Revisited: Income and the Quality of Life," *Social Indicators Research* 36, 1995: 275–86.

Diener, Ed; Marissa Diener; and Carol Diener, "Factors Predicting the Subjective Well-Being of Nations," *Journal of Personality and Social Psychology* 59, 1995: 851–64.

Diener, Ed, and Eunkook Suh. "Measuring Quality of Life: Economic, Social, and Subjective Indicators," *Social Indicators Research,* forthcoming.

Diener, Ed, and Eunkook Suh. "National Differences in Subjective Well-Being," in *Understanding Well-Being: Scientific Perspectives on Enjoyment and Suffering,* ed. Daniel Kahneman, Ed Diener, and Norbert Schwartz, New York: Russell Sage, 1998.

Diener, Ed, and Frank Fujita, "Social Comparisons and Subjective Well-Being," in *Health, Coping, and Social Comparison,* B. Buunk and R. Gibbons, Hillsdale, NJ: Erlbaum, forthcoming.

Diener, Ed, and Richard E. Lucas. "Personality and Subjective Well-Being," in *Understanding Well-Being: Scientific Perspectives on Enjoyment and Suffering,* ed. Daniel Kahneman, Ed Diener, and Norbert Schwartz, New York, Russell Sage, 1998.

Diener, Ed; Ed Sandvik; Larry Seidlitz; and Marissa Diener. "The Relationship Between Income and Subjective Well-Being: Relative or Absolute?" *Social Indicators Research* 28, 1993: 195–223.

DiRe, Elda. "Luxury Tax," *CPA Journal,* October 1991: 59–62.

Dominguez, Joe, and Vicki Robin. *Your Money or Your Life,* New York: Viking, 1992.

Donaldson, J.; F. S. Labella; and H. Gesser. "Enhanced Autooxidation of Dopamine as a Possible Basis of Manganese Neurotoxicity," *Neurotoxicology* 2, 1981: 2, 53.

Dorris, Gary W. *Redesigning Regulatory Policy: A Case Study in Urban Smog,* Ph.D. diss., Cornell University, 1996.

Duesenberry, James. *Income, Saving, and the Theory of Consumer Behavior,* Cambridge: Harvard University Press, 1949.

Duncan, Otis. "Does Money Buy Satisfaction?" *Social Indicators Research* 2, 1975–76: 267–74.

Dynan, Karen E.; Jonathan Skinner; and Stephen P. Zeldes. "Do the Rich Save More?" Columbia University Graduate School of Business, mimeographed, 1996.

Easterlin, Richard. "Does Economic Growth Improve the Human Lot?" in *Nations and Households in Economic Growth: Essays in Honor of Moses Abramovitz,* ed. Paul David and Melvin Reder, New York: Academic Press, 1974.

Easterlin, Richard. "Will Raising the Incomes of All Increase the Happiness of All?" *Journal of Economic Behavior and Organization* 27, 1995: 35–47.

Economist, The. "Bumper Profits, Sticker Shock," February 11, 1995: 57.

Economist, The. "Rising Tide, Falling Boats," December 20, 1997: 28.

Economist, The. "For Richer, For Poorer," November 5, 1994: 19–21.

Economist, The. "The Price of Beauty," January 11, 1992: 25–26.

Ehrenberg, Ronald G., and Paul Schuman. *Longer Hours or More Jobs? Amending Hours Legislation to Create Employment,* Ithaca, NY: ILR Press, 1982.

Ehrenberg, Ronald G., and Robert S. Smith. *Modern Labor Economics,* 3rd ed., New York: Harper Collins, 1994.

Elgin, Duane. *Voluntary Simplicity,* New York: Morrow, 1981.

Elias, M. "Serum Cortisol, Testosterone and Testosterone Binding Globulin Responses to Competitive Fighting in Human Males," *Aggressive Behavior* 7, 1981: 215–24.

Elias, Marilyn. "Looks Are a Plus, but Cash Is the King of Hearts," *Ithaca Journal,* August 19, 1997:B1.

Elmendorf, Douglas W. "The Effect of Interest-Rate Changes on Household Saving and Consumption: A Survey," Working Paper Number 96–27, Finance and Economics Discussion Series, Division of Research and Statistics, Division of Monetary Affairs, Federal Reserve Board, Washington, DC, July 1996.

Elster, Jon. "Social Norms and Economic Theory," *Journal of Economic Perspectives,* Fall 1989: 99–117.

Energy and Environmental Analysis, Inc., "Clearing the Air: An Updated Report on Emission Trends in Selected U.S. Cities," Washington, DC: AAA Association Communication, 1997.

Engen, Eric; William Gale; and John Karl Scholz. "The Illusory Effects of Saving Incentives on Savings," *Journal of Economic Perspectives* 10, Fall 1996: 113–38.

Engen, Eric; William Gale; and John Scholz. "Do Savings Incentives Work?" *Brookings Papers on Economic Activity* 1, 1994: 85–151.

European Foundation for the Improvement of Living and Working Conditions. "The Journey from Home to the Workplace: The Impact on the Safety and Health of the Commuters/Workers," Dublin: European Foundation for the Improvement of Living and Working Conditions, 1984.

Evans, G.; M. Palsane; and S. Carrere. "Type A Behavior and Occupational Stress: A Cross-Cultural Study of Blue-Collar Workers,"*Journal of Personality and Social Psychology* 52, 1987: 1002–7.

Evans, Gary W. "Working on the Hot Seat: Urban Bus Drivers," *Accident Analysis and Prevention* 26, 1994: 181–93.

Evans, Gary W., and S. Carrere. "Traffic Congestion, Perceived Control, and Psychophysiological Stress Among Urban Bus Drivers," *Journal of Applied Psychology* 76, 1991: 658–63.

Fairhall, L. T., and P. A. Neal. "Industrial Manganese Poisoning," National Institute of Health Bulletin No. 182: Washington, DC: U. S. Government Printing Office: 1943.

Faruqi, Anwar. "Gulf Is Big Market for Luxury Cars," *AP Online,* November 10, 1997.

Fatsis, Stefan. "Boomers Return to the Ski Slopes—To Nest," *Wall Street Journal,* January 17, 1997: B1, B10.

Fehr, Ernst, and G. Kirchsteiger "Insider Power, Wage Discrimination, and Fairness," *Economic Journal* 104, 1994: 571–83.

Fehr, Ernst; G. Kirchsteiger; and A. Riedl. "Does Fairness Prevent Market Clearing? An Experimental Investigation," *Quarterly Journal of Economics* 108, 1993: 439–59.

Feldstein, Martin. "Taxing Consumption," *New Republic,* February 28, 1976: 14–17.

Feldstein, Martin. "The Effect of Marginal Tax Rates on Taxable Income: A Panel Study of the 1986 Tax Reform Act," *Journal of Political Economy* 103, June 1995: 551–72.

Fergus, Mary Ann. "Life Unplugged: Americans Seek More Balance, Less Money," *The Pantagraph,* April 6, 1997: C2.

Fergus, Mary Ann. "Simple Living: Part II; Finding 'Bliss' in Simplicity; Living for a Simple Future," *The Pantagraph,* April 13, 1997: C1.

Fisher, Irving, and Herbert W. Fisher. *Constructive Income Taxation,* New York: Harper and Brothers, 1942.

Fletcher, June. "Withering Heights: Vying for the Views," *Wall Street Journal,* March 28, 1997: B8.

Fontane, Patrick E. "Exercise, Fitness, and Feeling Well," *American Behavioral Scientist* 39, January 1996: 288–305.

Frank, Robert H. "The Frame of Reference as a Public Good," *Economic Journal* 107, November 1997: 1832–47.

Frank, Robert H. "What Price the Moral High Ground?" *Southern Economic Journal,* July 1996: 1–17.

Frank, Robert H. "Positional Externalities," in *Strategy and Choice: Essays in Honor of Thomas C. Schelling,* ed., Richard Zeckhauser, Cambridge: MIT Press, 1992: 25–47.

Frank, Robert H. *Passions Within Reason: The Strategic Role of the Emotions,* New York: W. W. Norton, 1988.

Frank, Robert H. "The Demand for Unobservable and Other Nonpositional Goods," *American Economic Review* 75, March 1985a: 101–16.

Frank, Robert H. *Choosing the Right Pond,* New York: Oxford University Press, 1985b.

Frank, Robert H. "Are Workers Paid Their Marginal Products?" *American Economic Review* 74, September 1984: 549–71.

Frank, Robert H., and Philip J. Cook. *The Winner-Take-All Society,* New York: The Free Press, 1995.

Frank, Robert H., and Philip J. Cook. "Winner-Take-All Markets," Cornell University, 1993.

Frank, Robert H., and Robert Hutchens. "Wages, Seniority, and the Demand for Rising Consumption Profiles," *Journal of Economic Behavior and Organization* 21, 1993: 251–76.

Frey, Bruno, and Iris Bohnet. "Institutions Affect Fairness: Experimental Investigations," *Journal of Institutional and Theoretical Economics* 151, 1995: 286–303.

Fried, Y. "Meta-analytic Comparison of the Job Diagnostic Survey and Job Characteristics Inventory as Correlates of Work Satisfaction and Performance," *Journal of Applied Psychology* 76, 1991: 690–97.

Friedman, Benjamin. *Why Growth Matters: The Moral Consequences of Economic Growth* (working title), New York: Random House, forthcoming.

Friedman, Milton. *A Theory of the Consumption Function,* Princeton, NJ: Princeton University Press, 1957.

Friedman, Milton. "The Tax as a Wartime Measure," *American Economic Review* 33, March 1943: 50–62.

Frijda, Nico. "Emotions and Hedonic Experience," in *Understanding Well-Being: Scientific Perspectives on Enjoyment and Suffering,* ed. Daniel Kahneman, Ed Diener, and Norbert Schwartz, New York: Russell Sage, 1998.

Fronstin, Paul; Lawrence Goldberg; and Philip Robins. "An Analysis of the Decline in Private Health Insurance Coverage between 1988 and 1992," *Social Science Quarterly* 78, March 1997: 44–65.

Gabriel, Trip. "Six Figures of Fun," *New York Times,* February 12, 1997: B1, B8.

Gadomski, Nina. "Haute Couture; Harper College's Fashion Department Turns Out Winners," *Chicago Tribune,* March 2, 1997: 1.

Galbraith, John Kenneth. *The Affluent Society,* Boston: Houghton Mifflin, 1958.

Galbraith, John Kenneth. *The New Industrial State,* Boston: Houghton Mifflin, 1967.

Gallup, George, and Frank Newport. "Time at a Premium for Many Americans," *Gallup Poll Monthly,* November 1990: 43–56.

Galuska, Peter. "BMW, Mercedes, Rolls-Royce—Could This Be Russia?" *Business Week,* August 2, 1993.

Garrison, C., and F.-Y. Lee. "Taxation, Aggregate Activity and Growth," *Economic Inquiry* 20, 1992: 172–76.

Gerth, Jeff, and Tim Weiner. "Imports Swamp U.S. Food-Safety Efforts," *New York Times,* September 29, 1997: A1, A10.

Glass, D. C., and J. Singer. *Urban Stressors: Experiments on Noise and Social Stressors,* New York: Academic Press, 1972.

Glass, David C.; Jerome Singer; and James Pennegaker. "Behavioral and Physiological Effects of Uncontrollable Environmental Events," in *Perspectives on Environment and Behavior,* ed. Daniel Stokols, New York: Plenum, 1977.

Glyn, Andrew, and David Miliband, eds. *Paying for Inequality: The Economic Cost of Social Injustice,* London: Rivers Oram, 1994.

Gokhale, Jagdeesh; Erika Groshen; and David Neumark. "Do Hostile Takeovers Reduce Extramarginal Wages? An Establishment-Level Analysis," *Review of Economics and Statistics,* 1995: 713–40.

Goldstein, Marilyn. "It's Really Very Simple: Less Is Not Always More," *Newsday,* May 27, 1997: B2.

Goleman, Daniel. "Forget Money; Nothing Can Buy Happiness, Some Researchers Say," *New York Times,* July 16, 1996: C1, C3.

Gottschalk, L.; T. Rebello; M. S. Buchsbaum; H. G. Tucker; and E. L. Hodges. "Abnormalities in Trace Elements as Indicators of Aberrant Behavior, *Comprehensive Psychiatry* 32, 1991: 229–37.

Green, Douglas. "The Price of Being Too Busy," *Ithaca Journal,* June 1 1996: 8A.

Green, Francis, and Michael Potepan. "Vacation Time and Unionism in the U.S. and Europe," *Industrial Relations* 27, Spring 1988.

Greenspan, Alan, "Notable and Quotable," *Wall Street Journal,* March 26, 1997: A1.

Greist, J. H.; M. Klein; R. Eischens; J Faris; J. Gurman; A. Gurman; and W. Morgan. "Running as a Treatment for Depression," *Comparative Psychology* 20, 1979: 41–54.

Guardian, The. "Inequalities Rule Out Tax Cuts: Time to Help the Dispossessed," November 25, 1996: 12.

Guth, Werner; P. Ockenfels; and M. Wendel. "Efficiency by Trust in Fairness? Multiperiod Ultimatum Bargaining Experiments with an Increasing Cake," *International Journal of Game Theory* 22, 1993: 51–73.

Guth, Werner; Rolf Schmittberger; and Bernd Schwarze. "An Experimental Analysis of Ultimatum Bargaining," *Journal of Economic Behavior and Organization* 3, 1982: 367–88.

Hacker, Andrew. "Who They Are: The Upper Tail," *New York Times Magazine,* November 19, 1995: 70, 71.

Hagan, John. "Crime, Inequality, and Inefficiency," in *Paying for Inequality: The Economic Cost of Social Injustice,* ed. Andrew Glyn and David Miliband, London: Rivers Oram, 1994.

Hall, Robert E. "Why Is the Unemployment Rate So High at Full Employment?" *Brookings Papers on Economic Activity,* no. 3, 1970: 369–402.

Hall, Robert E., and Alvin Rabushka. *The Flat Tax,* 2nd ed., Stanford, CA: Hoover Institution, 1995.

Hamilton, W. D., and M. Zook. "Heritable True Fitness and Bright Birds: A Role for Parasites?" *Science* 218, 1982: 384–87.

Hardin, Garrett. "The Tragedy of the Commons," *Science* 162, 1968: 1243–48.

Hardy, Quentin. "Wine and Women," *Wall Street Journal,* April 7, 1997: A1, A5.

Hardy, Quentin. "Digital Gentry: Hot Young Companies, New Millionaires Fuel Silicon Valley Boom," *Wall Street Journal,* October 8, 1996: A1, A12.

Harte, Susan. "Today's Topic: Residential Real Estate," *Atlanta Journal,* January 31, 1997: G2.

Harty, Rosalynne. "Lack of Funds Cutting Meat Inspections," *State Journal-Register,* June 23, 1996: 47.

Hays, Laurie. "Banks' Marketing Blitz Yields Rash of Defaults," *Wall Street Journal,* September 25, 1996: B1, B6.

Headey, B., and A. Wearing. *Understanding Happiness,* Melbourne: Longman Cheshire, 1992.

Healey, James R., and Earle Eldridge. "Sport Utilities' Big Road Shcw," *USA Today,* January 5, 1996: 1B.

Heath, Rebecca Piirto. "Life on Easy Street," *American Demographics,* April 1997: 32–38.

Hedges, Janice Niepert. "Work and Leisure," *Monthly Labor Review,* May 1992: 43–54.

Helson, Harry. *Adaptation-Level Theory,* New York: Harper and Row, 1964.

Henderson, Angelo B. "U-Turn on Caddy Truck Detours GM Strategy," *Wall Street Journal,* March 26, 1998: B1, B13.

Hester, Luke C. "EPA Administrator Releases New Report on Environmental Health Threats to Children," Environmental Protection Agency, http://www.epa.gov, September 11, 1996.

Higgins, Benjamin. "Equity and Efficiency in Development," in *Equality and Efficiency in Economic Development,* ed. Donald J. Savoice and Irving Breecher, London: Intermediate Technology Publications, 1992.

Hirsch, Fred. *Social Limits to Growth,* Cambridge: Harvard University Press, 1976.

Hochman, Harold M., and J. D. Rogers. "Pareto Optimal Redistribution," *American Economic Review* 59, 1969: 542–57.

Hochschild, Arlie. *The Time Bind,* New York: Metropolitan Books, 1997.

Hoebel, Bartley. "Neural Systems for Reinforcement and Inhibition of Behavior," in *Understanding Well-Being: Scientific Perspectives on Enjoyment and Suffering,* ed. Daniel Kahneman, Ed Diener, and Norbert Schwartz, New York, Russell Sage, 1998.

House, James S.; C. Robbins; and H. M. Metzner. "The Association of Social Relationships and Activities with Mortality: Prospective Evidence from the Tecumsah Community Health Study," *American Journal of Epidemiology* 116, 1982: 123–40.

Hubbard, R. Glenn, and Jonathan Skinner. "Assessing the Effectiveness of Savings Incentives," *Journal of Economic Perspectives* 10, Fall 1996: 73–90.

Hubbard, Russell. "Forecast 1997: Luxury Purveyors Cater to Small Indulgences," *Birmingham Business Journal,* January 6, 1997: 5.

Hugick, Larry, and Jennifer Leonard. "Job Dissatisfaction Grows; 'Moonlighting' on the Rise," *Gallup Poll,* September 2, 1991.

Hunt, Alan. *Governance of the Consuming Passions,* New York: St. Martin's Press, 1996.

Huston, Margo. "Future Dim for Summer Stars," *Milwaukee Journal Sentinel,* June 10, 1996: 1.

Ireland, Norman. "On Limiting the Market for Status Signals," *Journal of Public Economics* 53, 1994: 91–110.

Ireland, Norman. "Status-Seeking, Income Taxation and Efficiency," *Journal of Public Economics,* forthcoming.

Joint Economic Committee. "U.S. Foreign Debt," hearing before the Joint Economic Committee of the United States, September 13, 1988.

Juster, F. Thomas, and Frank P. Stafford. "The Allocation of Time: Empirical Findings, Behavioral Models, and Problems of Measurement," *Journal of Economic Literature* 29, 1990: 471–522.

Kahn, Lawrence M., and J. Keith Murnighan. "A General Experimentation Bargaining in Demand Games with Outside Options, *American Economic Review* 83, December 1993: 1260–80.

Kahneman, Daniel. "Assessments of Individual Well-Being: A Bottom-Up Approach," in *Understanding Well-Being: Scientific Perspectives on Enjoyment and Suffering,* ed. Daniel Kahneman, Ed Diener, and Norbert Schwartz, New York: Russell Sage, 1998.

Kahneman, Daniel; Jack Knetsch; and Richard Thaler, "Perceptions of Unfairness: Constraints on Wealth-Seeking," *American Economic Review* 76, September 1986: 728–41.

Kahneman, Daniel; P. Slovic; and A. Tversky, eds. *Judgment Under Uncertainty: Heuristics and Biases,* New York: Cambridge University Press, 1982.

Kaldor, Nicholas. *An Expenditure Tax,* London: Allen and Unwin, 1955.

Kapteyn, Arie, and F. G. van Herwaarden. "Interdependent Welfare Functions and Optimal Income Distribution," *Journal of Public Economics* 14, 1980: 375–97.

Kapteyn, Arie, and B. M. S. van Praag. "A New Approach to the Construction of Family Equivalence Scales," *European Economic Review* 7, 1976: 313–35.

Keates, Nancy. "Sold-Out Swanky Resorts Chill Holidays for the Rich," *Wall Street Journal,* September 26, 1997: B1, B10.

Kelloway, E., and J. Barling. "Job Characteristics, Role Stress, and Mental Health," *Journal of Occupational Psychology* 1, 1991: 291–304.

Kessler, John. "From Nonna's Kitchen to Yours Cookbook: A Sampler from Italy," *Denver Post,* June 4, 1997.

Klepper, Michael, and Robert Gunther. *The Wealthy 100,* New York: Carol Publishing, 1996.

Knaff, Devorah. "Amazingly Intricate Miniature Sculptures," *Riverside Press-Enterprise,* March 16, 1997: E2.

Koford, Kenneth, and Adrian Tshoegl, "The Market Value of Rarity," *Journal of Economic Behavior and Organization* 34, March 1998: 445–58.

Kosicki, George, "Savings as a Nonpositional Good," *Eastern Economic Journal* 14, 1988: 271–76.

Kosicki, George. "A Test of the Relative Income Hypothesis," *Southern Economic Journal* 54, 1987: 422–34.

Koslowsky, Meni; Avraham N. Kluger; and Mordechai Reich. *Commuting Stress,* New York: Plenum, 1995.

Koslowsky, Meni, and Moshe Krausz. "On the Relationship Between Commuting, Stress Symptoms, and Attitudinal Measures," *Journal of Applied Behavioral Sciences,* December 1993: 485–92.

Koss-Feder, Laura. "6 Islands, 7 Days, 48 Monthly Payments: A Cruise Loan Buys a Dream, but at What Price?" *New York Times,* April 13, 1997: sec. 3, p. 10.

Kozol, Jonathan. *Amazing Grace,* New York: Crown, 1995.

Krugman, Paul. "The Right, the Rich, and the Facts," *The American Prospect* 11, Fall 1992: 19–31.

Kubovy, Michael. "Pleasures of the Mind," in *Understanding Well-Being: Scientific Perspectives on Enjoyment and Suffering,* ed. Daniel Kahneman, Ed Diener, and Norbert Schwartz, New York: Russell Sage, 1998.

Kuczynski, Alex. "A Benz for the Wrist," *New York Times,* March 8, 1998: sec. 9, pp. 1, 3.

Land, Kenneth; P. McCall; and L. Cohen. "Structural Co-variates of Homicide Rates: Are There Any Invariances Across Time and Space?" *American Journal of Sociology* 95, 1990: 922–63.

Landers, Renee M.; James B. Rebitzer; and Lowell J. Taylor. "Rate Race Redux: Adverse Selection in the Determination of Work Hours in Law Firms," *American Economic Review* 86, June 1996: 329–48.

Landers, Robert K. "America's Vacation Gap," *Congressional Quarterly's Editorial Research Reports* 1, no. 23, 1988: 314–22.

Lane, Robert E. *The Market Experience,* New York: Cambridge University Press, 1991.

Layard, Richard. "Human Satisfactions and Public Policy," *The Economic Journal* 90, December, 1980: 737–50.

LeBlanc, Aileen. "Historic Theater Sound Makers Found in Old Opera House," *Morning Edition,* National Public Radio, September 12, 1995.

Leete, L., and J. B. Schor. "Assessing the Time-Squeeze Hypothesis: Hours Worked in the United States, 1969–89," *Industrial Relations* 33, 1994: 25–43.

Lichtman, Sharla, and Ernest G. Poser. "The Effects of Exercise on Mood and Cognitive Functioning," *Journal of Psychosomatic Research* 27, 1983: 43–52.

Lienert, Anita. "Crowning Touch: Learning the Intracacies of Achieving, Maintaining the Sales Reign," *Chicago Tribune,* February 12, 1998: W3.

Linder, Staffan. *The Harried Leisure Class,* New York: Columbia University Press, 1970.

Lobsenz, George. "Erstwhile Ally Chafee Tells EPA to Back Off Soot Standards," *Energy Daily,* February 13, 1997.

Loeb, Susanna, and Marianne E. Page. "Examining the Link Between Wages and Quality in the Teacher Workforce," University of Michigan Department of Economics mimeograph, October 1997.

Loewenstein, George, and David Schkade. "Wouldn't It Be Nice? Predicting Future Feelings," in *Understanding Well-Being: Scientific Perspectives on Enjoyment and Suffering,* ed. Daniel Kahneman, Ed Diener, and Norbert Schwartz, New York: Russell Sage, 1998.

Loewenstein, George, and Shane Frederick. "Hedonic Adaptation: From the Bright Side to the Dark Side," in *Understanding Well-Being: Scientific Perspectives on Enjoyment and Suffering,* ed. Daniel Kahneman, Ed Diener, and Norbert Schwartz, New York: Russell Sage, 1998.

Long, L., and J. Perry. "Economic and Occupational Causes of Transit Operator Absenteeism: A Review of Research," *Transport Review* 5, 1985: 247–67.

Lowenstein, Roger. *Buffet: The Making of an American Capitalist,* New York: Random House, 1995.

Lucier, James P. "The Past and Future Collide in Moscow," *Washington Times,* December 1, 1997: 22.

Lykken, David, and Auke Tellegen. "Happiness Is a Stochastic Phenomenon," *Psychological Science* 7, May 1996: 186–89.

Maas, James. *Power Sleep,* New York: Villard, 1998.

Madsen, Douglas. "Serotonin and Social Rank Among Human Males," in *The Neuro-*

transmitter Revolution: Serotonin, Social Behavior, and the Law, ed. Roger Masters and Michael McGuire, Carbondale: Southern Illinois University Press, 1994: 146–58.

Manning, Anita. "Deadly Strain of Food Poisoning Is Hard to Defeat, Difficult to Track," *USA Today,* May 13, 1997: 1A.

Manning, F. J., and T. D. Fullerton. "Health and Well-Being in Highly Cohesive Units of the U.S. Army," *Journal of Applied Social Psychology* 18, 1988: 503–19.

Marmot, Michael G. "Contribution of Job Control and Other Risk Factors to Social Variation in Coronary Heart Disease Incidence," *Lancet,* July 26, 1997: 235.

Marmot, Michael. "Social Differentials in Mortality: The Whitehall Studies," in *Adult Mortality in Developed Countries: From Description to Explanation,* ed. A. Lopez et al., New York: Oxford University Press, 1995.

Marmot, Michael; Martin Bobak; and George Davey Smith. "Explanations for Social Inequalities in Health," in *Society and Health,* ed. B.C. Amick et al., Oxford University Press, 1995.

Marmot, Michael; G. Rose; M. Shipley; and P. J. S. Hamilton. "Employment Grade and Coronary Heart Disease," *British Medical Journal* 2, 1978: 1109–12.

Marmot, Michael; George Davey Smith; S. Stanfield, et al. "Health Inequalities among British Civil Servants: The Whitehall II Studies, *Lancet* 337, 1991: 1387–93.

Marmot, Michael G. "Social Differentials in Health Within and Between Populations," *Daedalus* 123, Fall 1994: 197–216.

Marmot, M. G.; M. Shipley; and G. Rose. "Inequalities in Death—Specific Explanations or General Pattern?" *Lancet* 1, 1984: 1003–6.

Martinsen, E. W. "Therapeutic Implications of Exercise for Clinically Anxious and Depressed Patients," *Journal of Sport Psychology* 24, 1993: 185–99.

Marwick, Charles. "Putting Money Where the U.S. Mouth Is," *Journal of the American Medical Association,* May 7, 1997: 1340–43.

Masters, Roger D.; Brian Hone; and Anil Doshi. "Environmental Pollution, Neurotoxicity, and Criminal Violence," in *Environmental Toxicology,* ed. J. Rose, London and New York: Gordon and Breach, 1998.

Mazur, Allan. "A Biosocial Model of Status in Face-to-Face Primate Groups," *Social Forces* 64, no. 2, December 1985: 377–402.

Mazur, Allan. "Physiology, Dominance, and Aggression in Humans," in *Prevention and Control of Aggression,* ed. A. Goldstein, New York: Pergamon, 1983.

Mazur, Allan, and T. Lamb. "Testosterone, Status, and Mood in Human Males," *Hormones and Behavior* 14, 1980: 236–46.

McCarty, Mary. "A Quick Look at the Slow Down Manifesto," *Cox News Service,* March 5, 1997.

McEwan, Ian. "Us or Me?" *The New Yorker,* May 19, 1997: 72–77.

McGeehan, Patrick. "Now Suddenly Rich, Wall Streeters Spark a Very Fancy Boom," *Wall Street Journal,* April 10, 1997: A1, A6.

McGuire, Mark. "A Rumble and Everything Went," *Albany Times Union,* March 30, 1997: A3.

McGuire, Michael; M. Raleigh; and G. Brammer. "Sociopharmacology," *Annual Review of Pharmacological Toxicology* 22, 1982: 643–61.

Meltzer, Peter D. "Grand Totals: Year-end Results for 1996 Show that Wine Auctions

Are Still Booming and Prices Continue to Rise," *Wine Spectator,* February 28, 1997: 32–35.

Modigliani, Franco, and R. Brumberg. "Utility Analysis and the Consumption Function: An Interpretation of Cross-Section Data," in *Post-Keynesian Economics,* ed. K. Kurihara, London: Allen and Unwin, 1955.

Moin, David. "Europe-Bound Buyers Eager to Open Wallets for More Daring Styles," *Capital Cities Media,* March 2, 1998: 1.

Molpus, David. "Voluntary Simplicity," Morning Edition, National Public Radio, February 25, 1997.

Moonan, Wendy. "Palm Beach High Rollers Get a Fair," *New York Times,* January 23, 1998: E37.

Mueller, Mark. "Americans Have Beaten the Clock," *Boston Herald,* June 5, 1997: 6.

Munk, Nina. "Rent-a-Cops," *Forbes,* October 10, 1994: 104–6.

Murphy, Kevin M.; Andrei Schleifer; and Robert W. Vishny. "The Allocation of Talent: Implications for Growth," *Quarterly Journal of Economics* 106, May 1991: 503–30.

Myers, David G. "Close Relationships and Quality of Life," in *Understanding Well-Being: Scientific Perspectives on Enjoyment and Suffering,* ed. Daniel Kahneman, Ed Diener, and Norbert Schwartz, New York: Russell Sage, 1998.

Myers, David G. *The Pursuit of Happiness: Who Is Happy and Why?* New York: Avon, 1993.

Myers, David G., and E. Diener. "Who Is Happy?" *Psychological Science* 6, 1995: 10–19.

Myers, Jim. "Inhofe Introduces Bill to Strangle Air Rules," *Tulsa World,* July 31, 1997: A1.

Nesse, Randolph. "Evolutionary Functions of Enjoyment and Suffering," in *Understanding Well-Being: Scientific Perspectives on Enjoyment and Suffering,* ed. Daniel Kahneman, Ed Diener, and Norbert Schwartz, New York: Russell Sage, 1998.

Neumark, David, and Andrew Postlewaite. "Relative Income Concerns and the Rise in Married Women's Employment," *Journal of Public Economics,* forthcoming.

Ng, Yew-Kwang. "Diamonds Are a Government's Best Friend: Burden-Free Taxes on Goods Valued for Their Values," *American Economic Review* 77, 1987: 186–91.

Noonan, David. "Really Big Football Players," *New York Times Magazine,* December 14, 1997: 64 ff.

Nozick, Robert. *Anarchy, State, and Utopia,* New York: Basic Books, 1974.

Okun, Arthur. *Equality and Efficiency: The Big Tradeoff,* Washington, DC: 1975.

Oswald, Andrew J. "Happiness and Economic Performance," University of Warwick, Department of Economics mimeograph, September 1996.

Oswald, Andrew J. "Altruism, Jealousy, and the Theory of Optimal Nonlinear Income Taxation," *Journal of Public Economics* 20, 1983: 77–87.

Othman, Muharyani. "Bright as Buttons," *New Straits Times,* April 12, 1997: 7.

Pacelle, Michelle. "In the Suburbs, Job Strife Starts in the Parking Lot," *Wall Street Journal,* October 25 1996: B1, B18.

Pacenti, John. "Forbidden Fruit: With the Popularity of Cigars, the Legendary But Illegal Variety Is Increasingly Being Smuggled into the United States," *Tampa Tribune,* September 22, 1996: 6.

Paik, Felicia. "Eccentric Homes Take Years to Build, Years to Sell," *Wall Street Journal,* October 4, 1996: B1, B6.

Paik, Felicia. "Huge Houses Squeeze into Tight Spaces," *Wall Street Journal,* November 22, 1996: B1, B14.

Paik, Felicia. "When Too Big Isn't Big Enough." *Wall Street Journal,* May 1, 1998: W10.

Palmer, Linda K. "Effects of a Walking Program on Attributional Style, Depression, and Self-Esteem in Women," *Perceptual and Motor Skills* 81, 1995: 891–98.

Parducci, A. *Happiness, Pleasure, and Judgment: The Contextual Theory and Its Applications,* Hillsdale, NJ: Erlbaum, 1995.

Pattison, E.; M. Sobell; and L. Sobell. *Emerging Concepts of Alcohol Dependence,* New York: Springer, 1977.

Pearlstein, Steven, and Paul Blustein. "In the Best of Both Worlds, Consider a Third Option," *Washington Post,* June 23, 1997: A12.

Pechman, Joseph. *Who Bears the Tax Burden?,* Washington, DC: The Brookings Institution, 1985.

Peers, Alexandra. "Hot Cellars: Wine Prices Are Soaring," *Wall Street Journal,* May 2, 1997: B8.

Perez-Pena, Richard. "Study Shows New York Has Greatest Income Gap," *New York Times,* December 17, 1997: A1.

Perkins, H. W. "Religious Commitment, Yuppie Values, and Well-Being in Post-Collegiate Life," *Review of Religious Research,* 32, 1991: 244–51.

Persson, T., and Guido Tabellini. "Growth, Distribution, and Politics," in *Political Economy, Growth, and Business Cycles,* ed. A. Cuckierman, Z. Hercowitz, and L. Leiderman, Cambridge: MIT Press, 1992: 3–22.

Pikus, W., and W. Tarranikova. "The Frequency of Hypertensive Diseases in Public Transportation," *Terapevischeskii Archives* 47, 1975: 135–37.

Pinker, Steven. *How the Mind Works,* New York: W. W. Norton, 1997.

Pitt, William. "The Capitalists of Imagery," *Director,* November 1991: 83–86.

Plante, Thomas G., and Judith Rodin. "Physical Fitness and Enhanced Psychological Health," *Current Psychology: Research and Reviews* 9, Spring 1990: 3–24.

Pope, C. Arden, III. "Respiratory Disease Associated with Community Air Pollution and a Steel Mill, Utah Valley," *American Journal of Public Health* 79, May 1989: 623ff.

Poterba, James; Steven Venti; and David Wise. "How Retirement Saving Programs Increase Savings," *Journal of Economic Perspectives* 10, Fall 1996: 91–112.

PR Newswire. "Oakland Road Comissioners Divert Money for 'Pothole Emergency'," April 19, 1997.

Pressler, Margaret Webb. "Hot Sales at the High End," *Washington Post,* January 26, 1997: H1.

Putnam, Robert D. "Bowling Alone: America's Declining Social Capital," *Journal of Democracy* 6, 1995: 65–78.

Ragland, D.; M. Winkleby; J. Schwalbe; B. Holman; L. Morse; L. Syme; and J. Fisher. "Prevalence of Hypertension in Bus Drivers," *International Journal of Epidemiology* 16, 1987: 208–14.

Raines, Franklin D. "Prepared Statement Before the Senate Budget Committee," *Federal News Service,* February 4, 1998.

Rainwater, Lee. "Poverty and Equivalence as Social Constructions," Luxembourg Income Study Working Paper 55, 1990.

Raleigh, Michael J., and Michael T. McGuire. "Serotonin, Aggression, and Violence in Vervet Monkeys," in *The Neurotransmitter Revolution: Serotonin, Social Behavor, and the Law,* ed. Roger Masters and Michael McGuire, Carbondale: Southern Illinois University Press, 1994: 146–58.

Raleigh, Michael J.; Gary Brammer; Edward Ritvo; and Edward Geller. "Effects of Chronic Fenfluramine on Blood Serotonin, Cerebrospinal Metabolites, and Behavior in Monkeys," *Psychopharmacology*, 90, November 1986: 503–8.

Rees, A. "The Role of Fairness in Wage Determination," *Journal of Labor Economics* 11, 1993: 243–52.

Rice, Dorothy; Sander Kelman; and Leonard Miller. "Estimates of Economic Costs of Alcohol and Drug Abuse and Mental Illness, 1985 and 1988," *Public Health Reports,* May–June 1991: 280–92.

Roberts, K., and P. Rupert. "The Myth of the Overworked American," *Economic Commentary: Federal Reserve Bank of Cleveland,* January 15, 1995.

Robinson, John P., and Geoffrey Godbey. *Time for Life,* State College: Pennsylvania State University Press, 1997.

Robson, Arthur J. "Status, the Distribution of Wealth, Private and Social Attitudes to Risk," *Econometrica* 60, 1992: 837–58.

Roche, William; Bryan Fines; and Terri Morrissey. "Working Time and Employment: A Review of International Evidence," *International Labor Review* 135, 1996: 129–57.

Rose, R.; I. Bernstein; and T. Gordon. "Consequences of Social Conflict on Plasma Testosterone Levels in Rhesus Monkeys," *Psychosomatic Medicine* 37, 1975: 50–61.

Rubenstein, Carin. "Vacations," *Psychology Today,* May 1980: 62–76.

Runciman, W. G. *Relative Deprivation and Social Justice,* New York: Penguin, 1966.

Sandvik, E.; E. Diener; and L. Seidlitz. "The Assessment of Well-Being: A Comparison of Self-Report and Nonself-Report Strategies," *Journal of Personality* 61, 1993: 317–42.

Schellhardt, Timothy D. "Company Memo to Stressed-Out Employees: 'Deal With It,'" *Wall Street Journal,* October 2, 1996: B1, B7.

Schelling, Thomas. "The Intimate Contest for Self-Command," *The Public Interest* 60, 1980: 94–118.

Schlesinger, Jacob M. "Card Games: As Bankruptcies Surge, Creditors Lobby Hard to Get Tougher Laws," *Wall Street Journal,* June 17, 1998: A1, A9.

Schor, Juliet. *The Overworked American,* New York: Basic Books, 1991.

Schwartz, Norbert, and Fritz Strack. "Reports of Subjective Well-Being: Judgmental Processes and Their Methodological Implications," in *Understanding Well-Being: Scientific Perspectives on Enjoyment and Suffering,* ed. Daniel Kahneman, Ed Diener, and Norbert Schwartz, New York: Russell Sage, 1998.

Scitovsky, Tibor. *The Joyless Economy,* New York: Oxford University Press, 1976.

Scott, S. P. *The Civil Law, Including the Twelve Tables, the Institutes of Gains, the Rules of Ulpian, the Opinions of Paulus, the Enactments of Justinian, and the Constitutions of Leo,* New York: AMS Press, 1973.

Segal, Jerome M. "The Politics of Simplicity," *Tikkun,* July 1996: 20 ff.

Seidlitz, L., and E. Diener, "Memory for Positive Versus Negative Life Events: Theories for the Differences Between Happy and Unhappy Persons," *Journal of Personality and Social Psychology* 64, 1993: 654–64.

Seidman, Laurence. *The USA Tax: A Progressive Consumption Tax,* Cambridge: MIT Press, 1997.

Seidman, Laurence, and Kenneth Lewis. "The Design of a Tax Rule for Housing Under a Personal Consumption Tax," *Public Finance Quarterly,* 1996a.

Seidman, Laurence S., and Kenneth A. Lewis. "Transition Protections During Conversion to a Personal Consumption Tax," University of Delaware Department of Economics Working Paper, 1996b.

Selz, Michael. "Lenders Find Niche in Cosmetic Surgery that Isn't Insured," *Wall Street Journal,* January 15, 1997, A1, A8.

Sen, Amartya. *The Standard of Living,* New York: Cambridge University Press, 1987.

Sen, Amartya. "Poor, Relatively Speaking," *Oxford Economics Papers* 35, July 1983: 153–67.

Sen, Amartya. *Poverty and Famines: An Essay on Entitlement and Deprivation,* Oxford: Clarendon Press, 1981.

Sharp, David. "Stress!" *The Buffalo News,* July 14, 1996: 4M.

Sharpe, Anita. "For $10 Million, It Better Have a Ballroom," *Wall Street Journal,* September 2, 1996: B1, B18.

Shellenbarger, Sue. "More Executives Cite Need for Family Time as Reason for Quitting," *Wall Street Journal,* March 11, 1998: B1.

Shellenbarger, Sue. "Work Hours Increasing? Well, More or Less," *San Diego Union Tribune,* August 10, 1997: D3.

Sherrod, D. R. "Crowding, Perceived Control, and Behavioral Aftereffects," *Journal of Applied Social Psychology* 4, 1974: 171–86.

Shin, D. C. "Does Rapid Economic Growth Improve the Human Lot?" *Social Indicators Research,* 8, 1980: 199–221.

Shnayerson, Michael. "The Champagne City," *Vanity Fair,* December 1997: 182–202.

Simmons, Matty. *The Credit Card Catastrophe,* New York: Barricade Books, 1995.

Simmons, Tim. "Teachers Stake Hopes on Bill," *Raleigh News and Observer,* March 29, 1997: A1.

Singer, Natasha. "The Rush to Russia; Luxury Goods Suppliers Gucci, Luis Vuitton, Hermes Establishing Presence in Moscow," *Capital Cities Media,* January 20, 1998: 6.

Sisolop, Sana. "It's Brand Over Bargain in the World of Cigars," *New York Times,* March 1, 1997: Business sec., 4.

Sjostrom, Joseph. "Projects' Delays Add to Expense Down Road; Stalled Projects Just Speed Deterioration of Crumbling Highways," *Chicago Tribune,* July 31, 1997: MC1.

Slemrod, Joel. "The Economic Impact of the Tax Reform Act of 1986," in *Do Taxes Matter? The Impact of the Tax Reform Act of 1986,* Joel Slemrod, Cambridge: MIT Press, 1990: 1–12.

Smith, Adam. *An Inquiry into the Nature and Causes of the Wealth of Nations,* Chicago: Encyclopedia Britannica, 1952 (1776).

Smith, Bruce H. "Anxiety as a Cost of Commuting to Work," *Journal of Urban Economics* 29, 1991: 260–66.

Smith, Robert L., and Robert J. Bush. "A Qualitative Evaluation of the U.S. Timber Bridge Market," *Forest Products Journal,* January 1997: 37–42.

Smolensky, Eugene. "The Past and Present Poor," in *The Concept of Poverty*, Task Force on Economic Growth and Opportunity, Washington, DC: Chamber of Commerce of the United States, 1965.

Snead, Elizabeth. "For Younger Patients, Aging Is an Unkinder Cut," *USA Today*, July 1, 1996: D1, D2.

Solnick, Sara J., and David Hemenway. "Is More Always Better? A Survey on Positional Concerns," *Journal of Economic Behavior and Organization*, forthcoming.

Spayd, Liz. "In Excess We Trust," *Washington Post*, May 26, 1996: C1.

Spector, P., and B. O'Connell. "The Contribution of Personality Traits, Negative Affectivity, Locus of Control and Type A to the Subsequent Reports of Job Stressors and Job Strains," *Journal of Occupational and Organizational Psychology* 67, 1994: 1–11.

Spector, P.; D. Dwyer; and S. Jex. "Relation of Job Stressors to Affective, Health, and Performance Outcomes: A Comparison of Multiple Data Sources," *Journal of Applied Psychology* 73, 1988: 11–19.

Stafford, Frank. "The Overworked American—A Book Review," *Journal of Economic Literature* 30, 1992: 1528–29.

Starr, John. "North Carolina's Grand Estate Tourists Made Biltmore a Success," *Arkansas Democrat-Gazette*, November 16, 1995: 7B.

Steinberg, Jacques. "Research Suggests the Fewer Students, the Better," *New York Times*, September 29, 1997: A40.

Stewart, Jr., Charles T. *Healthy, Wealthy, or Wise? Issues in American Health Care Policy*, Armonk, NY: M. E. Sharpe, 1995.

Stokols, Daniel; Raymond W. Novaco; Jeannette Stokols; and Joan Campbell. "Traffic Congestion, Type A Behavior, and Stress,"*Journal of Applied Psychology* 63, 1978: 467–80.

Strack, Fritz; N. Schwarz; B. Chassein; D. Kern; and D. Wagner. "The Salience of Comparison Standards and the Activation of Social Norms: Consequences for Judgments of Happiness and Their Communication," *British Journal of Social Psychology* 29, December 1990: 303–14.

Strauss, Gary. "Upscale Barbecue Grills Spark Hot New Market," *Ithaca Journal*, July 16, 1997: 7A.

Summers, Lawrence H. "An Equity Case for Consumption Taxation," in *New Directions in Federal Tax Policy for the 1980s*, ed. Charles E. Walker and Mark A. Bloomfield, Cambridge, MA: Ballinger, 1984.

Suris, Oscar. "Now, Mercedes Conveys a Sensible Image," *Wall Street Journal*, November 6, 1996: B1, B9.

Takahashi, Corey. "Crocodile Dandy: Detroiters Develop a Fetish for 'Gators'," *Wall Street Journal*, September 11, 1997: A1, A6.

Taylor, P., and C. Pocock. "Commuter Travel and Sickness: Absence of London Office Workers," *British Journal of Preventive and Social Medicine* 26, 1972: 165–72.

Taylor, Ralph, and J. Covington. "Neighborhood Changes in Ecology and Violence," *Criminology* 26, 1988: 553.

Tellegen, Auke, et al. "Personality Similarity in Twins Reared Apart and Together," *Journal of Personality and Social Psychology* 54, 1988: 1031–39.

Thaler, Richard. "Precommitment and the Value of a Life," in *The Value of Life and Safety*, ed. Michael Jones-Lee, Amsterdam: North Holland, 1982: 171–84.

Thaler, Richard. "Toward a Behavioral Theory of Consumer Choice," *Journal of Economic Behavior and Organization* 1, 1980: 39–60.

Thaler, Richard, and H. Shefrin. "An Economic Theory of Self-Control," *Journal of Political Economy* 89, April 1981: 392–405.

Tharpe, Gene. "Annual Bankruptcies Cross Million Mark for First Time," *The Atlanta Constitution,* March 21, 1997: 2G.

Thynne, Jane. "The Good Life Was the Rat Race All Along," *Sunday Times,* February 2, 1997.

Tierney, John. "Technology Makes Us Better," *New York Times Magazine,* September 28, 1997: 46 ff.

Townsend, Peter. "The Development of Research on Poverty," in *Social Security Research: The Definition and Measurement of Poverty,* Department of Health and Social Research, London: HMSO, 1979.

Troufexis, Anastasia. "Drowsy America," *Time,* December 17, 1990: 78.

Truell, Peter. "Another Year, Another Bundle," *New York Times,* December 5, 1997: D1, D4.

Tversky, Amos, and Dale Griffen. "Endowment and Contrast in Judgments of Well-being," in *Strategy and Choice,* ed. Richard Zeckhauser, Cambridge: MIT Press, 1991: 297–319.

Tversky, Amos, and Daniel Kahneman. "Judgment Under Uncertainty: Heuristics and Biases," in *Judgment Under Uncertainty: Heuristics and Biases,* ed. Daniel Kahneman, Paul Slovic, and Amos Tversky, New York: Cambridge University Press, 1982.

Uchitelle, Louis. "As Taste for Comfort Rises, So Do Corporations' Profits," *New York Times,* September 14, 1997: A1, A34.

U.S. Bureau of the Census. *Statistical Abstract of the United States: 1996 (116th ed.),* Washington, DC, 1996.

U.S. House of Representives, Committee on Ways and Means. *War Taxation of Incomes, Excess Profits, and Luxuries in Certain Foreign Countries,* Washington, DC: U.S. Government Printing Office, 1918.

U.S. National Institute on Drug Abuse and U.S. House Committee on Appropriations. *Departments of Labor, Health and Human Services, and Education Appropriation for 1996 Part 4 Hearing,* Washington, DC: 1995.

van Praag, Bernard M. S. "The Relativity of the Welfare Concept," in *The Quality of Life,* ed. Martha Nussbaum and Amartya Sen, Oxford: Clarendon, 1993: 363–92.

Van Voorst, Bruce. "Why America Has So Many Potholes," *Time,* May 4, 1992: 64, 65.

Veblen, Thorstein. *The Theory of the Leisure Class,* New York, Modern Library, 1899.

Veenhoven, Ruut. *Happiness in Nations: Subjective Appreciation of Life in 56 Nations,* Rotterdam: Erasmus University, 1993.

Venti, Steven F., and David A. Wise. "Have IRAs Increased U.S. Savings? Evidence from Consumer Expenditure Surveys," *Quarterly Journal of Economics* 105, 1990: 661–98.

Vincent, John Martin. Costume and Conduct in the Laws of Basel, Bern, and Zurich, *New York: Greenwood Press, 1969: 1370–1800.*

Wall, T.; P. Jackson; S. Mullarkey; and S. Parker. "The Demands-Control Model of Job

Strain: A More Specific Test," *Journal of Occupational and Organizational Psychology* 69, 1996: 153–66.

Wallich, Paul. "The Workaholic Economy," *Scientific American,* August 1994: 77.

Wallis, David. "Questions for Alan Wilzig," *New York Times Magazine,* August 17, 1997: 17.

Ward, Leah Beth. "Working Harder to Obtain the Same Vacation," *New York Times,* May 11, 1997: 12F.

Warr, Peter. "Well-Being and the Workplace," in *Understanding Well-Being: Scientific Perspectives on Enjoyment and Suffering,* ed. Daniel Kahneman, Ed Diener, and Norbert Schwartz, New York: Russell Sage, 1998.

Warr, Peter. "Decision Latitude, Job Demands, and Employee Well-Being," *Work and Stress* 4, 1990: 285–94.

Watson, Alan D. "Luxury Vehicles and Elitism in Colonial North Carolina," *Southern Studies* 19, Summer 1980: 147–56.

Weicher, John C. *The Distribution of Wealth: Increasing Inequality?* Washington, DC: American Enterprise Institute, 1996.

Weinstein, N. D. "Community Noise Problems: Evidence Against Adaptation," *Journal of Environmental Psychology* 2, 1982: 82–97.

Weiss, Manfred. "Legislation in the Federal Republic of Germany," *International Encyclopedia for Labor Law and Industrial Relations,* ed. R. Blanpain, Boston: Kluwer, 1991.

West, Debra. "Suburbs' Mass-Market Mansions," *New York Times,* March 18, 1998: B1, B6.

Wheeler, Larry. "Trouble on the Tracks," *Ithaca Journal,* December 8, 1997: 1A, 4A.

Whitaker, Barbara. "Wrapping Their Dreams Around Their Wrists," *New York Times,* March 2, 1997: 10F.

Wilkinson, Richard. "The Epidemiological Transition: From Material Scarcity to Social Disadvantage?" *Daedalus* 123, Fall 1994: 61–77.

Wilkinson, Richard. "Health, Redistribution, and Growth," in *Paying for Inequality,* ed. Andrew Glyn and David Miliband, London: Rivers Oram Press: 1994: 24–43.

Wilkinson, Richard G. *Unhealthy Societies: The Afflictions of Inequality,* London: Routledge, 1996.

Wilkinson, Richard G. "Income Distribution and Life Expectancy," *British Medical Journal* 304, 1992: 165–68.

Wilkinson, Richard G. "Income and Mortality: A Natural Experiment," *Sociology of Health and Illness* 12, 1990: 391–412.

Wilkinson, Richard G. "Socioeconommic Differences in Mortality: Interpreting the Data on Their Size and Trends," in *Class and Health: Research and Longitudinal Data,* ed. R. G. Wilkinson, London: Tavistock, 1986.

Williams, Heathcoate. *Whale Nation,* New York: Crown, 1989.

Wilson, William Julius. *When Work Disappears: The World of the New Urban Poor,* New York: Knopf, 1996.

Windsor, Robert, and Daniel Dumitru. "Anabolic Steroid Use by Athletes: How Serious Are the Health Hazards?" *Postgraduate Medicine* 84, 1988: 37–49.

Wright, Robert. *The Moral Animal,* New York: Pantheon, 1994.

Wuthnow, Robert. *Poor Richard's Principle: Rediscovering the American Dream Through the Moral Dimension of Work, Business, and Money,* Princeton: Princeton University Press, 1996.

Xie, J., and G. Johns. "Job Scope and Stress: Can Job Scope Be Too High?" *Academy of Management Journal* 38, 1995: 1288–1309.

Zahavi, Jacob. "Franklin Mint's Famous AMOS," *OR/MS Today* 22, 1995: 18–23.

Zizzo, Daniel J. "Relativity-Sensitive Behavior in Economics: An Overview with New Experimental Evidence," M. Phil. diss., Oxford University, 1997.

INDEX

Toll, Bruce, 29
Tooby, John, 125
Toxic metals, exposure to, 54–55
Toyota Corolla, 180
Traffic, commuting through, 80–83
Traffic congestion, sensitivity to interpersonal comparisons of, 164
Tragedy of the commons, 157, 237–38
Trickle-down economics
    fundamental premise of, 226, 227, 249
    on imposition of higher tax rates, 228–39
        effort–reward relationship and, 228–31
        tax avoidance and tax evasion and, 231–39
    reason for acceptance of, 242–43
    systematic challenge to, 243–45
Trophy homes, 21–22
Tshoegl, Adrian, 119
Turley, Helen, 30
Tuskus, William, 60
Tversky, Amos, 176

Uchitelle, Louis, 24
Ultimatum bargaining game, 116
Unemployment, psychological effects of, 265
Unemployment insurance, 246
Unger, William, 140
Unilateral action
    execution problem for, 183–86, 187
    limited potential for improvement through, 161
    voluntary simplicity movement and, 187–93
United Kingdom, income inequality in, 43
United States
    Department of Justice, 241
    luxury taxes in, 204, 205
    personal savings rate in, 5, 45, 96–98
USA tax (unlimited-savings-allowance tax), 224, 225

Vacation, 88–89
    regulation of, 275
Vacation homes, 20
Value-added taxes, 211–12
Vanderbilt clan, 14
Veblen, Thorstein, 14
Victoria's Secret, 25
Views, charm premium in houses with, 28
Viking-Frontgate Professional Grill, 1–2
Voluntary Simplicity Conference (1997), 188
Voluntary Simplicity (Elgin), 187
Voluntary simplicity movement, 7, 187–93
    downside of, 189–93

Wages for public-service jobs, 262
Wage structures, factors determining, 117–19
Wallich, Paul, 50
Wall Street professionals, incomes of, 34–35
Water systems, municipal, 54–55, 253–54
Wealth, environmental cleanup and, 106
Wealth of Nations, The (Smith), 147, 201
Weber-Stephens Summit Grill, 2
Weintraub, Alvin, 22
Welch, Jack, 39–40
Welfare
    public-service jobs as alternative to, 261–65
    reasons for failure of, 259–61
    reform of, 257–59
Well-being, subjective. *See* Subjective well-being
Whistler Village condominiums, 18
Whitehall Studies, 143–44
Whitetail Mountain, Pennsylvania, 20
Whole income, concept of, 241–42
Wilkinson, Richard, 142–43, 144–45, 239
Williams–Sonoma, 25
Wilson, William Julius, 261
Wilzig, Alan, 3
Wines, charm premium for ultrapremium, 29–30
Winner-take-all markets, 269, 276
    occupational choice in, 235–39
    spread of, 37–40
    technology and, 38–39
Within-group status, wage distribution and, 118–19
Women, working, 49
Woolman, John, 202
Worker stress, 52
Work–family balance, 52
Work hours, regulations limiting, 275
Workplace
    autonomy in, 89–90
    safety regulations for, 169–71, 275
    shrinking of, 52
Workweek, real wages and length of, 230
Wristwatches, luxury, 16–17, 18, 212, 221
Wuthnow, Robert, 50
Wyss, David, 46

Yachts, shortage of, 18
Your Money Or Your Life (Robin and Dominguez), 187

Zahavi, Jacob, 120
Zoning laws, 166